日本語 NOW!
NihonGO NOW!

NihonGO NOW! is a beginning-level courseware package that takes a performed-culture approach to learning Japanese. This innovative approach balances the need for an intellectual understanding of structural elements with multiple opportunities to experience the language within its cultural context.

From the outset, learners are presented with samples of authentic language that are context-sensitive and culturally coherent. Instructional time is used primarily to rehearse interactions that learners of Japanese are likely to encounter in the future, whether they involve speaking, listening, writing, or reading.

Level 1 comprises two textbooks with accompanying activity books. These four books in combination with audio files allow instructors to adapt a beginning-level course, such as the first year of college Japanese, to their students' needs. They focus on language and modeled behavior, providing opportunities for learners to acquire language through performance templates. Online resources provide additional support for both students and instructors. Audio files, videos, supplementary exercises, and a teachers' manual are available at www.routledge.com/9781138304147.

NihonGO NOW! Level 1 Volume 2 Textbook is ideally accompanied by the *Level 1 Volume 2 Activity Book*, which provides core texts and additional practice for beginning-level students.

Mari Noda is Professor of Japanese at The Ohio State University.

Patricia J. Wetzel is Emerita Professor of Japanese at Portland State University.

Ginger Marcus is Professor of the Practice of Japanese Language at Washington University in St. Louis.

Stephen D. Luft is Lecturer of Japanese at the University of Pittsburgh.

Shinsuke Tsuchiya is Assistant Professor of Japanese at Brigham Young University.

Masayuki Itomitsu is Associate Professor of Japanese at Linfield College.

日本語 NOW!
NihonGO NOW!

Performing Japanese Culture
Level 1 Volume 2
Textbook

Mari Noda, Patricia J. Wetzel, Ginger Marcus,
Stephen D. Luft, Shinsuke Tsuchiya,
and Masayuki Itomitsu

LONDON AND NEW YORK

First published 2021
by Routledge
2 Park Square, Milton Park, Abingdon, Oxon OX14 4RN

and by Routledge
52 Vanderbilt Avenue, New York, NY 10017

Routledge is an imprint of the Taylor & Francis Group, an informa business

© 2021 Mari Noda, Patricia J. Wetzel, Ginger Marcus, Stephen D. Luft, Shinsuke Tsuchiya, and Masayuki Itomitsu

The right of Mari Noda, Patricia J. Wetzel, Ginger Marcus, Stephen D. Luft, Shinsuke Tsuchiya, and Masayuki Itomitsu to be identified as authors of this work has been asserted by them in accordance with sections 77 and 78 of the Copyright, Designs and Patents Act 1988.

All rights reserved. No part of this book may be reprinted or reproduced or utilised in any form or by any electronic, mechanical, or other means, now known or hereafter invented, including photocopying and recording, or in any information storage or retrieval system, without permission in writing from the publishers.

Trademark notice: Product or corporate names may be trademarks or registered trademarks, and are used only for identification and explanation without intent to infringe.

British Library Cataloguing-in-Publication Data
A catalogue record for this book is available from the British Library

Library of Congress Cataloging-in-Publication Data
Names: Noda, Mari, author.
Title: Nihongo now! : performing Japanese culture / Mari Noda, Patricia J. Wetzel, Ginger Marcus, Stephen D. Luft, Shinsuke Tsuchiya, Masayuki Itomitsu.
Description: New York : Routledge, 2020. | Includes bibliographical references. | Contents: Level 1, volume 1. Textbook — Level 1, volume 1. Activity book — Level 1, volume 2. Textbook — Level 1, volume 2. Activity book. | In English and Japanese.
Identifiers: LCCN 2020026010 (print) | LCCN 2020026011 (ebook) | ISBN 9780367509279 (level 1, volume 1 ; set ; hardback) | ISBN 9780367508494 (level 1, volume 1 ; set ; paperback) | ISBN 9781138304123 (level 1, volume 1 ; textbook ; hardback) | ISBN 9781138304147 (level 1, volume 1 ; textbook ; paperback) | ISBN 9781138304277 (level 1, volume 1 ; activity book ; hardback) | ISBN 9781138304314 (level 1, volume 1 ; activity book ; paperback) | ISBN 9780367509309 (level 1, volume 2 ; set ; hardback) | ISBN 9780367508531 (level 1, volume 2 ; set ; paperback) | ISBN 9780367483241 (level 1, volume 2 ; textbook ; hardback) | ISBN 9780367483210 (level 1, volume 2 ; textbook ; paperback) | ISBN 9780367483494 (level 1, volume 2 ; activity book ; hardback) | ISBN 9780367483364 (level 1, volume 2 ; activity book ; paperback) | ISBN 9780203730249 (level 1, volume 1 ; ebook) | ISBN 9780203730362 (level 1, volume 1 ; ebook) | ISBN 9781003051855 (level 1, volume 1 ; ebook) | ISBN 9781003039334 (level 1, volume 2 ; ebook) | ISBN 9781003039471 (level 1, volume 2 ; ebook) | ISBN 9781003051879 (level 1, volume 2 ; ebook)
Subjects: LCSH: Japanese language—Textbooks for foreign speakers—English. | Japanese language—Study and teaching—English speakers.
Classification: LCC PL539.5.E5 N554 2020 (print) | LCC PL539.5.E5 (ebook) | DDC 495.682/421—dc23
LC record available at https://lccn.loc.gov/2020026010
LC ebook record available at https://lccn.loc.gov/2020026011

ISBN: 978-0-367-48324-1 (hbk)
ISBN: 978-0-367-48321-0 (pbk)
ISBN: 978-1-003-03933-4 (ebk)

Typeset in Times New Roman
by Apex CoVantage, LLC

Visit the eResources: www.routledge.com/9781138304147

Contents

Act 7　びっくりしました。
I was surprised. 1

話す・聞く　Speaking and listening 3

Scene 7-1　バスがあるから便利でいいです。There's a bus, so it's nice
　　　　　　and convenient. 3
　　　　BTS 1 Affirmative non-past informal Verb forms 6
　　　　BTS 2 Adjective ～さ: form 寒さ、広さ 8
　　　　BTS 3 Commuting in Japan 8

Scene 7-2　みんな上まで登るの？ Is everyone climbing to the top? 10
　　　　BTS 4 More on んです 12
　　　　BTS 5 Noun₁, Noun₂, それから Noun₃ 14
　　　　BTS 6 Family 14

Scene 7-3　先に始めてって。She said to go ahead and start. 16
　　　　BTS 7 Negative informal Verb (～ない・～なかった) 18
　　　　BTS 8 Affirmative past informal Verb forms 19
　　　　BTS 9 Quotations with と・(っ)て 21
　　　　BTS 10 More on informal style 22

Scene 7-4　もう大丈夫だと思います。I think she's all right now. 23
　　　　BTS 11 More on 思いやり 24
　　　　BTS 12 Sentence と思う 25

Scene 7-5　同じ電車の人は……。People on the same train 27
　　　　BTS 13 Verb stem as a Noun 28
　　　　BTS 14 Sentence modifiers (歩く人) 29
　　　　BTS 15 同じ 29
　　　　BTS 16 それに 30

v

Scene 7-6　あれ？まさか。Huh? Impossible. 31
　　　　BTS 17 Location を 33
　　　　BTS 18 Negative of んです 33
　　　　BTS 19 Referring without identifying: 何とかスーパー 34

読み書き　Reading and writing 35
　　　　BTL 1 Expanded spelling 35

Scene 7-7R　あしたのミーティング Tomorrow's meeting 36
　　　　BTL 2 Written forms of んです 36
　　　　BTL 3 /f/ 37
　　　　BTL 4 /w/ 37
　　　　BTL 5 /sh/, /j/, and /ch/ 38
　　　　BTL 6 /t/ and /d/ 38
　　　　BTL 7 /v/ 39
　　　　BTL 8 /kw/ 39
　　　　BTL 9 /ts/ 40
　　　　BTL 10 Introduction to kanji 40

Scene 7-8R　行きますか？ Are you going? 41
　　　　BTL 11 Stroke order 43
　　　　BTL 12 送りがな Okurigana 44
　　　　BTL 13 How many kanji? 44
　　　　BTL 14 Keyboard input 44

Scene 7-9R　何時までですか。 Until what time? 45
　　　　BTL 15 Radicals 46

Act 8　おめでとうございます。
Congratulations. 47

話す・聞く　Speaking and listening 49

Scene 8-1　おめでとう。Congratulations (happy X). 49
　　　　BTS 1 Verb〜てみる 51
　　　　BTS 2 The こんな series 52
　　　　BTS 3 毎日 'Every day' 53

Scene 8-2　そんなに急がないで。Don't be in such a rush. 54
　　　　BTS 4 Negative commands and requests: 急がないで！ 56
　　　　BTS 5 〜んだから Because, as you must surely know 56
　　　　BTS 6 Humor 57

Scene 8-3　お邪魔します。(Entering someone's space) Sorry to barge in. 58
　　　　　　BTS 7　Visiting someone's home 60
　　　　　　BTS 8　Polite prefixes お〜 and ご〜 60
　　　　　　BTS 9　Male and female speech style 61

Scene 8-4　いらしたこと、ありますか? Have you been there? 62
　　　　　　BTS 10　Sentence + ことがある 64
　　　　　　BTS 11　Giving and appreciating gifts 65

Scene 8-5　優しそうなお母さん Your mother seems nice. 67
　　　　　　BTS 12　優しそう Appearance 69
　　　　　　BTS 13　だろう 70
　　　　　　BTS 14　相槌: そうなんだ、なるほど、確かに、やっぱり、ふうん、へえ 70

Scene 8-6　一回も帰ってないなあ。I haven't gone back even once, I guess. 72
　　　　　　BTS 15　Frequency expressions 74
　　　　　　BTS 16　Approximation：2、3回 74
　　　　　　BTS 17　1回も: Quantity + も + negative or affirmative Sentence 75

読み書き　　Reading and writing 76

シーン 8-7R　日本人ではなくて、アメリカ人です。American, not Japanese 76
　　　　　　BTL 1　Conventions vs. actual use ラーメン・らぁめん・拉麺 81
　　　　　　BTL 2　Numerals and dates in kanji 81

シーン 8-8R　よろしくお願いします。Nice to meet you. 83
　　　　　　BTL 3　Kanji readings: きょう・今日 84

シーン 8-9R　先生がいらっしゃいます。The professor is coming. 86

Act 9　一番好きなのは……。
My favorite one is 89

話す・聞く　Speaking and listening 91

Scene 9-1　ここ掃除したの誰? Who is it that cleaned up here? 91
　　　　　　BTS 1　More on sentence modifiers 92
　　　　　　BTS 2　Sentence + の 94

vii

- BTS 3 Transitive Verb 〜てある 94
- BTS 4 まったく 95

Scene 9-2　できた! Done! 96
- BTS 5 Go for the purpose of X: 食べに行く 97
- BTS 6 Fractions: 3分の1 98

Scene 9-3　教えるの好きだし。And I like teaching. 99
- BTS 7 Discussing occupations 101
- BTS 8 どうして・なぜ〜んですか・なんで〜んですか 101
- BTS 9 Sentence + し: 教えるの好きだし 102

Scene 9-4　一番行ってみたいところは? (What is) the place that you want to go and see the most? 103
- BTS 10 Comparison of three or more things: 一番 most 105
- BTS 11 都道府県 105
- BTS 12 温泉 Hot springs 105

Scene 9-5　聞く方? それとも弾く方? Listening? Or playing? 107
- BTS 13 だって(さ) + Sentence 109
- BTS 14 Giving personal reasons: もん・もの 110

Scene 9-6　何倍も上手でしょう。You are probably many times better. 111
- BTS 15 Specifying order of events: Verb 〜てから 113
- BTS 16 Interjections: ハヤ! 113
- BTS 17 Multiplication: 何倍 114
- BTS 18 Compliments and encouragement 114

読み書き　Reading and writing 115

シーン 9-7R　火曜日のレセプション Reception on Tuesday 115

シーン 9-8R　高校の先生だよね? High school teacher, right? 119
- BTL 1 Quotation marks 120
- BTL 2 Small っ at the end of a word or phrase 120
- BTL 3 漢語 123

シーン 9-9R　オハイオ州立大学のブラウンさん Brown-san from The Ohio State University 124

Act 10 次回、頑張ろう。
Let's do our best next time 129

話す・聞く　　Speaking and listening 131

Scene 10-1　切符買っておきますので。Because I'll buy tickets ahead of time........ 131

    BTS 1 Verb 〜ておく 132
    BTS 2 Let's Verb: Verb 〜よう・〜おう 132
    BTS 3 Giving an explanation: Sentence ので 134

Scene 10-2　絶対仕上げたい論文なので。Since it's a paper I absolutely
　　　　　　want to finish. 135

    BTS 4 X〜中 137
    BTS 5 Apologizing 138

Scene 10-3　お決まりでしょうか。Have you decided? 139

    BTS 6 More on politeness 142
    BTS 7 Togetherness 144

Scene 10-4　……言うこともあるかもしれません。There may even be times
　　　　　　when I say 145

    BTS 8 Sentence + かもしれない 146

Scene 10-5　分からないことが多くて……。There are many things
　　　　　　I don't understand 148

    BTS 9 More on こと 149
    BTS 10 Restoring self-image after a mishap 150

Scene 10-6　がっかりしないで。Don't be disappointed 151

    BTS 11 Sentence とか 154
    BTS 12 Comparison of two activities 154
    BTS 13 Verb stem 〜方・〜かた 155
    BTS 14 Assertion + じゃない 156
    BTS 15 The こう series 156

読み書き　　Reading and writing 157

シーン 10-7R　英語を見ていただけないでしょうか。Would you check
　　　　　　the English? 157

ix

シーン 10-8R 昨日デパートで買ってきました。I bought it yesterday at a department store. 161

シーン 10-9R 会社のほうにTELください。Call me at work 166

    BTL 1 Punctuation in long Sentences 167

Act 11   どうしたらいい？
What shall I do? 171

話す・聞く   Speaking and listening 173

Scene 11-1 必要でしたらおっしゃってください。If you need it, please say so 173

    BTS 1 Conditional 〜たら + non-past Sentence 175
    BTS 2 Business phone conversation 175
    BTS 3 X と・に代わる 176

Scene 11-2 それにしたら？ If you do that? 177

    BTS 4 Clothing and Verbs for wearing 179
    BTS 5 Giving/seeking suggestions それにしたら？ 179
    BTS 6 Excess: 〜過ぎ（る） 179

Scene 11-3 10月になったら長袖 Long sleeves as soon as it's October 181

    BTS 7 〜ことにする 182

Scene 11-4 知っていたら持ってきたんですけど……。If I had known, I would have brought it, but 184

    BTS 8 More on compliments 187
    BTS 9 Conditional 〜たら + past Sentence 知っていたら 'if I had known' 187
    BTS 10 X 〜的 X-like 187
    BTS 11 Extended family and terms of address and reference 188

Scene 11-5 休んだらよくなりました。When I rested, it got better 190

    BTS 12 Sentence 〜たら + past sentence: 休んだら良くなりました when I rested it got better 193
    BTS 13 あまり・あんまり + Affirmative Sentence 193
    BTS 14 Onomatopoeia 194

Scene 11-6 そう言ったら笑ってた。When I said that they laughed 195

    BTS 15 Storytelling 196

読み書き　Reading and writing 198

シーン 11-7R　お世話になっております。Thank you for your support 198
　　　　　　BTL 1 Business emails: お世話になっております、お疲れ様です、よろしくお願いいたします 199

シーン 11-8R　東京駅から電話します。I'll call from Tokyo Station 203
　　　　　　BTL 2 Expressions with multiple meanings: 出る 204

シーン 11-9R　駅から歩いて5分です。About a five-minute walk from the station 208

Act 12　母が送ってくれたんだけど……。 My mom sent it to me 213

話す・聞く　Speaking and listening 215

Scene 12-1　くれるの？ You'll give it to me? 215
　　　　　　BTS 1 Verbs of giving (from そと to うち): くれる・くださる↑ and
　　　　　　　　　〜てくれる・くださる 216
　　　　　　BTS 2 Sentence って・ということ 217
　　　　　　BTS 3 Local promotional characters 218

Scene 12-2　ちゃんと食べて(い)るかどうか心配なんだね。She's worried
　　　　　　about whether you're eating right or not.....................................219
　　　　　　BTS 4 Embedded yes/no questions 220
　　　　　　BTS 5 Verb 〜てしまう・ちゃう 221

Scene 12-3　誰か知らないんだけど……。I don't know who that is, but 222
　　　　　　BTS 6 Embedded information questions 224
　　　　　　BTS 7 Sentence Particle さ 225
　　　　　　BTS 8 で at the beginning of a Sentence 225

Scene 12-4　2時を過ぎると…… When it gets past 2:00. 226
　　　　　　BTS 9 Verbs of receiving: もらう・いただく↓ and 〜てもらう・いただく↓ 228
　　　　　　BTS 10 Adjective 〜く forms as Nouns 229
　　　　　　BTS 11 ただ + Sentence 230
　　　　　　BTS 12 朝に強い・弱い 230
　　　　　　BTS 13 Affirmative non-past Sentence$_1$ と Sentence$_2$ 230
　　　　　　BTS 14 Successive んです: 寝不足なんじゃないの？ 231

xi

Scene 12-5 並んでいると似てるかな? Maybe when we're standing side
by side we look alike?..233

    BTS 15 More on families: birth order 235
    BTS 16 Description + まま 235
    BTS 17 Verb 〜てほしい 235

Scene 12-6 喜んで案内してあげるよ。I would be happy to show you around. 237

    BTS 18 Verbs of giving (from うち to そと): あげる・差し上げる↓ and
    〜てあげる・差し上げる↓ 239
    BTS 19 Sentence + ことになる 240
    BTS 20 もしかしたら・もしかすると 240

読み書き Reading and writing 241

シーン 12-7R 漢字を勉強してください。Please study kanji. 241

    BTL 1 Joining Sentences in written style 241

シーン 12-8R ハイキングに行きませんか。Won't you go hiking? 246

シーン 12-9R 晩ご飯、いっしょにどう? How about dinner together? 251

Appendix A: Japanese-English glossary in *gojuuon* order 255
Appendix B: Japanese-English glossary by Act and Scene 302
Index 327

第7幕
Act 7

びっくりしました。

I was surprised.

住(す)めば都(みやこ)
Home is where you make it.

◆ 話す・聞く　Speaking and listening

Scene 7-1　バスがあるから便利でいいです。
There's a bus, so it's nice and convenient.

Amy wants to know how Takashi, a student from Japan, is getting along in the United States.

The script

エイミー	孝
キャンパスが広いから大変でしょう？	うん、いや、広くてびっくりしました。でもバスがあるから便利でいいですね。
寒さにはもう慣れました？	ううん、それはまだ。でも部屋の中は暖かくて、とても気持ちがいいですよね。それより4時ごろ暗くなるでしょう？それがきつい！

Amy	Takashi
The campus is big (lit. 'spacious'), so it must be hard, right?	Yeah, gosh, I was surprised at how big it was. But there's a bus, so it's nice and convenient.
Have you gotten used to the cold yet?	Not yet. But my room is warm inside, so it feels cozy, you know. Leaving that aside, it gets dark at 4:00, you know? That is tough.

単語と表現 Vocabulary and expressions

Nouns

キャンパス	campus
遠く	distant
便利(な)	convenient
不便(な)	inconvenient
楽(な)	easy, comfortable
静か(な)	quiet
寒さ	the cold
気持ち	feeling, sensation
天気	weather
食堂	dining hall, cafeteria
カフェテリア	cafeteria
売店	shop, stand, kiosk
ＡＴＭ	ATM

Verbs

(Noun Xに) 慣れる (慣れない)	get used/accustomed to (X)
びっくりする	be surprised
通う(通わない)	commute

Adjectives

広い	spacious, wide

狭い	narrow, confined
寒い	cold (climate)
冷たい	cold (to the touch), cold (personality)
暑い	hot (climate)
熱い	hot (non-weather, non-climate)
暖かい・温かい	warm (climate, personality)
涼しい	cool (climate)
暗い	dark
明るい	bright
気持ちがいい	good feeling
天気がいい	the weather is good
きつい	severe, intense, tight
辛い	tough, bitter (experience), painful
うれしい・嬉しい	happy, glad
悲しい	sad
寂しい・寂しい	lonely
ありがたい	grateful, thankful

Special expressions

うん	yes (informal)
ううん	no (informal)
寒さ	coldness
寒さには慣れました。	I got used to the cold.
暖かくて気持ちがいい	warm and good feeling
バスがある	there's a bus
それより	leaving that aside, apart from that, more importantly
(Noun X に・Adjective X 〜くて)びっくりする	be surprised (at X)

拡張 Expansion

Find out what the buildings on your university campus are called in Japanese.

Behind the Scenes

BTS 1 Affirmative non-past informal Verb forms

You have seen the informal forms of Adjectives and Noun です already. In this Act you encounter Verbs in their non-past informal form. This is also often called the "citation" form because this is how Verbs appear (are cited) in dictionaries. This form will be used from here on to list Verbs in the vocabulary section. In Act 2 you saw that some negative forms of Verbs end in *–nai* and some end in *–anai* (also see BTS 7 below). In fact, these forms represent two classes of Verbs: -RU Verbs and –U Verbs respectively. From here on, we will use –RU and –U to refer to these two kinds of Verbs. We will call the part of the Verb that precedes –RU and –U the "root." Here is how each Verb class changes from citation form to 〜ます form. You can find a complete list of all Verbs that come up in this book by type on the website. The best way to learn the various forms of Verbs is to use them in context repeatedly, rather than trying to remember the grammatical rules.

-RU Verbs: drop *-ru* and add *-masu*

いる exist	います
考える consider, think	考えます
見る look	見ます

Note that the stem (〜ます form without 〜ます) of -RU Verbs ends in *-i-* or *-e-*. So all -RU Verbs end in *-iru* or *-eru*. But not all Verbs that end in *-iru* or *-eru* are -RU Verbs. See the list of -U Verbs below.

-U Verbs: drop *-u* and add *-imasu*

Here are the consonants that precede this final -u.

Final mora	Consonant in final mora	Non-past	〜ます form
〜つ	t-	待つ wait	待ちます
〜る	r-	帰る return, go home	帰ります
		ある have, exist	あります
		いる need	いります
〜う	w-*	使う use	使います
		会う meet, see	会います
〜く	k-	書く write	書きます

〜ぐ	g-	急ぐ hurry	急ぎます
〜ぶ	b-	喜ぶ be glad	喜びます
〜む	m-	飲む drink	飲みます
〜ぬ	n-	死ぬ die	死にます
〜す	s-	話す talk	話します

* Verbs such as 使う and 会う may look like there is no consonant before the final -u, but there is an underlying -w- in these Verbs that will come back in other conjugations. (See BTS 7.)

Note also that 帰る is a -U Verb, even though it ends in -eru. Thus it is not always possible to know the 〜ます form of a Verb simply by looking at it. Verbs that end in -eru and -iru may be -RU (iru 'be, exist') or -U Verbs (iru 'need').

Polite -ARU Verbs: drop -ru and add -imasu

There are five Verbs in this class, of which you have learned three. The other two are listed here for reference.

Non-past	〜ます form
いらっしゃる go, come↑	いらっしゃいます
おっしゃる say↑	おっしゃいます
ござる be, exist+	ございます
なさる do↑	なさいます
くださる give↑	くださいます

Notice what makes these polite Verbs special: you might expect the 〜ます form of いらっしゃる to be いらっしゃります. But for historical reasons, this isn't the case.

Irregular Verbs

Non-past	〜ます form
来る come	来ます
する do	します

Since Core Sentences precede でしょう, the informal Verb form is what you see in combination with でしょう. (Review Act 4 BTS 2.)

日本語、わかるでしょう。	They'll probably understand Japanese.
先生、いらっしゃるでしょうか。	Do you suppose the professor will go?
神田さん、喜ぶでしょう。	Kanda-san will probably be happy.

Note that Takashi goes back and forth between formal and informal forms in Scene 1, using the informal form as the final form when he is more emotionally involved in what he says. In general, when people let down their emotional guard, they are likely to speak less formally.

Note also that informal questions do not need か.

この漢字、わかる？	Do you understand this kanji?
明日のパーティーへは行く？	Are you going to tomorrow's party?

BTS 2 Adjective 〜さ: form 寒さ、広さ

Many (though not all) Adjectives have a Noun form that indicates the extent of the Adjective.

寒さ	cold
高さ	height
広さ	breadth, width
暑さ	heat
明るさ	brightness
ワイオミングは寒さが厳しかったです。	The cold in Wyoming was brutal.
京都の暑さにびっくりした。	I was surprised at the heat in Kyoto.

BTS 3 Commuting in Japan

Japan has an efficient transportation network that consists of trains, subways, buses, and taxis. The complexity of this system can be a little daunting at first, but it's actually quite user-friendly. Greater Tokyo has an extensive railway network with over 2000 stations. One hub, Shinjuku Station, has over 200 exits! Trains and subways can be crowded, especially during rush hour. Tokyo's transportation network carries 40 million passengers per day (that's 14 billion people annually!) on over 4000 kilometers of track. It isn't just Tokyo that is crowded; annual passenger ridership at Umeda Station in Osaka ranks 4th in the world. Despite the heavy use, public transportation in Japan is safe and punctual, making it the most convenient (and often the fastest) way to get around, especially if you have to commute.

Tickets and passes for rail lines and subways are sold through vending machines in most stations. There is often a system map or list of destinations above the ticket machines—telling riders how much each destination costs from the current location. Riders enter through an automated ticket gate like the one you see in Illustration X. If you have a ticket, you insert it into the slot at the entrance and it is returned almost instantaneously as you step through the wicket. If you use an electronic pass, you simply pass your phone or smart card over the sensor and the wicket opens to allow you to pass through. If you find yourself with a problem, most urban stations have someone posted at the wicket who can help you reconcile your ticket or figure out how to get where you are going.

One thing you may notice is that commuter trains in Japan are relatively free of chatter. Japanese commuters typically read (paper or online), text, or sleep on the train.

Bicycles are another viable means of transportation in Japan, although many people pedal as far as the station, park their bicycles, and use public transportation to the office or workplace, which can be quite far from where they live.

Now go to the Activity Book for 練習 Practice and 腕試し Tryout.

Scene 7-2 みんな上まで登るの？
Is everyone climbing to the top?

Brian and Ichiro are discussing their upcoming outing with their aikido club friends.

The script

ブライアン	一郎
富士山楽しみだね。	うん。みんな上まで登るの？
いや、一郎君と僕でしょう？それから鈴木さん、あと鈴木さんの弟さんも行くんだ。	ということは全部で4人なんだね。あ、鈴木さんの弟さんって何才ぐらい？
さあ。一郎君と同じぐらいじゃない？	ああ、そうなんだ。じゃあ大丈夫だね。

Brian	Ichiro
I'm looking forward to Mt. Fuji, aren't you?	Yeah. Is everyone going to climb to the top?
No, you (Ichiro) and I, right? Then Suzuki-san, and also her younger brother is going, too.	So that means four in all . . . How old is Suzuki-san's brother?
Hmmm. Isn't he about the same (age) as you, Ichiro?	Ah, so that's it. Then it should be OK, right?

単語と表現 Vocabulary and expressions

Nouns

富士山	Mount Fuji
プール	pool
カラオケ	karaoke
マラソン	marathon
楽しみ	enjoyment, looking forward to
弟さん	younger brother

妹さん	younger sister
(お)兄さん	older brother
(お)姉さん	older sister
(ご)兄弟	brothers, siblings
(お)母さん	mother
(お)父さん	father
奥さん	wife
(ご)主人	husband
娘さん	daughter
息子さん	son
(ご)家族	family
弟↓	younger brother (humble)
妹↓	younger sister (humble)
兄↓	older brother (humble)
姉↓	older sister (humble)
母↓	mother (humble)
父↓	father (humble)
妻↓	wife (humble)
夫↓	husband (humble)
娘↓	daughter (humble)
息子↓	son (humble)
大人・おとな	adult
子供・こども	child
赤ちゃん	baby
男の子	boy
女の子	girl
先輩	senior
後輩	junior
知り合い	acquaintance

Verbs

登るらない	climb
下るらない	come/go down from
走るらない	run
泳ぐがない	swim

Classifiers

1 歳・才	1 year old	7 歳・才	7 years old
2 歳・才	2 years old	8 歳・才	8 years old
3 歳・才	3 years old	9 歳・才	9 years old
4 歳・才	4 years old	10歳・１０歳・才	10 years old
5 歳・才	5 years old	20歳	20 years old
6 歳・才	6 years old	何歳・才	how (many years) old

Special expressions

ということは	that is to say
行くんだ。	The fact is I'm going.
そうなんだ。	So that's it; I get it now.

拡張 Expansion

Confirm how you should refer to each of your family members or significant others in Japanese.
　　Talk to a few of your Japanese friends who are married and ask how they address their husband/wife. Also ask how they talk about them when talking to their friends or co-workers.

Behind the Scenes

BTS 4 More on んです

In Act 6 you encountered Adjectives in combination with んです. Recall that this pattern is used to provide reasons, general rationale, as well as background information that is relevant to understanding the context.

a. Verb + んです

For Verbs, the informal Verb form combines with んです. In questions, you should have reason to believe that the Sentence before んです is true. Imagine that you see a small flower on the sushi selection that just arrived at your table. You might say to your Japanese friend:

　　これ、食べるんですか？　　　　　So do I eat this?

In statements (as opposed to questions), recall that a sentence ending in んです can be a reason or rationale. Imagine that your friend wants you to join a group hike on Friday. You might respond:

すみません、仕事があるんです。	Sorry, I have to work.

A sentence with んです can also be background information that sets the stage for what is to follow.

山田さんが中国語がわかるんですが、今いません。	Yamada-san understands Chinese, but she's not here now.
先生と相談したいんですが、何時にいらっしゃいますか?	You see, I'd like to consult with the professor, but what time will she be in?
この写真ではよく見えないんですけど、真ん中の人、川上さんです。	You can't see very well in this photo, but the person in the middle is Kawakami-san.

b. Noun な + んです

When [Noun だ] occurs before んです, だ changes to な. The past form and negative forms stay the same.

Affirmative		**Negative**	
上手なんです。	The fact is, he's good at it.	上手じゃないんです。	The fact is, he's not good at it.
上手だったんです。	The fact is, he was good at it.	上手じゃなかったんです。	The fact is, he wasn't good at it.

When Ichiro says そうなんだ at the end of this Scene, he is indicating that he has understood the whole situation.

c. Informal forms of んです

The ん of んです is an abbreviated form of the Noun の meaning something like 'fact, matter, (intangible) thing.' In informal speech you will find ん before all forms of だ (だ, じゃない, だった, じゃなかった, etc.), otherwise you will find の.

Formal	**Informal**	
使うんです。	使うんだ。 or 使うの。	The fact is, I'm going to use it.
高いんです。	高いんだ。 or 高いの。	The fact is, it's expensive.
そうなんです。	そうなんだ。 or そうなの。	The fact is, it's true.

In the informal alternatives above, recall that the Noun alone sounds a bit softer—and for this reason is perceived to be feminine—while a [Noun だ] sentence is a bit more forceful or assertive.

Finally, recall that だ doesn't occur in questions. So the informal form of んですか is simply a rising の.

Formal	Informal	
使(つか)うんですか？	使(つか)うの？	So you're going to use it?
高(たか)いんですか？	高(たか)いの？	So it's expensive?
そうなんですか？	そうなの？	So that's how it is?

BTS 5 Noun₁, Noun₂, それから Noun₃

You have seen series of Nouns connected by と 'and' as well as とか 'things like' and あと 'and then.' It is also possible to list Nouns and connect them with それから 'and then,' which you saw in earlier Acts. Unlike あと, which indicates that the list is ending, それから might even appear more than once to keep the list going. The list then might be followed by a Phrase Particle, as with any other Noun.

恵理(えり)さん、(それから)ブライアンさん、それからサーシャさんが上(うえ)まで登(のぼ)るんですね。
So Eri-san, and then Brian-san, and then Sasha-san will be climbing to the top, right?

デザイン、(それから)マーケティング、それから企画(きかく)を勉強(べんきょう)したかった。
I wanted to study design, and then marketing, and then planning.

それから is matched by other members of the こ-そ-あ-ど series for referring to the next in a sequence: これから 'after this,' あれから 'after that (thing/event that we both know about),' どれから 'from which?'

これからどこに行きますか。 Where are you going after this?
あれからどうしました？ What did you do after that?

BTS 6 Family

Japan is very much like other societies where family and gender roles are in a state of flux. You will see some generalizations here about traditional family terms and roles, but there is a great deal of variation that depends on region, socio-economic class, and individual preference—especially in terms of what people want to be called.

First, note in the vocabulary list above that there are polite and humble forms for most family roles. Someone else's parents are always お母(かあ)さん and お父(とう)さん. When addressing your own parents, you might use お母(かあ)さん and お父(とう)さん, but there is a good deal of variation in what people call their parents—one hears everything from ママ and パパ to dialect terms to given names in modern Japan. People never address their own parents as 母(はは) or 父(ちち). When referring to your own parents to someone else, the humble terms (母(はは) and 父(ちち)) are appropriate in formal situations. Among friends, you might hear うちのお母(かあ)さん・お父(とう)さん, お母(かあ)さん・お父(とう)さん, dialect terms, as well as ママ・パパ.

Now go to the Activity Book for 練習 Practice and 腕試し Tryout.

Scene 7-3 先に始めてって。
She said to go ahead and start.

Brian and Hiroshi Kawamura, Brian's language partner and *senpai*, are at a regular meeting at the International Office. Elizabeth seems to be late.

The script

川村	ブライアン
エリザベスさん来ないね。何か連絡あった？	あ、はい。すみません。
何て？	遅れるから先に始めてって言ってました。
へえ。めずらしいね。どうしてかな。	忙しいんじゃないでしょうか。試験がたくさんあるから。
そうか。ブライアンはいいの？テスト、あるんでしょう？	いや、実は僕もかなり厳しいです。

Kawamura	Brian
Elizabeth-san isn't here, is she? Was there any word from her?	Ah, yes. I'm sorry.
What did she say?	She said she'll be late, so (we should) go ahead and start.
Huh. Unusual, isn't it? I wonder why.	Isn't it that she's busy? Because she has a lot of tests.
I see. Are you okay? You have tests, don't you?	Well, actually, I'm also having a tough time.

単語と表現 Vocabulary and expressions

Nouns

| 試験 (しけん) | test, exam |

Verbs

| 遅れる (おくれる) (-RU; 遅れない) | become late, run late |

Adjectives

| 珍しい (めずらしい) | unusual, rare |
| 厳しい (きびしい) | strict, severe, intense |

Phrase particles

QUOTATION + って・と

Special expressions

かなり	quite, considerably
ま(あ)	hmmm, well, come now, you might say
そうか。	I see.
どうして	why (formal)
何故・なぜ	why
なんで	why (informal)

Behind the Scenes

BTS 7 Negative informal Verb (〜ない・〜なかった)

In Act 2 you learned that Verbs have two negative forms—one in 〜ません and one in 〜ないです, — and that the 〜ない form without です is the informal negative form of the Verb. Below you see how the four Verb groups form the informal non-past negative. You can find a complete list of all Verbs that come up in this book by type on the website.

-RU Verbs: drop *-ru* and add *-nai*

Citation Form	Informal non-past negative	Informal past negative
できる can do, be finished	できない can't do	できなかった couldn't do
始める start	始めない won't start	始めなかった wouldn't start
いる is, exists	いない isn't, doesn't exist	いなかった wasn't, didn't exist
考える consider, think	考えない doesn't think	考えなかった didn't think

-U Verbs: drop *-u* and add *-anai*

Citation Form	Informal non-past negative	Informal past negative
喜ぶ be glad, be pleased	喜ばない won't be glad, won't be pleased	喜ばなかった wasn't glad, wasn't pleased
急ぐ hurry	急がない isn't in a hurry	急がなかった wasn't in a hurry
行く go	行かない won't go	行かなかった didn't go
読む read	読まない won't/doesn't read	読まなかった didn't read
ある have, exist	ない doesn't have, doesn't exist	なかった didn't have, didn't exist
使う use	使わない won't/doesn't use	使わなかった didn't use

Notice that as mentioned in BTS 1, the negatives of Verbs ending in a vowel plus -u (会う、使う、手伝う) acquire a -w- in their negative form (会わない、使わない、手伝わない).

Polite -ARU Verbs: drop *-u* and add *-anai*

There are five Verbs in this category, of which you have learned three. The other two are listed here for reference.

Citation Form	Informal non-past negative	Informal past negative
いらっしゃる go, come↑	いらっしゃらない won't go, come↑	いらっしゃらなかった didn't go, come↑
おっしゃる say↑	おっしゃらない won't say↑	おっしゃらなかった didn't say↑
ござる be, exist (polite)	ござらない won't be, won't exist+ (rarely used)	ござらなかった wasn't didn't exist+ (rarely used)
なさる do↑	なさらない won't do↑	なさらなかった didn't do↑
くださる give↑	くださらない won't give↑	くださらなかった didn't give↑

Irregular Verbs

Citation Form	Informal non-past negative	Informal past negative
来る come	来ない won't come	来なかった didn't come
する do	しない won't/doesn't do	しなかった didn't do

This 〜ない form behaves like an Adjective (has an 〜い form and a 〜かった form) and combines with です for an alternative formal form of the Verb.

Citation form	Formal non-past negative	Formal past negative
できる can do, be finished	できません or できないです can't do	できませんでした or できないかったです couldn't do
行く go	いきません or 行かないです won't go	行きませんでした or 行かなかったです didn't go
する do	しません or しないです won't/doesn't do	しませんでした or しなかったです didn't do

BTS 8 Affirmative past informal Verb forms

In this Scene you also find Verbs in their past informal affirmative form. The past informal affirmative is similar to the 〜て form except that it ends with 〜た・だ instead of 〜て・で. Here is how each Verb class changes from citation form to past informal form. You can find a complete list of all Verbs that are introduced by type on the website.

-RU Verbs: drop -る and add -た

Citation form	〜た form
できる can do, be finished	できた
いる exist	いた
見る look	見た
食べる eat	食べた
出る leave, go out	出た

-U Verbs: the 〜た form depends on the consonant in the final mora of the citation form

Final mora	Changes to	Consonant in final mora	Citation form	〜た form
〜つ	〜った	t-	待つ wait	待った
〜る	〜った	r-	帰る return, go home	帰った
			ある have, exist	あった
〜う	〜った	w-	使う use	使った
			会う meet, see	会った
〜く	〜いた	k-	歩く walk	歩いた
			書く write	書いた
〜ぐ	〜いだ	g-	急ぐ hurry	急いだ
〜ぶ	〜んだ	b-	喜ぶ be glad, be pleased	喜んだ
〜む	〜んだ	m-	飲む drink	飲んだ
〜ぬ	〜んだ	n-	死ぬ die	死んだ
〜す	〜した	s-	話す talk	話した

The Verb 行く is slightly different from other –ku Verbs since its past form is 行った.

Polite -ARU Verbs: drop -る and adding -った

Remember, there are five Verbs in this category, of which you have learned three. The other two are listed here for reference.

Citation form	**〜た form**
いらっしゃる go, come↑	いらっしゃった or いらした
おっしゃる say↑	おっしゃった
ござる be, exist + (rarely used)	ござった (rarely used)
なさる do↑	なさった
くださる give↑	くださった

Irregular Verbs

Citation form	**〜た form**
来る come	来た
する do	した

Here is a chart with all forms of the three Core Sentences in formal and informal, affirmative and negative, and past and non-past forms.

	Formal, affirmative	Informal affirmative	Formal, negative	Informal, negative
Verb: non-past	見ます	見る	見ないです、見ません	見ない
Verb: past	見ました	見た	見ませんでした 見なかったです	見なかった
Adjective: non-past	古いです	古い	古くありません 古くないです	古くない
Adjective: past	古かったです	古かった	古くありませんでした 古くなかったです	古くなかった
Nounです: non-past	車です	車（だ）	車じゃありません 車じゃないです	車じゃない
Nounです: past	車でした	車だった	車じゃありませんでした 車じゃなかったです	車じゃなかった

BTS 9 Quotations with と・(っ)て

You have seen Phrase Particle と・(っ)て before with Verbs of saying such as 言う、申す、and おっしゃる used for telling what someone or something is called. In fact, this pattern can be used more generally for quoting what others have said, using other Verbs such as 聞く、読む, and 書く. Often the Verb is left out completely when context makes it clear whether the subject heard, read, or wrote the information. When reporting someone else's speech, speakers are likely to use the 言っています (when the speech is ongoing or when the speech has some sort of ongoing impact) or 言っていました (when the speech was in the past). When speakers report what they have heard, they are likely to use the 聞いています form rather than a simple past.

先に始めてって言っています。	She's telling us to go ahead and start.
先生も早く帰るとおしゃっていました。	The professor said she would go home early, too.
今学期はテストがあまりないって聞いています。	I've heard that there aren't going to be many tests this term.
明日は弟さん、来ないって。	Her younger brother wouldn't come tomorrow, she said.

Contrast this with a simple past form which presents something as a fact.

あした試験があるって聞いたよ。	I heard there's a test tomorrow!
先に始めてって言ったから始めたんです。	She said go ahead and start, so we did.

BTS 10 More on informal style

In this Scene you see a mix of formal and informal forms. Brian remains more formal than Hiroshi because he is younger (後輩) and a newcomer. Notice that he uses 〜ます・です throughout. Hiroshi's style is very relaxed. It includes:

a   the use of informal 来ないね 'She hasn't come' and あった 'there was (a phone call)'
b   the use of quotative て without a Verb such as 言いました. This use of （っ）て is extremely common in reporting or asking about what others said.
c   [Sentence + の] and [Sentence + んじゃない？], both informal forms of [Sentence + んです].
e   そうか—the informal version of そうですか.

Now go to the Activity Book for 練習 Practice and 腕試し Tryout.

Scene 7-4 もう大丈夫だと思います。
I think she's all right now.

Brian's mother is visiting from the U.S. and has come to an event with his aikido club, but became ill. Later, he thanks Suzuki-san for looking after her.

The script

ブライアン	鈴木
このあいだはありがとうございました。	楽しかったですね。
母がご迷惑をおかけして、すみませんでした。	とんでもない。お加減、どうですか?
はい、おかげさまで、もう大丈夫だと思います。	どうぞお大事になさってください。
ありがとうございます。すみませんでした。	いえいえ。

Brian	Suzuki
Thank you for the other day.	It was fun, wasn't it!
I'm sorry that my mother was a hassle for you.	Not at all. How is she feeling?
Yes, thanks to you, she's fine now, I think.	Please tell her to take care of herself.
Thank you. Again, I'm sorry.	No, no.

単語と表現 Vocabulary and expressions

Nouns

このあいだ	the other day, recently
(ご)迷惑(な)・(する)	trouble, bother
(お)加減	personal condition
具合	condition
(お)大事(な)	important, valuable

23

Verbs

かける (-RU; かけた)	cause (lit. 'hang (something)')
思う (-U; 思った)	think
なさる↑ (-ARU, なさった)	do (honorific)

Adjectives

楽しい	fun
悪い	bad
具合がいい・悪い	be in good/bad condition; feel well/unwell

Special expressions

(ご)迷惑をかける	cause someone trouble
(ご)迷惑になる	become an annoyance
とんでもない	not at all
おかげさまで	thanks to you
お大事に	take care

Behind the Scenes

BTS 11 More on 思いやり

Although this is not an extremely formal interaction, a good deal of ritual speech is used. At the same time that Brian thanks Suzuki-san for accommodating his mother (once at the beginning and again at the end of the exchange), he apologizes (twice!) for causing concern. He also gives credit to others as he reports his mother's improved condition. Suzuki-san is very solicitous of her welfare, asking if she is all right and encouraging her to take care of herself. These are not idle expressions on the part of these speakers. Recall from Act 3 that 思いやり (concern for others) is a highly valued trait in Japan. Noticing and using expressions of 思いやり are a signal that you understand Japanese culture.

BTS 12 Sentence と思う

An informal sentence plus the Phrase Particle と followed by 思う 'think' is used to express uncertainty or opinion:

時間がかかると思います。	I think it will take time.
悲しいと思う?	Do you think it's sad?
お姉さんだと思う。	I think it's her older sister.

When you are reporting or conjecturing what others think, it is best to use 思っている. 思う also sounds more definitive than 思っている, so if you are uncertain, the latter is preferable.

社長は何と思っているんでしょうか。	I wonder what the president is thinking.
9万円は高いと思っているけど。	I'm thinking ¥90,000 is expensive, but . . .

Either the sentence that precedes と思う or the Verb 思う might be in affirmative or negative, non-past or past. Consider the more common case where the sentence before と思う changes in each case:

学生は分かると思う。	I think the students do/will understand.
学生は分からないと思う。	I think the students don't/won't understand.
学生は分かったと思う。	I think the students understood.
学生は分からなかったと思う。	I think the students didn't understand.

Less common but also possible is that the form of 思う might change:

便利だと思う。	I think it's convenient.
便利だと思った。	I thought it was convenient.
便利だとは思わない。	I don't think it's convenient. (But the price is right, so it's up to you.)
便利だとは思わなかった。	I didn't think it would be convenient. (But the view may be worth the long walk to the subway.)

Also contrast:

| 来ないと思う。 | I think he won't come. (My opinion is that he will not come. What I think is that he will not come.) |
| 来ると<u>は</u>思わない。 | I don't think he will come. |

Note that Phrase Particle <u>は</u> (underlined above) occurs when the function of は is to carve out a subset from a larger circle of possibilities. 'I may think many things, but "convenient" is not among them.' Similarly, 'I may think many things but among them is not that he will show up.' This use is especially appropriate when you want to be vague and therefore more polite.

Note also that だ is normally required with a Noun before と思う (便利だと思う). You will hear native speakers drop this だ, but you should be cautious about doing so yourself. It is never dropped in formal writing.

Now go to the Activity Book for 練習 Practice and 腕試し Tryout.

Scene 7-5 同じ電車の人は……。
People on the same train

The aikido club outing is almost over. Suzuki-san is trying to organize the group of people into subgroups.

The script

鈴木	ブライアン
ええと、同じ電車の人は同じところに集まりましょう。	僕は母と歩きです。
え？歩くんですか？	近いですから。それに、雨ももう降らないと思いますから。
そうですか。えっと、ほかに歩く人、いますか？	

Suzuki	Brian
Ummm, let's have people on the same train all assemble at the same place.	I'll walk with my mother.
What? You're going to walk?	Because it's close. And besides, I don't think it's going to rain anymore, so . . .
I see. Well then, are there other people who will walk?	

単語と表現 Vocabulary and expressions

Nouns

歩き	walk

Verbs

集まる (-U; 集まった)	get together, assemble
降る (-U; 降った)	precipitate, fall (i.e. rain)

Special expressions

同じX	the same X
それに	what's more, besides
ほかに	in addition, besides
歩く人	people who (will) walk

Behind the Scenes

BTS 13 Verb stem as a Noun

In this Scene, Brian says that he and his mother will walk using 歩きです; that is, a Verb stem (〜ます form without 〜ます) used as a Noun and combined with です. Compared to 歩きます, this form sounds a bit more detached, as if it were a description of the Scene rather than an expression of a willful act. So it is a bit less confrontational when Brian tells Suzuki-san that he and his mother are not planning to do what the others do. Not all Verbs occur in this pattern, but below you see more examples.

月曜日は休みだと思います。	I think that Monday is a holiday.
行きは歩きで、帰りはバスです。	We're going on foot and returning on the bus.
読み書きの試験がありました。	We had a reading and writing test.

You have already seen 休み as a Noun. Can you tell the Verb from which it is derived?

BTS 14 Sentence modifiers (歩く人)

You have seen Adjectives modifying Nouns (広い部屋 'spacious room'). An Adjective is a Core Sentence, and, in fact, any Core Sentence can modify a Noun. In this Scene you see an informal Verb preceding a Noun in 歩く人 'people who are going to walk.' The Verb might be affirmative or negative, non-past or past. Here are other examples.

わからない学生	students who don't understand
作ったケーキ	the cake I made
集まる駅は新宿じゃないですか？	Isn't the station where we will gather Shinjuku?
急いでいる仕事	work that requires quick action

Actually, you have already seen what happens to [Noun だ] when it precedes a Noun. It changes either to の or な.

大丈夫な道	a street that is safe
課長の山田さん	the Yamada-san who is a section head
学生じゃない人	a person who isn't a student

Sentence modifiers can be much more complex than this, as you will discover in Act 10.

BTS 15 同じ

同じ is a unique Noun in that it connects directly to other Nouns without の or な.

同じ電車	the same train
同じ大学の先輩	a senior (to me) from the same university
同じスケジュールのクラスメート	a classmate with the same schedule

When something is the same as something else, you see [Noun と同じ].

神田さんと同じのにします。	I'll make mine the same as Kanda-san's.
先生と同じ電車です。	(I'm on) the same train as the professor.

BTS 16 それに

それに is used to list evidence or reasons in a sequence.

このアパート、きれいですね。それに地下鉄が近いから便利でいいですねえ。

This apartment is clean. What's more, it's close to the subway, so it's convenient, isn't it!

隣のらーめん、おいしいですよ。それに安いから、あそこに行きましょう。

The ramen next door is tasty! Besides that, it's cheap, so let's go there.

Now go to the Activity Book for 練習 Practice and 腕試し Tryout.

Scene 7-6 あれ？まさか。 Huh? Impossible

Brian and Kawamura-senpai thought they knew where they were going, but realize they are lost.

The script

ブライアン	川村
タウンシネマって、この道でしたよね？	うん、これをまっすぐ行って、二つ目の交差点で左へ曲がるんじゃない？……あれ？ナビがおかしい。
まさか。……あ、ほんとだ。変ですね。	ちょっと待って。……はい、直った。
あ、あった！あれですね？薬局と何とかスーパーの間。	スーパー？ああ、服部スーパーだね。分かった。行くよ！

Brian	Kawamura
Huh? Town Cinema was this way, wasn't it?	Yeah, you go straight along here, make a left at the second intersection . . . oh, the GPS is acting strange.
No way! . . . Oh, it really is weird.	Wait a minute . . . Oh, now it's OK.
Ah, there it is! That over there, right? Between the drug store and the something supermarket. I can't tell.	Supermarket? Ah, it's Hattori Supermarket. Got it. Let's go

単語と表現 Vocabulary and expressions

Nouns

| タウンシネマ | Town Cinema |
| 映画館 | movie theater |

道	street
通り	way, road, street, avenue
(この・その・あの)辺	area, vicinity
まっすぐ	straight
交差点	intersection
信号	traffic light
突き当たり	end (of a street, hallway, etc.)
角	corner
ナビ	GPS, navigator
変(な)	weird, odd, strange
ほんと	really (short, informal form of ほんとう)
薬局	pharmacy
交番	police box
服部スーパー	Hattori Supermarket
マンション	condominium
間	interval, space between

Verbs

曲がる (-U; 曲がった)	turn, make a turn
戻る (-U; 戻った)	go back
着く (-U; 着いた)	arrive
直る・治る (-U; 直った・治った)	get better, get fixed; restore (itself)

Adjectives

おかしい	funny, weird, odd, strange
危ない	dangerous

Special expressions

あれ?	What? Huh?
まさか。	No way. Never. (interjection)

何<ruby>なん</ruby>とかスーパー	such-and-such/something-or-other supermarket
XとYの間<ruby>あいだ</ruby>	between X and Y

拡張 Expansion

Find out what various landmarks near your university campus, workplace, and home would be called in Japanese.

Behind the Scenes

BTS 17 Location を

A place Noun followed by Phrase Particle を indicates the area or range through which a motion (such as 行く, 来る, 帰る, 通る, 歩く, 登る, etc.) takes place.

これをまっすぐ行くんですね?	We go straight along here, right?
コンビニの交差点を曲がってください。	Please turn at the intersection where there's a convenience store

BTS 18 Negative of んです

You have seen んです in both formal and informal style:

ちょっとわからないんです。	I don't quite understand.
ちょっとわからないの。 or ちょっとわからないんだ。	

Remember that the ん・の of んです is a Noun, so it also has a negative form in じゃない・じゃありません. This is most commonly seen in questions when you want to confirm your opinion, meaning (literally) 'isn't it the case that . . .?'

2万円って、高いんじゃない?	Isn't ¥20,000 a lot?
すみません。これ、ちょっと違うんじゃないでしょうか。	Sorry. Wouldn't this be wrong?

33

サイズ、ダブルXですよ。大きいんじゃないですか？

It's size extra extra large! Isn't that big?

鈴木さんには2週間ぐらい会ってないけど、大変なんじゃない？今の仕事。

We haven't seen Suzuki-san for two weeks, but isn't it tough—the work he has now?

BTS 19 Referring without identifying: 何とかスーパー

There are many ways to refer to something without identifying it by name. 何とか in place of a Noun signals that there is something you cannot recall, identify, or read. In this Scene, Brian can read "スーパー" on the sign, but cannot read the kanji combination before that. Given the extraordinary number of compound words that contain katakana and kanji components, you can see that using 何とか appropriately is a useful learning strategy.

A: 新しいインターンの名前、知っていますか？
B: ええと、山本さんですよね。山本何とかさん。
A: 日本語で何とかっていいますけど、ええと……
B: 交番ですか？
A: そう、そう。交番！交番に行ってね……

A: Do you know the name of the new intern?
B: Uhh, It's Yamamoto-san. Yamamoto something-or-other.
A: You call it so-and-so in Japanese, but uhh . . .
B: You mean *kooban*?
A: Right, right. *Kooban!* You go as far as the *kooban* . . .

Now go to the Activity Book for 練習 Practice and 腕試し Tryout.

Then do 評価 Assessment activities.

◆ 読み書き Reading and writing

Between the lines

BTL 1 Expanded spelling

Often, Japan imports words that contain sounds not found in Japanese. For the most part, pronunciation of those words is adapted to the closest Japanese alternative. You saw, for example, that English /v/ can be represented in Japanese by /b/ morae バン for *van*. More recently, Japan has adapted katakana to represent those sounds that do not exist in Japanese. This will be called here "expanded spelling."

Scene 7-7R あしたのミーティング Tomorrow's meeting

Kanda-san was copied on an email message from Division Chief Yagi regarding a meeting on July 6th.

テキスト Text

From: Reiko Yagi <ryagi@ogaki.co.jp>
Date: Tuesday, July 5, 2020 at 10:32 PM
To: John Williams <jwilliams@ogaki.co.jp>
CC: Kenta Kanda <kkanda@ogaki.co.jp >
Subject: RE: Meeting

ウィリアムズさん

あしたのミーティングなのですが、１２：００からジェイソンさんのオフィスでします。よろしくお願いします。

八木

From: Reiko Yagi <ryagi@ogaki.co.jp>
Date: Tuesday, July 5, 2020 at 10:32 PM
To: John William <jwilliam@ogaki.co.jp>
CC: Kenta Kanda <kkanda@ogaki.co.jp >
Subject: RE: Meeting

Williams-san,
About tomorrow's meeting, it will be held at 12:00 in Jason-san's office. Thank you.
Yagi

BTL 2 Written forms of んです

You have seen formal and informal forms of んです in spoken style, and in this Act learned that ん is a contracted form of の that occurs before forms of です. In formal written

Japanese, の does not contract. So while in spoken style you might hear あしたのミーティングなんですが, in formal written style (such as the foregoing email) you are more likely to see あしたのミーティングなのですが. Note that in casual written style such as interactions on social media, you may still see ん instead of の.

BTL 3 /f/

Morae beginning with an /f/ sound (other than those represented by フ) are represented by フ + small ア, イ, エ, or オ. Thus ファ フィ フェ フォ.

Examples

Names

1. クリストファーがしますが、いいですか。 Christopher will do it. Is it okay?
2. フォードさんがするのですが、いいですか。 It's that Ford-san will do it. Is it okay?

Places

1. カフェテリアのおいしさ the cafeteria's tastiness
2. フィンランドのさむさ Finland's cold (weather)
3. ハートフォードのよさ Hartford's good quality
4. カリフォルニアのあたたかさ California's warm (weather)

Others

1. メンズファッションは３Ｆでしょうか。 Is men's fashion on the third floor?
2. オフィスは３Ｆなのでしょうか。 So the office is on the third floor, right?
3. ファストフードにしてもいいでしょうか。 Is it okay to decide on fast food (for a meal)?
4. フォローしてもいいのでしょうか。 So is it okay to follow?

BTL 4 /w/

Morae beginning with a /w/ sound (other than those represented by ワ or ウ) are represented by ウ + small イ, エ, or オ. Thus ウィ ウェ ウォ.

Examples

Names

1. ウィリアムさんのよさ William-san's good quality
2. ダーウィンさんのいいところ Darwin-san's good quality

Places

1. ウィーンにはウィーンのよさがある から……。 Vienna has it's good qualities, so . . .
2. デラウェアのさむさにびっくりしました。 I was surprised by the cold in Delaware.
3. ウィスコンシンのひろさはどのぐらい ですか。 About how big is Wisconsin?

Others

1. ビールよりウォッカでしょう。 Vodka is probably (better) than beer.
2. ウェイトレスよりウェイターのほうがお おい。 There are more waiters than waitresses.

BTL 5 /sh/, /j/, and /ch/

Morae /sh/, /j/, and /ch/ before what is called "long a" (as in *day*) or "short e" (as in *check*) are represented by シェ、ジェ、and チェ, respectively.

Examples

Names

1. シェーンさんはジェーンさんよりあかるい。 Shane-san is more cheerful than Jane-san.
2. ジェシカのアパートよりチェスターのアパ ートのほうがせまい。 Chester's apartment is smaller than Jessica's.
3. ジェイソンよりシェーンのほうがおとなしいです。 Shane is more quiet/mature than Jason.

Other

1. シェフをしている。 I'm working as a chef.
2. なにをチェックしているんですか。 What are you checking?
3. なにをシェアしているのでしょうか。 What is he sharing?
4. ジャーマンシェパードがはしっているよ。 That German shepherd is running (away).

BTL 6 /t/ and /d/

Words with /t/ or /d/ before "long e" or "short i" (as in *teak* or *tick*) are represented by ティ and ディ, while /du/ (as in *due*) is represented by デュ.

Examples

Names

1. ディーンがするよ。　　　　　　　　Dean will do this.
2. デュークがしているよ。　　　　　　Duke is doing that.
3. マーティンがしているんだよ。　　　It's that Martin is doing it.

Others

1. アンディーはありますか。　　　　　　Does Andy have it?
2. ＤＶＤディスクはあるのですか。　　　Is it that you have the DVD disks?
3. パーティーがあるんでしょう。　　　　It's probably that there's a party.
4. デュエットするんですか。　　　　　　Is it that you are doing a duet?
5. ウィキペディアだよ。　　　　　　　　It's Wikipedia.
6. インディアナなんだよ。　　　　　　　It's in Indiana, you see.
7. デューティーフリーなのでしょうか。　I wonder if it's that it's duty-free?

BTL 7 /v/

/v/ morae may be represented by バ, ビ, ブ, ベ, or ボ. But they may also be represented by ヴ + small ア, イ, エ, or オ.

Examples

Names

1. ヴィヴィアン(ビビアン)です。　　　　It's Vivian.
2. ベートーヴェン(ベートーベン)なんです。　It's that it's Beethoven.

Other

1. ベニス(ヴェニス)のまんなかだよ。　　It's in the middle of Venice.
2. １００ヴォルト(ボルト)なんだよ。　　So it's 100 volts.
3. ヴィーガン(ビーガン)なのです。　　　I'm a vegan, you see.
4. ミロのヴィーナス(ビーナス)ってなんでしょう。　What is the Venus de Milo?
5. ヴァイオリン(バイオリン)なんでしょう。　So it's a violin.
6. ヴォルヴォ(ボルボ)２０１９なんだ。　It's a 2019 Volvo, you see.

BTL 8 /kw/

Words with /kw/ (as in *quick*) will be represented by ク + small ア, イ, エ, or オ.

39

Examples

1. クォーターがいるんだ。   It's that I need a quarter/there is a quarter of it.
2. フレンチクォーターです。   It's the French Quarter (in New Orleans).
3. クェスチョンマークがいるんです。   It's that you need a question mark.
4. クォーテーションマークがいるんでしょう?   So I need quotation marks, right?

BTL 9 /ts/

Words with /ts/ before /a/, /i/, /e/, or /o/ (as in Mozart) are represented by ツ+ small ア, イ, エ, or オ.

Examples

1. フィレンツェよりヴェネツィアのほうがいいんです。   It's that Venice is better than Florence.
3. モーツァルトのメロディーのかなしさ   the sadness of Mozart's melodies
4. イタリアのカンツォーネ、知ってる?   Do you know what an Italian canzone is?

Now go to the Activity Book for 練習 Practice.

BTL 10 Introduction to kanji

In the next section you will begin the study of kanji. Eight characters will be introduced in this Act, and approximately twenty-five in each Act that follows. Each entry will provide the character with a number, the Japanese pronunciation(s) or "reading(s)" (*kunyomi*) in hiragana, the pronunciation(s) or "reading(s)" based on the original Chinese (*onyomi*) in katakana, and a translation, along with examples. The symbols #, +, and ¥ mark new kanji readings or usages that are not introduced in the Speaking/Listening portion prior to the lesson.

- #: for your reference only. These expressions won't appear in practice activities until they are introduced in the Speaking and Listening portion.
- +: new expression that is to be learned. These may appear in practice activities.
- ¥: for those expressions that have already been introduced but when written in Japanese include kanji that have not yet been introduced. The kanji representation is for reference only.

Note that kanji readings that are introduced in this textbook are not exhaustive.
    Sometimes additional kanji readings are included with a reference to the lessons where they will appear in parentheses. This occurs when certain readings require the introduction of additional vocabulary or kanji.

Scene 7-8R 行(い)きますか？ Are you going?

Kanda-san received an email message from his supervisor at Ogaki Trading, Yagi-bucho.

テキスト Text

From: Reiko Yagi <ryagi@ogaki.co.jp>
Date: Tuesday, February 27, 2019 at 11:06 AM
To: Kenta Kanda kkanda@ogaki.co.jp
Subject: RE: バースデーパーティー

サーシャさんのバースデーパーティーは３月１８日だったと思います*。
行きますか？

八木

*思(おも)います. You will learn this kanji in 10-8R (#69).

From: Reiko Yagi <ryagi@ogaki.co.jp>
Date: Tuesday, February 27, 2019 at 11:06 AM
To: Kenta Kanda <kkanda@ogaki.co.jp >
Subject: RE: バースデーパーティー

I think Sasha-san's birthday party was on March 18th.
Will you go?
Yagi

文字と例　**Kanji with examples**

Common font　　　　　　　　　　　　　　　　**Handwritten version**

#1.　日　ひ か　ニチ　　　　　　sun, [naming and　
　　　　　ジツ (See kanji #9)　　counting classifier
　　　　　　　　　　　　　　　　for days of the
　　　　　　　　　　　　　　　　month and week]

1.　＋日　　　　　　　　　　　　day
2.　あの日　　　　　　　　　　　that day
3.　まだ６日です。　　　　　　　It's still the sixth (or six days).
4.　１８日　　　　　　　　　　　the eighteenth, eighteen days
5.　もう２日になりますよ。　　　It's already the second (or two days).
6.　２０日にしましょう。　　　　Let's decide on the twentieth.
7.　２０日¹しましょう。　　　　Let's do it for twenty days.
8.　１日あると思うけど……。　　I think it's one day long.
9.　１日にあると思うけど……。　I think it's on the first of the month.

#2.　月　つき　ガツ　ゲツ　　　moon, [naming and　月
　　　　　　　　　　　　　　　　counting classifier
　　　　　　　　　　　　　　　　for months]

1.　＋月　　　　　　　　　　　　moon, month
2.　２月にします。　　　　　　　I decided on February./I will do it in
　　　　　　　　　　　　　　　　February.
3.　３か月²　　　　　　　　　　three months
4.　（月）　　　　　　　　　　　Monday (abbreviation)
5.　＃月日　　　　　　　　　　　date

#3.　行　い（く）　ギョウ　　　go, line　
　　　　　コウ (See kanji #103)

1.　行くんですか。　　　　　　　So you'll go?
2.　行かない月　　　　　　　　　the month I won't go
3.　行った日　　　　　　　　　　the day I went
4.　行かなかった。　　　　　　　I didn't go.
5.　行ってきます。³　　　　　　See you later.
6.　行ってらっしゃい。　　　　　See you later.
7.　行きです。　　　　　　　　　It's on the way.
8.　行きにしたんだよ。　　　　　It's that I did that on the way.
9.　＃行　　　　　　　　　　　　10 lines

42

Additional kanji with examples

#4. 来　く(る)　き(た)　　　come, (up)coming　　　　　来
　　　　こ(ない)　ライ

1. 来る月　　　　　　　the month I come
2. 来ないから……。　　He won't come here, so . . .
3. 来たと思います。　　I think he came.
4. 来なかった日　　　　the day I didn't come
5. 来てください。　　　Please come.
6. 来月しましょう。　　Let's do this next month.
7. 来月にしましょう。　Let's decide on next month.

BTL 11 Stroke order

As with hiragana and katakana, stroke order is extremely important when writing kanji. For kanji, the cursive version of a character can look quite different from its original shape. Take a good look at the handwritten models below. All represent 来月日本に行きます。 'I will go to Japan next month.' in vertical writing. If the writer does not use correct stroke order, the cursive version is impossible to write. More practically, online dictionaries and apps allow you to use a stylus to write characters in order to look them up. The app will not recognize a character if the strokes are in the wrong order. (Remember also that hiragana characters actually derive from the cursive version of kanji. Look again at the chart in BTL 1, Act 1.)

The same sentence (来月日本にいきます。) written in 楷書 (printed style), 行書 (semi-cursive style), and 草書 (cursive or 'grass style'). (courtesy of Ayako Horii)

BTL 12 送りがな *Okurigana*

Hiragana that are used to write the endings for Verbs and Adjectives (for example 食べました or 高かった) are called 送りがな. Word processing will provide the correct 送りがな in most instances, but sometimes 送りがな distinguishes words that are related but different in meaning. For example, 話 (with no 送りがな) is a Noun meaning 'story,' while 話し is a form of the Verb 話します and means 'talk' or 'spoken words.' When you write by hand, it is important to use the correct 送りがな, much as it is important to spell correctly in English.

BTL 13 How many kanji?

People often ask how many kanji there are. In the case of Japanese, there is a list of 2136 characters 常用漢字 that are taught in grades 1 through 12 in Japan. Most people know more than this, especially if they go to college where specialized vocabulary is required for various fields of study.

BTL 14 Keyboard input

You learned how to input Japanese kana syllabaries in earlier lessons. When you input text on a computer, you have two options. If you press the Return/Enter key, the conversion process ends and you have kana. (Presumably this is what you have been doing so far.) If you press the 変換 'change' key (usually the space bar), you will see a selection of possible realizations for your input. Select the one that is correct, and press return. Many machines (especially phones) allow you to input using a stylus. Whether you use text or a stylus, your input must be accurate (long vowels and consonants for text, stroke order for a stylus) in order to get the correct output.

If you input text on a phone, you should see possible realizations for the text that you enter as you type.

If the foregoing does not work, check online for Japanese input on the word processing software or computer/phone that you are using.

Now go to the Activity Book for 練習 Practice.

Notes

1. Young people are starting to use にじゅうにち for both naming and counting. When counting, some people choose to use にじゅうにち to differentiate it from naming (はつか).
2. This can also be written using katakana: ３カ月 or ３ケ月 (reduced or full size). The reading is the same for all options.
3. Note that きます 'come' is usually written in hiragana when it follows a 〜て form. Otherwise it is written in kanji: 来ます (see kanji #4).

Scene 7-9R 何時(なんじ)までですか。 Until what time?

Here is a message from Sasha to Kanda-san. Before you look at the translation, can you guess what Sasha wants to know?

テキスト Text

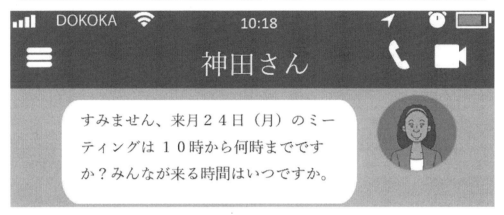

Sorry to bother you, but the meeting next month on the 24th (Monday) is from 10:00 to what time? What is the time when everyone will come?

文字と例 Kanji with examples

#5. 時　とき ジ　　　time, [naming classifier for hours of the day]　時

1. 4時(よじ) — four o'clock
2. まだ7時です。 — It's still seven o'clock.
3. 17時になった。 — It's five p.m.
4. もう23時だよ。 — It's already eleven o'clock.
5. + 日時(にちじ) — date and time
6. + 時(とき) — time
7. つまらない時 — when it's boring
8. 来る時 — when I come here

#6. 何　なに　なん　　　　　what　　　何

1. 何がありますか。　　　　　What is there?
2. 何ですか。　　　　　　　　What is it?
3. 何時までしないんですか。　So until what time will you not do it?
4. 何月　　　　　　　　　　　what month?
5. 何日いないんですか。　　　How many days will you be gone?
6. 何かあるんですか。　　　　It there something (I can do)?
7. 何とかスーパー　　　　　　supermarket something or other

Additional kanji with examples

#7. 半　ハン　　　　　half　　　半

1. 半日　　　　　　　　　　　half a day
2. 半月行ってた。　　　　　　I was gone for half the month.
3. ２時半からだと思います。　I think it's from 2:30.

#8. 間　あいだ　カン　　　interval, space　　間

1. XとYの間　　　　　　　　between X and Y
2. 来た時間　　　　　　　　　the time I came
3. 半時間なんでしょう？　　　It's that it takes half an hour, right?
4. ３時間半かかるんです。　　It's that it takes three and a half hours.

BTL 15 Radicals

You can already see that kanji are made up of repeating parts. The character 日 'day,' for example, can be seen on the left hand side of 時 'time, hour.' These repeating parts are called "radicals" and they are what will allow you to look up characters when you don't know them. The radicals have names based on where they appear in the character (left side, right side, top, bottom, etc.). The name of this radical is *hi-hen* 'day radical'; *hen* means that it appears on the left side of the character. If you use a stylus on an interactive screen to write characters in order to look them up, when you write 日 a list of characters with that radical will appear.

Now go to the Activity Book for 練習 Practice.

Then do 評価 Assessment activities, including 読んでみよう Contextualized reading, 書き取り Dictation, and 書いてみよう Contextualized writing.

第8幕
Act 8

おめでとうございます。
Congratulations.

類(るい)は友(とも)を呼(よ)ぶ
Birds of a feather flock together.

◆ 話す・聞く　Speaking and listening

Scene 8-1　おめでとう。　Congratulations (happy X).

Sasha comes back from work on her birthday to see her roommate Eri greet her with a big smile and a gift.

The script

サーシャ	恵理
ただいま。	お帰り。サーシャ、お誕生日おめでとう！はい、これ。私から。
わあ、ありがとう。	よかったら開けてみて。
何かな～。(開けて)あ、目覚ましだ。	当たり！サーシャなかなか起きないから。
すごい！いろいろな声も出る！	でしょう？
こんなの欲しかったんだ。ありがとう。あしたからは毎日これでバッチリだね。	一人でちゃんと起きてよね。

Sasha	Eri
I'm home!	Welcome back. Sasha, happy birthday! Here you go. From me.
Wow, thanks.	If you want to, open it and see.
What could it be. (opening present) Oh, it's an alarm clock!	You got it! Because you have a hard time waking up.

49

| Amazing! It produces different voices! | Right? |
| I've wanted something like this. Thanks! Starting tomorrow I'll be right on time every day with this, won't I. | Wake up on your own, okay? |

単語と表現 Vocabulary and expressions

Nouns

(お)誕生日	birthday
(ご)卒業(する)	graduation
(ご)結婚(する)	wedding, marriage
(ご)就職(する)	employment, getting a job
目覚まし(時計)	alarm (clock)
いろいろ(な)	various
声	voice
音	sound

Time expressions

毎日	every day	毎年・毎年	every year
毎週	every week	毎回	every time
毎月	every month	毎朝	every morning
毎時間	every hour	毎晩	every evening
毎学期	every academic term, semester		

Verbs

開ける (-RU; 開けた)	open (something)
当たる (-U; 当たった)	hit on target
起きる (-RU; 起きた)	wake up, rise
寝る (-RU; 寝た)	sleep, go to bed, lie down
聞こえる (-RU; 聞こえた)	be audible

Adjectives

欲しい (欲しかった)	want

Special expressions

お誕生日おめでとう(ございます)。	Happy Birthday! (lit. 'Congratulations on your birthday.')
開けてみる	try opening and see
当たり!	right (on target)!; you got it!
こんな	this kind of
そんな	that kind of
あんな	that kind over there
どんな	what kind of
こんなの	this kind (of thing)
バッチリ	perfectly, properly, sure thing (informal)
一人で	by oneself, alone (lit. as one person)
なかなか	quite, considerably, rather
ちゃんと	properly, reliably, satisfactorily

Behind the Scenes

BTS 1 Verb 〜てみる

A Verb in its 〜て form combines with various forms of みる to mean 'try doing X and see what it's like.'

すしを食べてみました。	I tried eating sushi (to see what it was like).
このナビを使ってみてください。	Try using this navigation system (and see if it works).
スペイン語を勉強してみたけど、だめでした。	I tried studying Spanish, but it didn't work out.
難しいと思うでしょうけど、やってみましょう。	You may think it's hard, but let's give it a go.

BTS 2 The こんな series

The words こんな、そんな、あんな、どんな are members of the *ko-so-a-do* series introduced earlier. Members of this new series modify Nouns and describe the "kind of" Noun:

こんな + Noun_X	this kind of X
そんな + Noun_X	that kind (near you) of X; that kind of X that was just mentioned
あんな + Noun_X	that kind (over there) of X; that kind of X that we both know about
どんな + Noun_X	what kind of X

Note that neither the これ nor the この series can combine with Noun の, but the こんな series can: こんなの 'this kind of one,' そんなの 'that kind of one,' あんなの 'that (over there) kind of one,' and どんなの 'what kind of one?'

どんな本が好きですか？	What kind of books do you like?
ここにはそんな人はいなかったと思いますが……。	I don't think such a person was here, but . . .
あんなところがいいって、だれが言ったんですか？	Who is it that said a place like that is good?
こんなの、もっと読みたいでしょう？	You probably want to read more like this kind, right?
そんなこと聞いていないですよ。	I've not heard that sort of thing!
プレゼントはどんなものがいいでしょうか。	What kind of thing do you suppose would be good for a present?
こんなことがあるとは、思ってもいませんでした。	I never even thought that such a thing would occur. (a common way to express surprise at what has happened—natural disaster, winning a Nobel prize)

In a manner expression with Phrase Particle に, this word group is used to suggest that the thing/situation at hand is a rather extreme case.

大丈夫ですよ。こんなに一生懸命勉強したんですから。	It will be fine. Because you have studied your heart out like this.
そんなに大きくなくてもいいでしょう。	It will probably be fine if it's not that big.

Note that the こんな series sometimes suggests that the extreme case is insignificant or undesirable.

こんなものでいいですか。	Is a (little) thing like this all right?
こんなもの、いらないです。	I don't need a (useless, unwelcome) thing like this.
あんなもの、読みたくない。	I don't want to read a thing like that (that we both know about, much less comment about it, for example).
そんなことないですよ。	It's not like that (often used in response to a self-deprecating comment, as an encouragement).

BTS 3 毎日 'Every day'

The prefix 毎〜 before a time word means 'every.'

毎日暑いから、きつい。	It's hot every day, so it's intense.
毎学期試験が難しくなるでしょう。	Probably the tests get harder every term.
毎月お父さんと話しますか。	Do you talk to your father every month?
毎晩何時まで起きてるの？	So how late (until what time) are you up every night?
このクラスだけは毎回本当に楽しみにしています。	This is the only class I look forward to every time. (I really look forward only to this class every time.)
このサイトはほとんど毎日見てます。	We look at this website almost every day.

Now go to the Activity Book for 練習 Practice and 腕試し Tryout.

Scene 8-2　そんなに急がないで。
Don't be in such a rush.

Sasha and Eri are using a long weekend to visit Eri's family in Kyoto. As they leave, they have a playful argument.

The script

恵理	サーシャ
出ますよ〜！	そんなに急がないでよ。駅まで近いんだから。
まあ、そうだけど。忘れ物ないよね。	あ、切符！
え？嘘！	冗談、冗談。
もう！やめてよ。嫌だなあ。	晴れてよかったね、今日。
またすぐ話題を変える。	

Eri	Sasha
We're leaving!	Don't be in such a rush! 'Cause it's not far to the station, as you must know.
Well, that's true but . . . Nothing forgotten, right?	Oh, the tickets!
What? No way! (lit. 'it's a lie!')	It's a joke, it's a joke.
Enough already. Stop it. I hate that.	Good thing it cleared up today, huh.
There you go changing the subject again.	

単語と表現 Vocabulary and expressions

Nouns

(お)忘れ物	forgotten item
切符	ticket
嘘	lie
(ご)冗談	joke
嫌(な)	disagreeable, unpleasant
話題	subject, topic of conversation

Verbs

止・辞・やめる(-RU; 止・辞・やめた)	stop, quit (something)
忘れる (-RU; 忘れた)	forget
覚える (-RU; 覚えた)	remember, memorize
笑う (-U; 笑った)	laugh
泣く (-U; 泣いた)	cry, weep
晴れる(-RU; 晴れた)	clear up (of weather)
曇る (-U; 曇った)	get cloudy
変える(-RU; 変えた)	change (something)

Special expressions

そんなに	to that extent; so X/such a X
もう！	enough already!

拡張 Expansion

Listen to a casual conversation where people are joking with each other. Pay attention to when and why people laugh (i.e., what makes it funny). Are people laughing at things you don't find as funny? Are there types of humor you're used to that don't show up? If you can, when someone makes a joke try to remember exactly what they said.

Behind the Scenes

BTS 4 Negative commands and requests: 急がないで！

Recall that Verbs in the 〜て form can be used as commands, or as requests with ください（ませんか）or いただけませんか。

どうぞ座ってください。	Please have a seat.
みんな立って！	Everyone stand up!

A negative command is formed by adding で to the 〜ない form of a Verb. Note that these commands are often followed by よ or ね. As with affirmative commands, 〜ないで can be made into a request with ください（ませんか）or いただけませんか。

切符、忘れないでね。	Don't forget the tickets, okay?
ここを歩かないでください。	Please do not walk through here.
携帯を持ってこないでください。	Please do not bring cell phones.
そう言わないでよ！	Don't say that!
あしたまで使わないでいただけませんか。	Can we have you not use this until tomorrow?

BTS 5 〜んだから Because, as you must surely know...

Recall that a Sentence plus から constitutes an explicit reason.

怖いから行きたくない。	It's scary so I don't want to go.
きれいで、気持ちがいいから。	Because it's pretty and has a nice feeling.

Sentence plus んです also often functions as a reason, though the causal connection may be less obvious, and this is not the only function of this pattern.

先生と相談してみたいんです。	(The reason I'm here is that) I'd like to try consulting with the professor.
A: これを三つください。	A: I'd like three of these.
B: あ、そんなのは一つだけなんです。	B: Oh, we only have one of those (so I can't give you three).

When the two of these are combined, there is a strong sense of 'you must surely know this.' This can sound like an accusation. In fact, mothers often use this form to their children. In many situations this is just fine, but beware of using this with superiors or in situations where the other person may not actually be aware of the circumstances.

時間ないんだから、今食べて。	There is no time (as you surely know), so eat.
先生がそうおっしゃったんだから、平気ですよ。	The professor said so, so it's bound to be okay.

BTS 6 Humor

There is teasing humor here between Sasha and Eri, who are roommates and friends. But humor does not translate easily from one language or culture to another, so use caution when you try to make a joke.

Now go to the Activity Book for 練習 Practice and 腕試し Tryout.

Scene 8-3　お邪魔します。(Entering someone's space) Sorry to barge in.

Sasha and Eri have arrived at Eri's family home in Kyoto and are being greeted by Eri's mother.

The script

恵理	サーシャ
どうぞ上がって。	お邪魔します。
母です。ルームメイトのサーシャさん。	

山田久美子（恵理の母）	サーシャ
	サーシャモリスです。よろしくお願いします。
まあ、ようこそ。お疲れ様でした。恵理がいつもお世話になっております。	いえいえ、こちらこそ。
ご遠慮なく、ゆっくりなさってくださいね。	ありがとうございます。お世話になります。

Eri	Sasha
Come on in.	Sorry to barge in.
This is my mother. This is my roommate Sasha-san.	

Kumiko Yamada (Eri's mother)	Sasha
	I'm Sasha Morris. Nice to meet you.
Welcome. You must be tired. We appreciate you always looking after Eri.	No, no. I am the one who is looked after.
Please feel free to take it easy, okay?	Thank you. For looking after me.

単語と表現 Vocabulary and expressions

Nouns

(お)邪魔(する)	a bother, a nuisance, an obstacle
(ご)遠慮(する)	restraint
(ご)ゆっくり	slow, relaxed

Verbs

上がる (-U; 上がった)	rise, go up, enter a house
ゆっくりする	relax, take it easy

Special expressions

ようこそ	welcome (greeting)
ご遠慮なく	without reservation

Behind the Scenes

BTS 7 Visiting someone's home

In this Scene you find many ritual expressions and behaviors that are associated with visiting someone's home. Ritual expressions include:

ようこそ, used when welcoming guests when they arrive at your home, the airport, or station. You may also hear a longer form ようこそいらっしゃいました。

お邪魔します, used when you go into someone else's home as a guest. Literally, it means 'I am going to be a nuisance,' and it indicates that you recognize the bother that you might pose as an outsider. The word 邪魔 can be used in reference to any obstacle: 邪魔になるから、捨てましょう。 'It will get in the way, so let's throw it out.'

ご遠慮なく, used to encourage guests to relax. Keep in mind that this does not mean you can "relax" in the same way you would in your home culture. There are limits on how intrusive you can be in other people's space, especially when visiting for the first time.

You have also seen こちらこそ, ありがとうございます, お世話になる and よろしくお願いします in other contexts that call for ritual expressions.

BTS 8 Polite prefixes お〜 and ご〜

You have seen two polite prefixes so far: お〜 and ご〜. There are no hard and fast rules for using these prefixes and native speakers do not always agree, but in general:

- お〜 attaches to words of Japanese origin, while ご〜 attaches to words of Chinese origin. As you learn more Japanese you will acquire a sense for which words are which, but Verbs and Adjectives are usually of Japanese origin. In Act 6 you saw お〜 attached to some Adjectives to be polite (お忙しい 'busy,' お早い 'fast, early'). お〜 also attaches to some Verb stems with です in an honorific form:

  部長、お帰りですか。　　　　　Division Chief, are you going home?
  ２０日まで、お休みでしたね。　You had a holiday through the 20th, didn't you.

Words of Chinese origin that take ご〜 include ご遠慮 ('restraint'), ご冗談 ('joke'), ご卒業 ('graduation'), ご迷惑 ('bother'), ご相談 ('consult'), ご報告 ('report'), ご連絡 ('contact'), ご専門 ('specialization'), and ご専攻 ('academic major'). Some obvious counter-examples to this are お電話 ('telephone') and お元気 ('healthy'), which are of

Chinese origin but take お〜, and ごゆっくり ('leisurely'), which is of Japanese origin but takes ご〜.
- Since they are polite, these prefixes can be used in one of two ways. Either the word refers to someone else (not yourself) or the action affects someone toward whom you want to show deference. When you want to politely ask someone's specialization, you should use ご専門 or ご専攻; you would never use the polite form to talk about your own major or specialization. But when you have to make a report to or get in touch with colleagues, you can show respect for them by being polite: ご報告します ('I will make a report'), ご連絡します ('I will contact you').

BTS 9 Male and female speech style

You have seen that certain speech forms sound soft or gentle while others sound abrupt or blunt. Specifically, a Noun by itself as a sentence (本当。) sounds softer than a Noun plus だ (本当だ。) These tendencies are strongly associated with gender in Japanese, where it is said that men tend to use the blunter sounding alternatives. Women are less constrained by "feminine speech" than they have been in the past, but still use softer sounding forms in certain contexts. This Scene is a good example of that. Eri's mother uses softer, more tentative language than her father might. Here are some changes that male students might want to consider when playing the role of Eri's father:

恵理の父	サーシャ
ああ、ようこそ。お疲れ様。恵理がいつもお世話になっております。	いえいえ、こちらこそ。
遠慮なく、ゆっくりしていってくださいね。	ありがとうございます。お世話になります。

Now go to the Activity Book for 練習 Practice and 腕試し Tryout.

Scene 8-4　いらしたこと、ありますか？
Have you been there?

Sasha presents Eri's mother a souvenir from St. Louis, her hometown.

The script

サーシャ	山田久美子（恵理の母）
あの、これ、おみやげです。どうぞ。	まあ！何でしょう。
アメリカのお菓子です。	アメリカのもの？わざわざありがとうございます。サーシャさんはアメリカのどちらのご出身？
ミズーリのセントルイスです。いらしたことありますか？	いや、行ったことはないわねえ。ご家族はセントルイスにいらっしゃるの？
はい、両親はセントルイスに住んでいます。	そう。あ、喉乾いたでしょう。お茶いれましょうね。
あ、どうぞお構いなく。	

Sasha	Kumiko Yamada (Eri's mother)
Umm, this is a gift. Please (take it).	My goodness! What could it be.
It's sweets from America.	Something from America? Thank you for going to all that trouble. Where were you born (are you from) in America?
St. Louis in Missouri. Have you been there?	No, I've never been (there). So your family is in St. Louis?
Yes, my parents live in St. Louis.	I see. Ah, you must be thirsty. I'll make some tea, OK?
Oh, please don't go to any trouble.	

単語と表現 Vocabulary and expressions

Nouns

お土産・おみやげ	souvenir, gift
ヨーロッパ	Europe
アフリカ	Africa
オーストラリア	Australia
(お)祝い	congratulations, celebration
(お)菓子	sweets, candy
(ご)出身	birthplace
ミズーリ州	Missouri
セントルイス	St. Louis
(ご)両親	parents
喉	throat
お腹	stomach

Verbs

住む (-U; 住んだ)	reside
渇く・乾く (-U; かわいた)	become dry
空く (-U; 空いた)	become empty
入れる・いれる (-RU; いれた)	put (something) in; brew or infuse (tea)
淹れる・いれる (-RU; いれた)	brew or infuse (tea)

Classifiers

〜度	times, degrees

Final particles

わ	particle used for emphasis

8-4 おめでとうございます。

63

Special expressions

まあ！	oh my, oh!
わざわざ	specially
いらしたこと	have gone; the experience of having gone
お茶を淹れる	brew or infuse tea
喉が渇く	get thirsty
お腹が空く	get hungry
お構いなく	don't go to any bother

Behind the Scenes

BTS 10 Sentence + ことがある

Recall from previous Acts that the Noun こと means 'matter' or '(intangible) thing.' A past Verb with ことがある means something like 'times' or 'occasions,' or 'have done X' in the sense of having the experience of X-ing. In the negative (ことが・はない) it means 'have never done X.'

新幹線で行ったことがあります。	I have (at some time) gone by Shinkansen.
ここへは前に一度だけ来たことがあります。	I have been here at least once before.
その本のこと、聞いたことはありますけど、まだ読んだことはないです。	I have heard about that book, but I've never read it.
そんな人、会ったことありません。名前を聞いたこともないと思います。	I've never met a person like that. I think I've never even heard his name.
こんな魚は食べたことがない。	I have never eaten this kind of fish.

If you usually go by train but have on occasion used other transportation, you can also use a negative Verb before ことがある.

電車で行かなかったことがあります。	I have (at times) not gone by train (taking the bus instead).
勉強しなかったこともありますか。	Are there also times when you didn't study?

When the Verb is in the non-past form, this combination means 'there are times when I do' (or 'do not do') X.

電車で行くことがあります。	There are times when I go by train.
漢字を使わないこともあります。	There are also times when we don't use kanji.

Finally, both parts of the Sentence may be negative, meaning 'it is never the case that I don't do X.'

電車で行かないことはありません。	There are never times when I don't go by train.

This is very close to いつも電車で行きます。 'I always go by train.'

Less common but nonetheless possible are other kinds of Sentences (Adjectives, Noun だ) with ことがある:

あのレストランで食べて、まずかったことはないです。	I have never had an unpleasant experience eating at that restaurant.
ブライアンが遅れた？へえ、珍しいことがありますね。	Brian is late? Huh, unusual things happen, don't they.
たくさん人が来て忙しいこともありますが、誰も来ないこともあります。	There are times when it's busy because a lot of people come, but there are also times when nobody comes.
あの人の話は、本当だったことがありません。	That person has never told the truth. (What that person says has never been the truth.)
頑張ってもダメなことはありますよ。大丈夫。次はもっと良くなりますよ。	There are times when I fail even if I do my best! It's all right. It will be better next time.

BTS 11 Giving and appreciating gifts

Giving gifts is an important way of cementing relationships in Japan. A gift indicates that you recognize the value of the other person in your life. People give gifts when they meet for the first time. They also give gifts on returning from being away—even if it was for a short time. Workers who stay late at the office often buy something small to take home to show their concern for those who are waiting. What makes a good gift? Things that represent the place you come from or visited are very common. Consumables (such as sweets) are generally safe. It isn't always the value of the thing that you give so much as a beautiful presentation; gifts are almost always nicely wrapped in Japan. Here are some sample expressions that are frequently used in association with gift giving and receiving.

つまらないものですが……。	It's a small (lit. 'boring') thing, but . . .
PLACEのものです。	It's a thing from PLACE.
PLACEから持ってきました。	I brought it from PLACE.
わざわざありがとうございます。	Thank you for going to all the trouble.
ありがたくいただきます。	I gratefully accept it.

Now go to the Activity Book for 練習 Practice and 腕試し Tryout.

Scene 8-5　優しそうなお母さん
Your mother seems nice.

Sasha and Eri talk about their respective takes on Eri's mother.

The script

サーシャ	恵理
優しそうなお母さんだね。	実は結構こわいんだから。
へえ、そうなんだ。全然そうは見えないけどね。	初めて会うお客様の前だからね。
ふうん。	いつも「結婚は？」とか「就職は？」とか、うるさいんだ。
うちも！まあ、親ってみんなそうなんだろうね。	確かにね。

Sasha	Eri
Your mother seems really nice.	No, in fact she's pretty scary.
Really, is that so. She doesn't look that way at all, but . . .	Because she's in front of a guest she's meeting for the first time!
No kidding.	It's always "How about getting married?" and "How about getting a job?" and such, it's annoying.
Mine too! Well, maybe all parents are that way, you know.	For sure.

単語と表現 Vocabulary and expressions

Nouns

優しそう（な）	looks nice, looks kind
元気（な）	healthy, energetic

元気そう(な)	looks healthy, energetic
真面目(な)	diligent, serious
真面目そう(な)	looks diligent, serious
(ご)親切(な)	kind, gentle
親切そう(な)	looks kind
面倒(な)	trouble(some), care, attention
面倒そう(な)	looks troublesome
初めて	first time
大切(な)	important, necessary
(お)客(様)	guest, customer, client
お客さん	guest, customer, client
うち	(my) family; in-group
親	parent
母親	mother
父親	father
確か(な)	sure, certain

Adjectives

優しい	kind, nice, gentle
恐い・怖い	scary, frightening
うるさい	annoying, loud, noisy, tiresome
やかましい	noisy, boisterous, annoying
面倒くさい・めんどくさい	bothersome, tiresome
うざい	annoying (slang)

Special expressions

実は	actually, in fact
ふうん	hmmm
確かに	for sure, certainly

拡張 Expansion

Listen to a conversation in Japanese, and pay attention to the 相槌 (BTS 14). How frequently does it occur? Is it more or less than what you expected? Write down the 5 words or phrases you hear used as 相槌 most frequently during the conversation. Also, write down how many times the 相槌 consists of repetition or rephrasing of content that the listener heard.

Behind the Scenes

BTS 12 優しそう Appearance

In Act 2 you learned the word おいしそう 'looks delicious.' The suffix 〜そう attaches to Adjective and Verb stems as well as な Nouns to mean 'looks/sounds/smells/seems like.' Here are some points to remember:

- Verbs in this pattern always refer to the future.
- The よ〜 stem of いい and negative forms of Adjectives and な Nouns always add さ before 〜そう. Thus よさそう 'looks good,' 高くなさそう 'doesn't look expensive,' and 元気じゃなさそう 'doesn't look healthy.'
- For negative Verbs this さ is usually optional (except for する which is always しなさそう). Thus both 食べなさそう and 食べなそう are acceptable.
- Adjectives such as 危ない, つまらない, and 少ない are not negative, so there should be no さ: 危なそう, つまらなそう, and 少なそう. However, sometimes native speakers inadvertently add さ for these words.

	Affirmative		Negative	
Adjective	優しそう	looks kind	優しくなさそう	doesn't look kind
Noun	元気そう	looks healthy	元気じゃなさそう	doesn't look healthy
Verb	晴れそう	looks like it will clear up	晴れな(さ)そう	looks like it won't clear up

These forms act like な Nouns—that is, they can be followed by です in all its forms, and when they modify other Nouns they take な.

新しいインターンの人、あんまり真面目じゃなさそうですね。　The new intern seems to be not very serious.

この本、どうですか？あまり難しくなさそうだから。	How is this book? It doesn't look very difficult, so . . .
まだ降らなそうだから、今出ませんか？	It still looks like it's not going to rain, so why don't we leave now?

BTS 13 だろう

The informal of でしょう is だろう. Recall that this tentative form can occur after an Adjective, Verb, or Noun:

恐かっただろう。	It was probably scary.
晴れるだろう。	It'll probably clear up.
おみやげだろう。	It's probably a gift.
日本語がわからないからだろう。	It's probably because they don't understand Japanese.

And when the Sentence Particle か is added to だろう, it becomes even less sure:

恐いだろうか。	Do you suppose it's scary?
晴れるだろうか。	Do you think it will clear up?
おみやげだろうか。	Do you suppose it's a gift?

Like だ (the informal form of です), だろう at the end of a Sentence can be a bit blunt. But the informal form is the one you will find preceding と思う.

うるさいだろうと思います。	I think it will probably be loud.
構わないだろうと思いました。	I thought it probably wouldn't be a problem.
忘れ物だろうと思いませんか。	Don't you think it's probably something someone forgot?

BTS 14 相槌：そうなんだ、なるほど、確かに、やっぱり、ふうん、へえ

相槌 refers to frequent, short responses during a conversation that indicate you are listening or paying attention to what the other person is saying. These responses are a powerful tool in keeping the conversation going smoothly; they are critical if you want to be a good listener. An absence of 相槌(あいづち) can be interpreted as defiance, rejection, disinterest, etc. Simple 相槌(あいづち) include a nod (at the right time), and phrases such as そうですか, which you have seen before. In this Scene you see そうなんだ, なるほど, 確(たし)かに, やっぱり, ふうん, and へえ. You can signal more active engagement and even modify the direction of the conversation by using the appropriate 相槌(あいづち).

Now go to the Activity Book for 練習 Practice and 腕試し Tryout.

8-5 おめでとうございます。

Scene 8-6 一回（いっかい）も帰（かえ）ってないなあ。
I haven't gone back even once, I guess.

Sasha and Eri talk about how frequently they visit their families.

The script

サーシャ	恵理（えり）
休（やす）みの時（とき）はよく京都（きょうと）に帰（かえ）ってくるの？	そうだね。お正月（しょうがつ）は必（かなら）ず。夏休（なつやす）みの間（あいだ）とかにも時々（ときどき）帰（かえ）るから、年（ねん）に2、3回（かい）ぐらいかな。
そう。私（わたし）より親孝行（おやこうこう）だね。私（わたし）はこの2年（ねん）ぐらい1回（かい）も帰（かえ）ってないなあ。	そう。寂（さび）しくならない？
まあ、ほとんど毎週話（まいしゅうはなし）はしてるからね。	

Sasha	Eri
When you have a vacation, do you often come home to Kyoto?	Let's see. Always for the New Year, and sometimes I come home during the summer break, so maybe two or three times a year.
I see. You're better to your parents than I am, aren't you. I haven't gone home even once in about two years, I guess.	Really. Don't you miss them?
Well, we talk almost every week, so you know.	

単語と表現 Vocabulary and expressions

Nouns

時（とき）・とき	time, occasion
（お）正月（しょうがつ）	New Year

夏休み（なつやすみ）	summer vacation, holiday
春（はる）	spring
夏（なつ）	summer
秋（あき）	autumn, fall
冬（ふゆ）	winter
間（あいだ）	during, between
休暇（きゅうか）	break, holiday
出張（しゅっちょう）（する）	business trip
親孝行（おやこうこう）	filial piety (a Confucian virtue); dedication to parents
親不孝（おやふこう）	lack of filial piety
暇（ひま）（な）	free (time)

Classifiers

回（かい）	times, instances

Special expressions

休みの時（やすみのとき）	during one's vacation, when one is on vacation
必ず（かならず）	without fail, always, without exception
たいてい	usually, as a rule
時々（ときどき）	sometimes
たまに	once in a while
夏休みの間（なつやすみのあいだ）	during summer vacation
年に2、3回（ねんにに、さんかい）	two or three times a year
1回も（いっかいも）	not a single time

拡張 Expansion

Find out what the major holidays are that you get vacation for at a Japanese workplace or university.

Behind the Scenes

BTS 15 Frequency expressions

You have seen a variety of expressions that can be used to tell frequency. These give you a range of possibilities for telling about your own activities as well as asking about others. Below is a chart for review.

Expression		Example	
いつも	always	日曜はいつも家にいます。	I'm always at home on Sunday.
必ず	without fail	必ず勉強してください。	Please don't fail to study.
時々	sometimes	ときどき学校まで歩いていきます。	Sometimes I walk to school.
たまに	occasionally	いつも忙しいからたまにはゆっくりしたい。	I'm always busy, so occasionally I want to take it easy.
よく	often	傘、よく忘れていきます。	I often forget my umbrella.
たいてい	as a rule, usually	日本語の試験は、たいてい金曜日にあります。	Our Japanese tests are usually on Fridays.
ほとんど + TIME	almost every TIME	ほとんど毎週両親と話します。	I talk to my parents almost every week.
TIME にX回	X times per TIME	年に4回大阪に行きます。	I go to Osaka four times a year.
X、Y回 (see next BTS)	X or Y times	2、3回食べてみました。	I tried it two or three times.

BTS 16 Approximation: 2、3回

Two consecutive numbers (between 1 and 9) plus a classifier (or a number in the tens, hundreds, etc.) indicates approximation.

2、3回食べてみました。　　　　　I tried eating it two or three times.
4、5時間待っていました。　　　　We waited for four or five hours.

７、８ヶ月札幌にいました。　　　　　We were in Sapporo for seven or eight months.
６、７０ドルかかりそうです。　　　　It looks like it'll cost sixty or seventy dollars.
１５、６日休みます。　　　　　　　　We'll be on vacation for fifteen or sixteen days.

BTS 17 1回も : Quantity + も + negative or affirmative Sentence

A quantity expression followed by も plus an affirmative means 'as much as' or 'as many as,' and in the context indicates that the quantity is large.

そのクッキー、５つも食べた。　　　　I ate FIVE of those cookies.
２時間も待っていたんです。　　　　　So we waited for all of TWO hours.
２時間も電話で話していた。　　　　　We talked on the phone for all of TWO hours.

A quantity expression followed by も plus a negative means 'not even,' and in the context indicates that the quantity is small.

１回も会っていない。　　　　　　　　I haven't even met him once.
少しもわからないから……。　　　　　I don't understand even a little so . . .
試験は１つもない。　　　　　　　　　There's not a single test.

Now go to the Activity Book for 練習 Practice and 腕試し Tryout.

Then do 評価 Assessment activities.

◆ 読み書き Reading and writing

シーン 8-7R 日本人ではなくて、アメリカ人です。
American, not Japanese.

Sasha received a text message from Ikeda-san in HR regarding a candidate for a job interview.

 テキスト Text

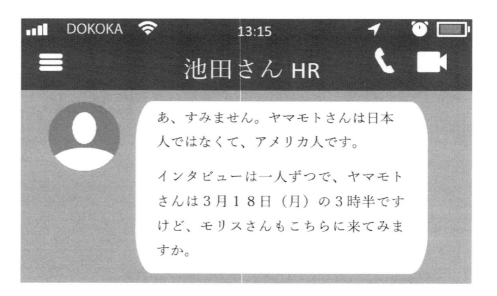

あ、すみません。ヤマモトさんは日本人ではなくて、アメリカ人です。

インタビューは一人ずつで、ヤマモトさんは3月18日（月）の3時半ですけど、モリスさんもこちらに来てみますか。

Oh, sorry, Yamamoto-san is American, not Japanese.
　We'll do the interviews individually and Yamamoto-san's (turn) will be at 3:30 on March 18 (Monday). Would you like to try and come, too?

文字と例 Kanji with examples

#9. 本 　もと(see kanji #56)　　book, [classifier　本
　　　　ホン　ボン　ポン　　for long objects]

1. どんな本？ — What kind of book is it?
2. 日本に行ってみたい。 — I want to try and go to Japan someday.
3. １本 — one cylindrical object
4. ２本 — two cylindrical objects
5. あんなのは３本だけですか。 — There are just three of that kind of thing?
6. 何本あるんですか。 — So how many are there?
7. + 本日 — today (formal)
8. 本日はよくいらっしゃいました。 — Thank you very much for coming today.

#10. 人 　ひと　　　　　　　person, [classifier　人
　　　　ジン　ニン　　　for people]

1. こんな人 — this kind of person
2. そんな日本人 — that kind of Japanese person
3. あんなアメリカ人 — that kind of American person
4. １人 — one person
5. ２人 — two people
6. ３人 — three people
7. 何人来るんですか。 — How many people are coming?
8. 何人が来るんですか。 — People of what nationality are coming?

#11. 一 　ひと　ひと(つ)　　one　　　　　　　一
　　　　イチ　イツ

1. 一 — one
2. 一人 — one person
3. 一時 — one o'clock
4. 一時間半 — one hour and a half
5. 一日にいました。 — I was here on the first of the month.
6. 一日いました。 — I was here for one day.
7. 一月に行きます。 — I will go in January.
8. 一月行きます。 — I will go for one month.
9. まだ一か月もあるんだからいそがないで。 — It's that there is still one month, so don't hurry.

Additional kanji with examples

#12. 円　まる(い)　エン　　　　yen (Japanese currency), circle　　円

1. ３５０円　　　　　　　　¥350
2. 何円　　　　　　　　　　how many yen?
3. １ドル110円ぐらい　　　$1 is about ¥110

#13. 年　とし　ネン　　　　　year　　年

1. 年　　　　　　　　　　　year
2. いい年　　　　　　　　　a good year
3. ２０２０年はどんな年？　What kind of year was the year 2020?
4. 何年　　　　　　　　　　what year? how many years?
5. 何年間　　　　　　　　　how many years?

#14. 二　ふた　ふた(つ)　ニ　　two　　二

1. 二日　　　　　　　　　　the second of the month, two days
2. 二日間　　　　　　　　　two days
3. 二月にします。　　　　　I'll do it in February
4. 二か月します。　　　　　I do it for two months.
5. 二時　　　　　　　　　　two o'clock
6. 二時半　　　　　　　　　2:30
7. 二人で行ってみたいなあ。　I want to try and go as a couple.

#15. 三　み　み(つ)　みっ(つ)　サン　　three　　三

1. 三日　　　　　　　　　　three days, the third of the month
2. 三日間　　　　　　　　　three days
3. まだ三月です。　　　　　It's still March.
4. 三か月　　　　　　　　　three months
5. 三時半にしてみました。　I tried it at 3:30.
6. 三人　　　　　　　　　　three people

#16. 四　よ　よ(つ)
　　　　　よっ(つ)　よ(ん)
　　　　　シ

1. 四日 (よっか) — four days, the fourth of the month
2. 四日間 — four days
3. 四月 (しがつ) — April
4. もう四か月(げつ)だよ。 — It has been four months already.
5. 四時半 (よじはん) — 4:30
6. 四人(よにん)なんだからいいでしょう。 — So it's probably okay because there are four people.
7. 四円 (よえん) — ¥4

#17. 五　いつ　いつ(つ)　ゴ

1. 五日 (いつか) — five days, the fifth of the month
2. 五日間 — five days
3. まだ五月(ごがつ)になってませんよ。 — It isn't (hasn't become) May yet!
W4. え、五か月(げつ)？そんなに！ — What, five months? That long?
5. 五時半 — 5:30
6. 五人 (にん) — five people

#18. 六　む　むい　む(つ)
　　　　　むっ(つ)　ロク

1. 六日 (むいか) — six days, the sixth of the month
2. 六日間 — six days
3. 六月(ろくがつ)に行ってみたかったなあ。 — I wanted to try going in June.
4. 六か月 — six months
5. 六時半 — 6:30
6. もう六人(にん)もいますよ。 — There are as many as six people already.

#19. 七　なな　なな(つ)
　　　　　なの　シチ

1. 七日 (なのか) — seven days, the seventh of the month
2. 七日間 — seven days
3. 七月(しちがつ)にしてみる？ — Should we try doing it in/try and decide on July?
4. 七か月 (なな　げつ) — seven months

79

5.	七時半 (しち・なな)	7:30	
6.	七人来ていますよ。(しち・ななにん)	Seven people are here.	

#20. 八 や や(つ) よう ハチ　　eight　　八

1. 八日 (ようか) — eight days, the eighth of the month
2. 八日間行ってました。— I was gone for eight days.
3. 八月 (はちがつ) — August
4. 八か月 (はっ・げつ) — eight months
5. 八時半にあるんだからまだいいよ。— It's at 8:30, so it is still okay.
6. もう八人いりますね。(にん) — I need eight more people.
7. テストはまだ八つある。— There are still eight tests (left).

#21. 九 ここの ク キュウ　　nine　　九

1. 九日 (ここのか) — nine days, the ninth of the month
2. 九日間 — nine days
3. 九月にまいりました。(くがつ) — I came here in September.
4. 九か月 (きゅう・げつ) — nine months
5. 九時半だからそんなにいそがないで。— It's 9:30, so don't hurry so much.
6. もう九人来ます。(きゅう・くにん) — Nine more people are coming.
7. 九円 (きゅうえん) — ¥9

#22. 十 と とお ジッ ジュウ　　ten　　十

1. 十日 (とおか) — ten days, the tenth of the month
2. 十日間 — ten days
3. 十月にいらしてみますか。(じゅうがつ) — Would you like to try and come in October?
4. 十か月 (じゅ・じっ) — ten months
5. 十時半 — 10:30
6. 十人も来ないでください。(にん) — Don't come with as many as ten people.

#23. 百 ヒャク ビャク ピャク　　hundred　　百

1. 百 (ひゃく) — hundred
2. 百円 (えん) — ¥100

3. 三百円 ¥300
4. おめでとう。六百ドルです。 Congratulations. Here is $600.
5. 何百円 how many hundreds of yen?

#24. 千　ち　セン　ゼン　thousand　千

1. 千 thousand
2. 千円 ¥1,000
3. 二千円 ¥2,000
4. 三千円 ¥3,000
5. 八千ドルもあるんだからもういいかな。 I have as much as $8,000, so I guess I am already okay.
6. 何千円 how many thousands of yen?
7.# 千歳飴 candy stick sold at children's festival

#25. 万　マン　バン　ten thousand　万

1. 一万円 ¥10,000
2. 三万ドル $30,000
3. 一万人も来たんですか？ So as many as 10,000 people came (to the rally)?

BTL 1 Conventions vs. actual use ラーメン・らぁめん・拉麺

Although there are agreed-on conventions for using kanji, hiragana and katakana, in actual practice these conventions are often disregarded for stylistic reasons. This is especially true in signs and advertising, where alternative script is used for effect. Katakana, for example, is regularly used in advertising for company names such as ホンダ 'Honda,' マツダ 'Mazda,' or サッポロ(ビール) 'Sapporo (Beer),' all of which would normally be written in kanji. Ramen shops might use katakana (ラーメン), hiragana (らぁめん), or kanji (拉麺) to identify themselves. Don't be surprised when you see these alternatives.

BTL 2 Numerals and dates in kanji

The use of kanji for numerals is usually limited to vertical writing and more traditional contexts. Arabic numerals appear elsewhere. Kanji numerals are also used in horizontal writing when they occur in proper names (三井さん 'Ms. Mitsui') and set phrases (一人で 'on one's own,' 三日月 'crescent moon,' 日本一 'Japan's No.1,' or 'best in Japan,' etc.). You saw them in the *kotowaza* of Act 1 and Act 2:

一期一会 'Once In a Lifetime' or '*Carpe Diem*' ('Seize the day')

千里の道も一歩から 'A journey of a thousand miles begins with a single step'

The character 〇（ゼロ、まる、れい）is sometimes used to indicate the numeral 0, especially for years and prices in vertical writing.

Example

一月二日

七月六日

四月三日（日）

五月八日（日）七時

九月九日（月）九時半

2004年9月5日

二〇〇四年八月一日

一九七〇年三月三〇日

Now go to the Activity Book for 練習 Practice.

シーン 8-8R よろしくお願(ねが)いします。 Nice to meet you.

Brian is reading an entry on an online discussion board for international students.

 テキスト Text

> How do you do, I'm Christina Natalov.
> Has anyone gone to Ukraine?
> I came from Kiev in Ukraine.
> This year will be my third year in Japan. Nice to meet you!

文字と例 Kanji with examples

#26. 目 め モク eye, [ordinal number classifier] 目

1. ＋目(め) — eye
2. 五年目(ごねんめ) — fifth year
3. 三日目(みっか)に行ったことがありますか。 — Have you been there on day three?
4. これで四人目(よにん)です。 — This is the fourth person.
5. 六本目(ろっぽん)のビール — sixth bottle of beer
6. 二時間目(に)になりました。 — It was changed to (became) the second hour.
7. ＃目次(もくじ) — table of contents

#27. 今 いま コン now 今

1. 今(いま) — now
2. 今日(きょう・こんにち) — today
3. 今月(こんげつ)は何かすることがありますか。 — Do you have something to do this month?
4. 今年(ことし)も行ってみたいですね。 — I would like to try and go this year, too.

BTL 3 Kanji readings: きょう・今日(きょう)

Sometimes, kanji are used purely for their pronunciation regardless of meaning. The word *sushi,* for example, can be written in kanji using 寿司, in which case the pronunciation matches the word but has little to do with the meaning of the characters (寿 means 'longevity' and 司 means 'government office'). In other cases, kanji combinations might be assigned readings that can't be broken into units. The combination 今日, read *kyoo*, can be inferred from the meaning of the kanji ('now day' or 'today') but this is the only time these characters will have this pronunciation and neither kanji can be assigned a reading. Similarly, 一日 and 二十日 are read *tsuitachi* and *hatsuka,* respectively, based purely on the coinciding meaning of these words and what the character combinations suggest. Place names are frequently assigned kanji on the basis of pronunciation. The city of Sapporo, for example, is written 札幌 which is made up of two characters pronounced *satsu* 'paper bill (in currency)' and *horo* 'curtain.' The meaning of these characters has little to do with the city, but is an approximation of the original Ainu name for the area: *sat-poro-pet* 'big dry river.' Your friends may want to assign kanji to your non-kanji-based name. You can't use this name officially, but it is a fun exercise that most people find entertaining. If you already use Chinese characters to write your name, find out how your name is pronounced in Japanese.

#28. 語　ゴ　　　　　　　language　語

1. 日本語 (にほんご) — Japanese (language)
2. + タイ語 — Thai (language)
3. ロシア語 — Russian (language)
4. + ベトナム語 — Vietnamese (language)
5. こんなフランス語ってわかりますか。 — Do you understand this kind of French?
6. スペイン語でしないでください。 — Please don't do this in Spanish.
7. + インドネシア語 — Indonesian (language
8. 何語 (なにご) — what language?

#29. 願　ねが(う)　ガン　　wish　願

1. お願いします。 — Please give me a hand.
2. お願いがあります。 — I have a favor (to ask).
3. お願いって何ですか。 — What do you mean by *onegai*?
4. お願いしてもいいですか。 — Is it all right to ask a favor?
5. リーさんにお願いできますか。 — Can I ask Lee-san a favor?
6. モリスさんにお願いできないでしょうか。 — Couldn't I perhaps ask Morris-san a favor?
7. ワンさんにお願いしたことがありますか。 — Have you asked Wang-san to do it before?
8. # 祈願 (きがん) — pray

Now go to Activity Book for 練習 Practice.

おめでとうございます。

シーン 8-9R 先生(せんせい)がいらっしゃいます。
The professor is coming.

A fellow international student of Brian Wang at Fukuzawa University forwarded him the following message.

テキスト Text

Subject: Fwd: レクチャーシリーズ

日本語１０２の学生のみなさん

来月の８日（月）２時半からのセミナーに、スタンフォード大学の
ピーター・リチャードソン先生がいらっしゃいます。その日は１時間ぐらいの
パネルディスカッション（テーマ：「今、どうしてアメリカの大学へ？」）もあります。
リフレッシュメントもあるだろうからみなさん、ぜひ来てくださいね！

Subject: Fwd: Lecture Series

To all students in Japanese 102

Professor Peter Richardson from Stanford University will be at the 2:30 seminar on the 8th of next month (Monday). There will also be a panel discussion of about one hour on that day on the theme of "Why (go) to an American university now?" There will probably be some refreshments, so everyone, please be sure to come!

文字と例 Kanji with examples

#30.	大	おお(きい) ダイ	big, large	大
1.		大(おお)きい	big, large	
2.		やさしそうな大人(おとな)	an adult who seems nice	
3.		大きさ	size	

#31. 学　まな(ぶ)　ガク　　　　　learn, school　　　学

1. 大学（だいがく）　　　　　　university
2. むずかしそうな大学　　　　　university that seems difficult
3. #語学（ごがく）　　　　　　(foreign) language study
4. #学ぶ（まな）　　　　　　　learn

#32. 生　い(きる)　セイ　　　　life　　　生

1. 学生（がくせい）　　　　　　(college) student
2. いそがしそうな学生　　　　　student who seems to be busy
3. 大学生、一人も来ないだろうなあ。　　I bet there will be not even a single university student.
4. 大学生　　　　　　　　　　university student
5. #生きる（い）　　　　　　　live

#33. 先　さき　セン　　　　　　previous, ahead　　　先

1. もっと先（さき）だろう。　　　It's probably farther ahead.
2. お先に。　　　　　　　　　　(I will go) ahead (of you).
3. いそがしそうな先生（せんせい）　　a teacher who seems busy
4. 先月（せんげつ）だろう。　　　It was probably last month.
5. 先日（せんじつ）行ったことがある。　I was (there) the other day.

Now go to Activity Book for 練習 Practice.

Then do 評価 Assessment activities, including 読んでみよう Contextualized reading, 書き取り Dictation, and 書いてみよう Contextualized writing.

おめでとうございます。

第 9 幕
Act 9

一番好きなのは ……。

My favorite one is . . .

好きこそものの上手なれ

What one likes, one does well.

◆ 話す・聞く　Speaking and listening

Scene 9-1　ここ掃除したの誰？
Who is it that cleaned up here?

Kawakami-san, the leader of the aikido club, is not happy about the state of an area in the dojo.

The script

川上	ブライアン
きのう、ここ掃除したの誰？	さあ、僕は昨日は来てなかったんですが。
ゴミ、捨ててなかったよ。	すみません。
ブライアンが謝らなくてもいいよ。	捨ててきます。
あ、じゃ、悪いけど頼む。袋はあそこにおいてあるから。	はい。
でも誰だろう、まったく。	

Kawakami	Brian
Who is it that cleaned up in here yesterday?	Gosh, I didn't come in yesterday, so . . .
The trash wasn't thrown away, you know.	Oh, sorry.
There's nothing for you to apologize for.	I'll go and throw it out.
Ah, well then, it's awful to ask but I will. The bags are stored over there.	Okay.
But who could it have been, good grief.	

91

単語と表現 Vocabulary and expressions

Nouns

ゴミ	trash, garbage
掃除(する)	cleaning
整理(する)	sorting, putting in order
夜	evening
袋	bag

Verbs

捨てる (-RU; 捨てた)	throw away
片付ける (-RU; 片付けた)	clean (something) up, tidy up
洗う (-U; 洗った)	wash
謝る (-U; 謝った)	apologize
置く (-U; 置いた)	put, place, position

Special expressions

掃除したの 誰?	Who is it that cleaned up?
まったく	good grief (expression of exasperation)

Behind the Scenes

BTS 1 More on sentence modifiers

You encountered Sentence Modifiers in Act 7 with 歩く人 'people who walk.' In fact, Sentence Modifiers can be quite complex, consisting of much longer sequences. In the following examples, the modifying Sentences are underlined.

地下鉄の駅まで行くバス	the bus that goes as far as the subway station
来学期日本語の授業で使う教科書	the textbook that we're going to use in Japanese class next term
大丈夫だと思ったけどやっぱり危ない道	the street that I thought was safe but is dangerous after all

Remember that the Sentence Modifier may be non-past or past, affirmative or negative. It is usually, but not always, informal. Compare the following.

今年卒業する学生	the students who are going to graduate this year
今年卒業した学生	the students who graduated this year
今年卒業しない学生	the students who are not going to graduate this year
今年卒業しなかった学生	the students who didn't graduate this year

When the subject is overtly mentioned within the modifying Sentence, Phrase Particle が or its special alternate, の, is used rather than は.

ブライアンが (or の) 間違えた漢字	the kanji that Brian made a mistake on
サーシャさんが掃除しておいた会議室	the conference room that Sasha-san cleaned up

A topic of a conversation may be introduced with complex modification, sometimes involving multiple Sentence Modifiers.

去年ニューヨークから来て今月までここで研修していた、張さんっていう人、覚えていますか。すごく日本語の上手な人。あの張さんがね。	Do you remember Cho-san who came from New York for training last year through this month? The person who's really good at Japanese. That Cho-san, right?
３０歳ぐらいで、仕事をしていても親と一緒に住んでいる人は結構多い。	There are quite a lot of people about age thirty who live with their parents even though they're working.
ブライアンが知っている好きな歌を教えてください。	Please tell me songs that Brian knows and likes.
お母さんが昨日新しいお店で買ってきたケーキ、すごく美味しかったよ。	The cake that your mother bought at the new shop yesterday was really delicious.
課長が一人で書いたこのレポートですけどね、違っているところがあるんです。	About this report that the section chief wrote by himself, but . . . it's that there are some discrepancies in it.

This is particularly common in self-introductions.

クリントン大学から福沢大学に留学しているブライアン・ワンといいます。	I am Brian Wang, studying abroad at Fukuzawa University from Clinton College.
今日からこちらでお世話になります、アメリカから参りましたモリスと申します。	My name is Morris. (I) came here from America, and will be relying on your assistance starting today.

93

<u>中国から来て先月からこちらの研修プログラムでお世話になっている</u>、張です。

I am Cho. I came from China, and will be relying on your assistance in this training program.

BTS 2 Sentence + の

When you add Noun の to a Sentence, it turns that Sentence into a Noun. You already saw すしが好きです 'I like sushi.' But you can also say すしを食べるのが好きです 'I like eating sushi,' where the Sentence Modifier すしを食べる precedes の.

いろいろなところのラーメン食べるのが大好きなんです。 What I love is to eat ramen at various places.
謝るのは、難しいです。 It's hard to apologize.

In this Scene you see nominalizer の used <u>before</u> the meaning of の is known or becomes clear: ここ掃除したの誰? 'Who is it that cleaned up in here?' Here are other examples of this use of の.

背が高いのは誰?	Who is it that's tall?
始めるのはいつから?	What time is it that you're starting?
嫌いなのはあまりないです。	There aren't many things I don't like.
宿題の中で大変だったのはどれでしたか?	Which is the one that was hard in the homework?
これを買ったのは私じゃないです。	I'm not the one who bought this.
このかばんをよく使うのはね、これが使いやすいからですよ。	The reason I use this bag a lot, you know, is because this is easy to use.
持ってきたのはこっちのお菓子ですよ。	The one that I brought is this cake, you know.

BTS 3 Transitive verb 〜てある

You have seen Verbs in their 〜て form combined with いる, indicating either a continuing action (テレビを見ています。'She is watching television.') or a completed action (日本に行っています。'She has gone to Japan.'). Here you see transitive Verbs in their 〜て form combined with some form of ある. A transitive Verb is any Verb that can take an object (an を phrase). Examples of transitive Verbs include 食べる、片付ける、捨てる、and 決める. In this pattern, there is a definite sense that someone did something, but either we don't know or we can't say who that someone is. The object becomes the subject and the resulting phrase means that something has been done to it.

ゴミ、捨ててある？	Has the trash been thrown out?
部屋はちゃんと片付けてありますか。	Has the room been cleaned up as it should?
あそこに置いてあるのは何？	What is it that's been put over there?

ある may be negative (something hasn't been done) or past (something had been done).

ゴミ、捨ててなかったよ。	The trash hadn't been thrown out, you know.
先生の傘、隣には置いてないんです。	The professor's umbrella isn't (hasn't been placed) next door.
来学期のスケジュール、決めてあった。	The schedule for next semester had been decided.

Remember that the い of いる is often deleted, so that 食べてない may be the negative of 食べてある 'it hasn't been eaten' or it may be a short form of 食べていない 'I haven't eaten.'

BTS 4 まったく

In this Scene Kawakami-san is frustrated at the mess that the aikido club members left in their meeting room. He signals this by saying まったく, which in this context means 'good grief, honestly, I'm sick of this.'

まったく、いつ掃除するんだ？！	Just when is it that they're going to clean up?!

まったく literally means 'really, entirely' and you will also see it in combination with Sentences having this meaning.

昨日の授業、まったくわからなかったんだけど、どうしよう。	I didn't understand a thing in yesterday's class—what shall I do?
鈴木くんの企画、まったくだめなのね。	Suzuki-kun's design is completely ridiculous, isn't it.

Now go to the Activity Book for 練習 Practice and 腕試し Tryout.

Scene 9-2 できた！ Done!

Brian and Kawamura-senpai are helping out with a task that requires repetition at the International Student office.

The script

ブライアン	川村
あとどのぐらいですか。	まだ3分の1も片付いてないよ。
それだけ？半分は行ったと思ったんですけど。	とんでもない。さ、どんどんやって。
……できた！終わり！	やった！お疲れ様。ちょうどお昼だね。何か食べに行く？
いいですね！行きましょう。	

Brian	Kawamura
About how much longer will it be?	We haven't even done a third of it yet, you know.
That's it? I thought we'd gone through half, but . . .	No way! So keep at it.
. . . Done! The end!	We did it! Good job. It's just noon. Shall we go get something to eat?
Good idea! Let's go.	

単語と表現 Vocabulary and expressions

Nouns

半分	half (of something)
点	point(s), score
パーセント	percent

終わり	the end
お昼	noon, lunch time, lunch
夕方	evening

Verbs

行く (-U; 行った)	cover (as in a task)
片付く (-U; 片付いた)	be in order; be finished; be taken care of
Verb stem + おわる (-U; おわった)	finish X-ing
始める (-RU; 始めた)	begin
Verb stem + はじめる (-RU; はじめた)	begin X-ing

Special expressions

3分の1	one-third
だいぶ	a fair amount
さ、さあ	well, well now, so, go on
どんどん	rapidly, steadily
ちょうど	exactly, precisely, just
食べに行く	go to eat

Behind the Scenes

BTS 5 Go for the purpose of X: 食べに行く

A Verb stem (〜ます form without the ます) in combination with に行く (or other motion Verb such as 帰る) means 'go for the purpose of' or 'go (in order) to.'

先生に頼みに行ったのは今朝です。	The time that I went to ask the professor was this morning.
忘れ物を取りに戻りました。	I went back to get something I forgot.
本を借りに図書館に寄りました。	I stopped at the library to borrow a book.
熊本に3ヶ月間、勉強しに参りました。	I came to Kumamoto to study for three months.
先生と相談しに帰りました。	I went back to consult with the professor.

BTS 6 Fractions: 3分の1

Fractions are counted using [number + 分] for the denominator, which comes before the numerator in Japanese. So one-third is 3分の1, two-thirds is 3分の2, etc. (A more technical way to say 半分 'half' is 2分の1.)

8分の7	seven-eighths
5分の1	three-fifths
3/6 イコール 1/2。	Three-sixths equals one-half.
3分の2の人が「いい」と言っています。	Two-thirds of the people are saying it's fine.

Of course, Japanese also uses the decimal system. The decimal point is called 点 and numbers are read in succession. 5.324 is read ごう-てん-さんにいよん. Numbers less than one are always read with a zero, whether it appears or not. Thus both 0.675 and .675 are read れい-てん-ろくななご.

Now go to the Activity Book for 練習 Practice and 腕試し Tryout.

Scene 9-3 教えるの好きだし。 And I like teaching.

After training at Brian's aikido dojo, several people go out. After toasting, Brian and Suzuki-san, his fellow club member, begin a conversation.

The script

ブライアン	鈴木
じゃあ、乾杯!	[みんな] 乾杯!
鈴木さんは高校の先生をしているんですよね。	そう。本当はね、旅行関係の仕事に興味があったんですけど。
ふ〜ん、じゃあどうして先生になったんですか。	教えるの好きだし、旅行はね、仕事より遊びで行きたかったし。
ああ、だから。なるほど。	

Brian	Suzuki
Okay, cheers!	[everyone] Cheers!
Suzuki-san, you're a high school teacher, right?	Right. Actually, I was interested in doing travel-related work, but . . .

Huh, so why is it that you become a teacher?	I like teaching, and when it came to travel, you know, I wanted to go for fun, not for work.
Oh, that's why. I get it.	

単語と表現 Vocabulary and expressions

Nouns

乾杯(する)	toast
事務所	(business) office
研究所	research institute
公務員	public employee
会社員	company employee
アルバイト(する)	part-time work, part-timer
フリーランス	freelance, freelancer
弁護士	lawyer, attorney
エンジニア	engineer
フリーター	non-permanent worker
旅行(する)	travel
関係(する)	relationship
建築	architecture
教育(する)	education
ＩＴ	IT
法律	law
興味	interest (in something)
分析(する)	analysis
説明(する)	explanation
遊び	play, fun

Verbs

遊ぶ (-U; 遊んだ)	play
(Xに)勤める (-RU; 勤めた)	be employed (at X)

Special expressions

乾杯! (かんぱい)	Cheers!
X 関係のY (かんけい)	Y related to X
X に興味がある (きょうみ)	have an interest in X
だから	that's why

拡張 Expansion

Learn how to describe your current or past work, or your future career goals. What is the general area? (何関係?) (なにかんけい) What is your occupational title? (教師 (きょうし), エンジニア, コンサルタント, etc.) In what kind of organization do you work?

Find out what the occupations of your family and friends would be called in Japanese.

Behind the Scenes

BTS 7 Discussing occupations

When discussing what you do for a living, all occupations take です: 事務所です (じむしょ); 公務員です (こうむいん); エンジニアです. Most also combine with する: 事務所をしています (じむしょ); 公務員をしています (こうむいん); エンジニアをしています. Some take [……の仕事をしています (しごと)]: 法律の仕事をしています (ほうりつ・しごと); 建築(関係)の仕事をしています (けんちく・かんけい・しごと). Be careful about using high-ranking professions such as 先生 (せんせい), 教授 (きょうじゅ), 医者 (いしゃ), 学長 (がくちょう), 所長 (しょちょう) to talk about yourself. Similarly, ranks such as 課長 (かちょう) and 部長 (ぶちょう) are not normally used in talking about yourself.

BTS 8 どうして・なぜ〜んですか・なんで〜んですか

When asking for reason or motivation, a common pattern you will hear is [どうして + Sentence + 〜んですか], [なんで + Sentence 〜んですか] or [なぜ + Sentence + 〜んですか]. (The なぜ equivalent for 'why' is a bit more formal. The なんで equivalent is informal.) Answers must be marked as reasons—that is, using [Sentence + から] or [Sentence + んです], unless you don't know why as shown in the last example.

A: どうして部屋 (へや) をちゃんと掃除 (そうじ) しないの!
B: 面倒 (めんどう) だからね。

A: Why don't you clean up your room as you're supposed to?
B: Because it's a drag.

A: 山田君はどうして冬が好きなんでしょうね。

B: 出身が北海道でね、スキーが大好きなんですよ。だからじゃないですかね。

A: お昼ご飯からまだ 1 時間ですよ。なんでもうお腹が空くんですか。

B: 僕はお昼あまり食べなかったんですよ。

A: どうして私が謝るんですか。悪いのは部長なんですよ。

B: まあ、そう言わないで。部長は部長だからね。

A: この 2、3 年、どうしてこんなに出張がたくさんあるんでしょうかね。

B: どうしてでしょうねえ。まあ、悪いことじゃないでしょう？

A: Why do you suppose Yamada-kun likes winter?

B: She was born in Hokkaido, right? So she likes skiing! Isn't that why?

A: It hasn't been an hour since lunch! How can you be hungry already?

B: Because I didn't eat much for lunch!

A: Why am I the one to apologize? The one in the wrong is the division chief!

B: Come on, don't say that. 'Cause the division chief is the division chief.

A: What would be the reason for having so many business trips in these two or three years?

B: I wonder why that would be. Well, it's not a bad thing, right?

BTS 9 Sentence + し：教えるの好きだし

The Sentence Particle し is used when listing evidence or reasons to illustrate a point. We might think of this as 'and what's more' or '…and so on.' As often as not, the list is often truncated to a single item or remains unfinished, implying that there may be even more evidence to present and that the listener should draw some conclusion.

A: 今年もヨーロッパに行きますか。

B: いや、ユーロが高いし……。

A: 隣の喫茶によく行きますねえ。

B: ええ、オフィスに近いし、コーヒーがおいしいし。

A: あのアプリ買った？

B: うん。便利だし。

部屋片付いたし、料理もバッチリだし、いつお客様が見えても平気だね。

夏は暑いし、冬は寒いし、住みにくいところです。

勉強？とんでもない。外はやかましいし、子供はうるさいし……。

Are you going to Europe again this year?

No, the euro is expensive, and (what's more)…

You go to the coffee shop next door a lot, don't you.

Yes, it's close to the office and the coffee is delicious.

Did you buy that app?

Yeah, it's convenient and all that.

The room's been cleaned up, and the food's also ready, so whenever guests arrive it's not a problem.

Summer is hot, and winter is cold, (so) it's just a hard place to live.

Study? Heck no. It's loud outside, the children are noisy, and . . .

Now go to the Activity Book for 練習 Practice and 腕試し Tryout.

Scene 9-4 一番行ってみたいところは？
(What is) the place that you want to go and see the most?

Suzuki-san and Brian are looking at travel pamphlets for various locations that Brian picked up.

The script

鈴木	ブライアン
この中で一番行ってみたいのはどこですか。	北海道、四国、九州のうちで、ですか。
そう。この3つのうちでどこに一番行きたいですか？	う〜ん、四国かなあ。松山とか、温泉でリラックスできそうですよね。
ああ、いいですねえ、松山。『坊ちゃん』でも有名ですし。	「坊ちゃん」って、夏目漱石の？へえ、知らなかった。ますます行きたくなりますね。

Suzuki	Brian
Among these, where do you want to go the most?	You mean among Hokkaido, Shikoku, and Kyushu?
Right. Among these three, where do you want to go most?	Hmmm, maybe Shikoku. (At places) like Matsuyama it seems like you can relax at hot springs.
Ah, that's nice, Matsuyama. It's also famous for *Botchan*.	You mean Natsume Soseki's *Botchan*? I didn't know that. I want to go even more.

単語と表現 Vocabulary and expressions

Nouns

世界	the world
国	the nation
四国	Shikoku

103

本州（ほんしゅう）	Honshu
九州（きゅうしゅう）	Kyushu
北海道（ほっかいどう）	Hokkaido
沖縄（おきなわ）	Okinawa
松山（まつやま）	Matsuyama (a city in Ehime Prefecture)
札幌（さっぽろ）	Sapporo
仙台（せんだい）	Sendai
金沢（かなざわ）	Kanazawa
福岡（ふくおか）	Fukuoka
大阪（おおさか）	Osaka
京都（きょうと）	Kyoto
那覇（なは）	Naha
温泉（おんせん）	hot spring
リラックス(する)	relax
有名（ゆうめい）(な)	famous
『坊（ぼっ）ちゃん』	*Botchan* (novel by Natsume Soseki)
夏目漱石（なつめそうせき）	Natsume Soseki (author, 1867-1916)

Special expressions

CATEGORYの中（なか）で一番（いちばん）行（い）ってみたいの	within/among CATEGORY the one I want to go to most
X, Y, Zのうちで	among X, Y, and Z
3つのうちで	among three
う〜ん	u-m-m
Xで有名（ゆうめい）	well-known for X
ますます	more and more, less and less

拡張 Expansion

1. Learn how a Japanese person would say the city name and the larger governmental unit (e.g., state, province) where your school/work is located outside of Japan.
2. If you are in Japan, learn the names of five prefectures around where you are.

Behind the Scenes

BTS 10 Comparison of three or more things: 一番 most

You have seen comparisons of two things in earlier Acts. When you want to compare three or more things, you can define the set using A、B、C (の中・うち)で 'among A, B, and C' or Quantity (の中・うち) で 'among this group.' (The list of nouns might also be connected with と: AとBとC (の中・うち)で.) Either 中 or うち is acceptable, but they are optional. One member of the set is then designated as the most X using 一番 plus a sentence: AとBとC (の中・うち)で、Aが一番好きです。 'Among A, B, and C, A is my favorite.'

この４人の中で一番優しいのは誰ですか。	Who is the nicest among these four people?
京都、奈良、神戸の中では京都の秋が一番好きです。	Among Kyoto, Nara, and Kobe, I like autumn in Kyoto best.
いろいろやってみましたが、一番よくできたのはテニスでしょう。	I tried various things, but probably tennis is what I did best.
青と赤と紫のうちで、一番好きなのはどの色ですか。	Among blue, red, and purple, which color do you like best?
一日のうちで、一番大事なのは朝ごはんだって、知ってた？	Did you know that the most important (meal) of the day is breakfast?

BTS 11 都道府県

For the purposes of governance, Japan is subdivided into forty-seven units: one 都 (the large metropolis of Tokyo), one 道 (Hokkaido), two 府 (Osaka and Kyoto), and forty-three 県 (prefectures). For reference, these are grouped together under the term 都道府県.

BTS 12 温泉 Hot springs

In Japan, inns and resorts are often built around *onsen*, or 'hot springs.' Japan's many volcanos are matched by an abundance of geothermal springs. There are many kinds of *onsen*—outdoor and indoor, public and private, expensive and less expensive. At an *onsen* (and at public baths, which are rare these days), guests are expected to wash themselves (being careful not to splash water over neighboring guests) before going into the hot-spring bath. On entering the bath area (often a large tiled room), you will find washing stations with faucets, stools for sitting, and pails for pouring water over yourself, as well as soap, shampoo, and other toiletries. There are co-ed *onsen*, but for the most part, areas for men and women are separated. Guests do not wear swimsuits and are often provided with a small towel that protects modesty when going from the washing area to the bath. If you stay at an inn attached to an *onsen*, two meals (breakfast and dinner) are usually included in the price. A common morale builder for student groups and office get-togethers is a weekend at an *onsen* where everyone gets to relax and enjoy natural scenery.

Now go to the Activity Book for 練習 Practice and 腕試し Tryout.

Scene 9-5 聞く方？それとも弾く方？
Listening? Or playing?

Brian is talking to Ichiro about his hobbies.

The script

ブライアン	一郎
一郎は趣味は合気道だけ？	いや、音楽とかスポーツとか旅行とか、まあ、いろいろね。
ふぅん。音楽は、聞く方？それとも弾く方？	あ、弾くのは無理、無理。僕は聞くの(が)専門。
僕も音楽好きだよ。	知ってるよ。演歌でしょう？
え？どうして知ってるの？	だっていつもお風呂で歌ってるもん。
えぇぇ？やばい！	自分では気がつかなかった？

Brian	Ichiro
Aikido is your only hobby?	No. (I like) music and travel, all kinds of things.
Wow. Do you listen to music? Or play it?	Oh, no, no way do I play. My specialty is listening.
I like music, too, you know.	I know. Enka, right?
Huh? How do you know?	Because you're always singing in the bath.
Wha-a-t? Oh no!	You never noticed it yourself?

単語と表現 Vocabulary and expressions

Nouns

趣味	hobby
剣道	kendo
音楽	music
スポーツ	sport(s)
山登り	mountain climbing
(お)料理(する)	cooking
読書(する)	reading
ゲーム(する)	game(s)
絵	drawing, picture
演歌	enka (a popular ballad style of singing)
歌	song
ジャズ	jazz
クラシック	classical (music)
無理(な)(する)	impossible, unreasonable
(お)風呂	bath
シャワー	shower
台所	kitchen
庭	garden
リビング	living room
洗面所	washroom
玄関	entry way
自分	self, oneself

Verbs

弾く (-U; 弾いた)	play (a stringed instrument)
習う (-U; 習った)	learn
歌う (-U; 歌った)	sing
描く (-U; 描いた)	draw, paint, sketch

浴びる (-RU; 浴びた)	take (a shower) (lit. 'bathe in' or 'be covered in')
X に気がつく (-U; 気がついた)	notice X
思い出す (-U; 思い出した)	remember

Adjectives

| やばい | troublesome, dangerous, awesome, extreme (as an interjection, awful, crap, oh no) |
| まずい | awkward, unappetizing, unpleasant |

Special expressions

それとも	or (else)
聞くの(が)専門	listening is my specialty
だって……ってるもん・もの	because you're singing
自分で(は)	on one's own, by oneself (without help)

拡張 Expansion

1. Find out what your hobbies are called in Japanese. Also find out what the hobbies of your friends are called.

Behind the Scenes

BTS 13 だって（さ）+ Sentence

だって (often followed by the particle さ) is used as a conversational strategy to reduce the speaker's responsibility for a problematic situation and thus to ease the degree of anger or misunderstanding on the other person's part. This kind of explanation is used only when the problem is not serious. In this Scene, Ichiro is aware of Brian's preference in music, which may be surprising to Brian, perhaps slightly embarrassing, but not a serious offense. Using this expression with superiors may be viewed as childish.

| 何がおかしいの？だって本当のことよ。 | What's so funny? It's true! |
| わからないよ。だってさ、説明が悪いんだ。 | I don't get it. 'Cause the explanation is lousy. |

BTS 14 Giving personal reasons: もん・もの

You have seen many ways to provide reasons and explanation: [Sentence + から], [Sentence + んです], [Sentence + し], and now, [Sentence + もの] (or a more informal equivalent, もん). In an informal situation, an explanation may be followed by もん to underscore the speaker's feeling that the reason is justified. Small children often use this pattern to justify mishaps. By extension it is not always appropriate to provide an explanation, especially to superiors, when you are the cause of something going wrong—it can sound childish. Often, it is better to simply accept responsibility (no excuses) and promise to try harder next time. Notice that もの statements are often preceded by だって.

A: 昨日なんで練習休んだの？
B: だって宿題が大変だったんだもん。

A: Why did you miss practice yesterday?
B: Because my homework was so hard.

A: 欲しいなあ、このゲーム。
B: だってそれは無理でしょう。今月もうお金ないんだもん。

A: I want this game!
B: But that's not possible, right? 'Cause we don't have any more money this month.

今日は誰も来ないでしょう。だって学校がお休みだもの。

No one will come today. Because it's a school holiday.

Now go to the Activity Book for 練習 Practice and 腕試し Tryout.

110

Scene 9-6 何倍も上手でしょう。
You are probably many times better.

Ichiro is curious about Brian's Japanese language study.

The script

一郎	ブライアン
日本語はもうどのぐらい？	大学に入ってからだから、3年間ぐらい。
ハヤっ！マジ？どうやって3年でこんなに上手くなるの？	いや、まだまだ。
いや、すっごい上手いよ。	どうかなあ。一郎の英語は僕の日本語の何倍も上手でしょう。
いやいや、発音メッチャひどいし。	そんなことないよ。

Ichiro	Brian
How long is it now (that you've studied) Japanese?	Since I entered the university, so about three years.
Already! Really? How did you get this good in three years?	No, there's still a ways to go.
No, really it's amazing.	I wonder. Your English is probably many times better than my Japanese.
No, no, my pronunciation is really awful, and . . .	No such thing!

単語と表現 Vocabulary and expressions

Nouns

小学校 (しょうがっこう)　　elementary school
中学(中学校) (ちゅうがく／ちゅうがっこう)　　middle school

倍(ばい)	double, -fold
発音(はつおん)(する)	pronunciation

Verbs

入る(はいる) (-U; 入った(はいった))	go in, enter

Adjectives

速い(はやい)	speedy
上手い(うまい)	delicious, skillful
偉い(えらい)	excellent, distinguished, admirable
まずい	awful, disgusting, unappetizing
ひどい	cruel, harsh, severe
すっごい	really

Classifiers

〜倍(ばい)	multiple, -fold

Special expressions

Verb 〜てから	after X-ing
ハヤっ！	Already? So fast? (slang)
マジ？	Really? Truly? (slang)
どうやって	(doing) how
３年(ねん)で	in three years
こんなに	to this extent
どうかなあ。	I wonder
何倍(なんばい)も上手(じょうず)	many times better at
メッチャ	absurd, really, extreme (slang)

112

Behind the Scenes

BTS 15 Specifying order of events: Verb 〜てから

A Verb in the 〜て form plus から means 'after doing X' or since doing X.' What follows may be non-past, past, or some other form of Core Sentence.

日本に来てから、友だちがだいぶできました。	Since coming to Japan I've made a fair number of friends.
バックしてから、右に行きました。	After backing up, I went right.
『坊ちゃん』を読んでから、宿題してください。	Please do the homework after reading *Botchan*.
課長に相談してから決めましょう。	Let's decide after consulting with the section chief.

Note that the 〜てから combination focuses on the question of <u>when</u> something happened or will happen, while a simple 〜て form shows sequence or answers a question of <u>how</u>. Compare B's responses in the examples below.

A: 晩ご飯作る？	A: Are you going to make dinner?
B: いや、コンビニで買って食べる。	B: No, I'll buy (something) at the convenience store and eat.
A: いつ食べる？	A: When will you eat?
B: みんな来てから食べる。	B: I'll eat after everyone gets here.

When the 〜てから combination modifies another Noun, the two phrases are connected by の:

日本に来てからの仕事	work that I've done since coming to Japan

BTS 16 Interjections: ハヤ！

In informal situations, the final 〜い of Adjectives is dropped in interjections. This only happens among friends, so be cautious.

スゴっ！	Amazing!
タカっ！	Expensive!
ヤバっ！すごいうまくできてる。	No way! It's done really well.

BTS 17 Multiplication: 何倍(なんばい)

The mathematical operation of multiplication in Japanese is indicated by the word 倍(ばい) 'times.'

10は5の2倍(ばい)だね。	Ten is two times five, right?
12の6倍(ばい)はいくら？	How much is six times twelve?

This term is also used in conversation, as you see in this Scene when Brian says 何倍(なんばい)も上手(じょうず) 'many times better' in reference to Ichiro's English. By itself, 倍(ばい) means 'twice as much.'

人(ひと)の何倍(なんばい)も仕事(しごと)して、それでもサラリーは上(あ)がらない。それってひどくないですか。	I work many times harder than other people, and still my salary doesn't go up. Don't you think that's terrible?
今年(ことし)の8月(がつ)から新(あたら)しい仕事始(しごとはじ)めましたが、前(まえ)より百倍(ひゃくばい)ぐらい楽(たの)しいです。	I started a new job in August of this year, and it's a hundred times more enjoyable than the one before.
私(わたし)の倍(ばい)ぐらい食(た)べた。	He ate twice as much as I did.

BTS 18 Compliments and encouragement

In this Scene you find Ichiro complimenting Brian on his Japanese. These kinds of compliments are often meant as encouragement as much as actual admiration. Brian deflects the compliment by saying いや、まだまだ。 'No, not yet, not yet' and by complimenting Ichiro's English in turn. The exchange turns into one of mutual encouragement. This kind of humility, along with the ability to turn encouragement of your work into encouragement for the other person's, is viewed very positively in Japan. But be cautious about complimenting or encouraging higher-ups; as a rule, lower-ranking people do not have the right to judge their superiors in any way.

Now go to the Activity Book for 練習 Practice and 腕試し Tryout.

Then do 評価 Assessment activities.

◆ 読み書き Reading and writing

シーン 9-7R 火曜日のレセプション Reception on Tuesday

Brian is reading an email from Sakamoto-sensei at Fukuzawa University.

テキスト Text

Subject: レセプション

学生のみなさん

来週１４日（火曜日）のレセプションは７時からですが、６時半までにはホテルの
ロビーに来ていてください。
フォーマルなイベントですから男の人はスーツです（ネクタイはオーダーしてあります）。

よろしくお願いします。

坂本

Subject: Reception

Dear students,
The reception on the 14th (Tuesday) starts at 7:00, but please come to the hotel lobby by 6:30.
It's a formal event, so a suit is a must for men (neckties have been ordered).
Please dress appropriately.
Sakamoto

文字と例 Kanji with examples

#34.	週	シュウ		week	週
1.	今週			this week	
2.	来週行くのはわたしです。			The one who is going next week is me.	

115

3.	先週(せん)来たのはだれ？		Who was the one that came last week?
4.	1週間まったくしていません。		I haven't done it at all for one week.
4.	2週目		second week
5.	3週		three weeks or third week
6.	何週間		how many weeks

#35. 火　ひ　カ　(#36)　fire　　火

1.	#　火(ひ)	fire

#36. 曜　ヨウ　　　　　-day　　曜

1.	月曜(げつよう)	Monday
2.	火曜(か)	Tuesday
3.	日曜(にち)	Sunday
4.	月曜日に来るのはスミスさんです。	The one that's coming on Monday is Smith-san.
5.	火曜日にはしてあった。	It had been done on Tuesday.
6.	日曜日にはもうしてありました。	It had already been done on Sunday.
7.	何曜日	what day of the week?

#37. 男　おとこ　ダン (#43)　male, man　男

1.	男(おとこ)	male
2.	男の人	man
3.	まったくできないのはあの男の人です。	The one who can't do it at all is that man.

Additional Kanji with examples

#38. 水　みず　スイ　water　　水

1.	水(みず)	water
2.	水曜(すいよう)	Wednesday
3.	水曜日に行くのは3人だけです。	Those who are going on Wednesday are just three people.

#39. 木　き　モク　wood, tree　　木

1.	+	木 (き)	wood, tree
2.		レモンの木	lemon tree
3.		木曜 (もくよう)	Thursday
4.		木曜日はテニスしに行きますけど……。	I will go play tennis on Thursday, but . . .
5.	#	三木 (みき)	[family name]
6.	#	五木 (いつき)	[family name]
6.		八木 (やぎ)	[family name]
7.	#	六本木 (ろっぽんぎ)	[place name in Tokyo]

#40. 金　かね　キン　　gold, money　　金

1.	#	金 (きん)	gold
2.	+	お金 (かね)	money
3.		金曜 (よう)	Friday
4.		金曜日に行ったのはあの人だけです。	The only person who went on Friday is that person.

#41. 土　つち　ド　　earth　　土

1.	#	土 (つち)	dirt
2.		土曜 (どよう)	Saturday
3.		土曜日	Saturday
4.		土日 (どにち) にあったのはあのイベントです。	The event that was held on Saturday and Sunday is that one.

#42. 女　おんな　　female, woman　　女
　　　　ジョ　(#43)

1.	女 (おんな)	female
2.	女の人	woman
3.	今日行くのはあの女の人だったんですけど……。	The one who is going today was that woman, but . . .

117

#43. 子　こ　シ　　　child　　　子

1.		子ども	child
2.		来るのは男の子だけです。	Those who are coming are just boys.
3.		女の子	girl
4.		男の子がゲームしに来ますよ。	A boy is coming to play some games.
5.	+	男子	young man
6.	+	女子	young woman
7.	+	今日子	[female given name]

Now go to the Activity Book for 練習 Practice.

シーン 9-8R 高校(こうこう)の先生(せんせい)だよね？
High school teacher, right?

Brian is responding to Kawamura-senpai (川村センパイ), who is asking about Suzuki-san (鈴木さん) a fellow aikido club member.

テキスト Text

How about "Ninja Kid" for a movie night next week?	
	That's good.
Is Suzuki-san coming?	
	I don't know.
Suzuki-san is a high school teacher, right?	
	Yes.
Do you know the name of her high school?	
	No, I don't . . .
I see. I see.	
	Well, isn't it already Saturday today?
Oh no!	

BTL 1 Quotation marks

Japanese indicates quotations with square brackets: 「土日にあった。」って坂本先生がおっしゃいました。 Prof. Sakamoto said, "It was on Saturday." Book titles and the like (movies, television programs, etc.) are marked with heavier brackets: 『ニンジャキッド』.

BTL 2 Small っ at the end of a word or phrase

You may see a small っ at the end of a Japanese word or phrase. This indicates that the sound is cut off abruptly, and usually indicates excitement or slight irritation.

Examples

やばっ！もう11時だよ。	No way! It's already 11 o'clock.
もう全部食べたの？うそっ！マジっ？	You already ate it all? Unbelievable! Really?

文字と例 Kanji with examples

#44. 校　コウ　　　　school　　　校

1. 学校　　　　school
2. 日本語学校　　Japanese language school

120

3.	# 語学学校	(foreign) language school	
4.	どうしてこの学校にしたんですか。	Why did you decide on this school?	

#45. 高　たか(い)　コウ　　high, expensive　　高

1.	高い	expensive
2.	高さ	height
3.	+ 高校生	high school student
4.	まだ高校生だし……。	I'm still a high school student, so...
5.	高いし、やっぱりいらない。	It is expensive, so I don't need it after all.

#46. 川　かわ　　river, creek　　川

1.	# 川	river

#47. 上　うえ　かみ　ジョウ　　top, above　　上

1.	テーブルの上	on top of the table
2.	+ 目上	superior, senior, elder
3.	+ 川上	[family name]
4.	どうして川上さんがするんですか。	Why is Kawakami-san doing it?
5.	# 以上	above

#48. 名　な　メイ　　(given) name　　名

1.	+ 名	name
2.	あの人の名は何ですか。	
3.	# 人名	name of the person
4.	# 名人	master

#49. 前　まえ　ゼン　　front, before　　前

1.	ビルの前	in front of a building
2.	名前	name

3.	１か月前		one month ago/prior
4.	２年前にもう行ったことあるし……。		I've already been (there) two years ago, so...
5.	人前 (ひとまえ)		in front of people
6.	前日 (ぜんじつ)		the other day

#50. 分　わ（かる）　フン　プン　ブン　understand, divide, share, minutes　分

1.	５分 (ふん)	five minutes
2.	１０分 (じっ・じゅっぷん)	ten minutes
3.	半分 (はんぶん)	half
4.	５分前 (ふんまえ)	5 minutes before, 5 minutes prior
5.	３分の１ (ぶん)	one-third
6.	分かる (わ)	understand
7.	もういいよ。分からないだろうし……。	It's okay now. You probably don't understand it, so...
8.	＋分 (ぶん)	portion
9.	川上さんの分 (かわかみ)	Kawakami-san's portion

Additional kanji with examples

#51. 下　した　カ　ゲ　down, below, under　下

1.	下 (した)	under
2.	＋目下 (めした)	subordinate, junior, younger
3.	＋木下 (きのした)	[family name]
4.	どうしてテーブルの下にあるんですか。	Why is it underneath the table?
5.	＃上下 (じょうげ)	up and down
6.	＃下宿 (げしゅく)	lodging house
7.	＃以下 (いか)	below

#52. 聞　き(く)　ブン　　　listen, ask　　　　聞

1. 聞く — listen, ask
2. 木下さんに聞く。 — ask Kinoshita-san
3. お願いを聞く。 — grant someone's request
4. 先生に聞いたのはいつ? — When is it that (you) asked the teacher?

BTL 3 漢語

You read about 外来語 'borrowed words' in Act 3. There is another category of Japanese vocabulary called 漢語 (literally 'Chinese words,' but usually called 'Sino-Japanese vocabulary' in English). You should associate 漢語 with the 音読み of characters. These are words that are built from Chinese elements—though interestingly, they are not all Chinese. Many of them were invented in Japan, especially during the Meiji Era when Japan embarked on the process of translating scientific and technical vocabulary from the west. Just as English uses Latin and Greek elements to create technical vocabulary, Japanese uses Chinese elements to create technical vocabulary for Japanese. Like 外来語, 漢語 are almost always Nouns. It is also the case that 漢語 are more prevalent in written style than in spoken.

Spoken version	Written version
前の日 previous day	前日 previous day
日にち date	日時 date and time
日本に来る come to Japan	来日する come to Japan
急ぎ in a hurry	至急 urgent
忙しい busy	多忙 busy
大きい big	特大 enormous (size), 膨大 massive (quantity), 甚大 severe (impact)

Now go to the Activity book for 練習 Practice.

シーン 9-9R オハイオ州立大学(しゅうりつだいがく)のブラウンさん
Brown-san from The Ohio State University

Kawamura-san is reading an email he received from a staff member at the International Student Office of Fukuzawa University.

テキスト Text

Subject: ブラウンさん

川村さん

オハイオ州立大学のスー・ブラウンさんは川村さんのカンバセーションパートナーですよね?
ブラウンさんの日本語はどうですか?コミュニケーションはうまくいっていますか?

今月はブラウンさんがそちらに行くほうですか。それとも川村さんがこちらに来るほうですか。
ブラウンさんが来てからまたメールしますね。

ISO 山上

Subject: Brown-san

Kawamura-san,
Sue Brown from The Ohio State University is your conversation partner, right? How is her Japanese? Is the communication going well (between the two of you)?

Is Brown-san going there this month? Or are you coming here? I will email you again after Brown-san comes.

ISO Yamagami

文字と例 Kanji with examples

#53. 村　むら　ソン(#55)　village　村

1. 川村(かわむら)　[family name]
2. ＋ 村上(むらかみ)　[family name]
3. ＋ 上村(かみ・うえむら)　[family name]

4.	+ 木村(きむら)		[family name]
5.	村上さん、すごっ！		Murakami-san, you're great!
6.	だって川村さんってうまいんだもん。		You see, Kawamura-san is so good at it.

#54. 州　シュウ　　state (political entity)　州

1.	オハイオ州(しゅう)	state of Ohio
2.	オハイオ州に来てからまだ２か月です。	It's been two months since I came to Ohio.
3.	本(ほん)州	[island in Japan]
4.	日本で行ってみたいところは九(きゅう)州です。	The place I want to go in Japan is Kyushu.

#55. 立　た(つ)　リツ　　stand, establish　立

1.	立(た)つ	stand
2.	立ってください。	Please stand up.
3.	+ 立川(たちかわ)	[place name in Tokyo]
4.	州立大学(しゅうりつ)	state university
5.	# 村立(そんりつ)	established by a village
6.	立つほう？それともすわるほう？	Are you standing? Or are you sitting?

Additional kanji with examples

#56. 山　やま　サン　　mountain　山

1.	+ 山(やま)	mountain
2.	+ 山下(やました)	[family name]
3.	+ 上山(うえ・かみやま)	[family name]
4.	山本(やまもと)	[family name]

125

5.	¥[1]	富士山(ふじさん)	Mt. Fuji
6.	#	エベレスト山(ざん)	Mt. Everest
7.	#	山上(やまのうえ)ホテル	Mountain Top Hotel
8.		今日は山本さんがこちらに来るほうですか。それともこちらから行くほうですか。	Is Yamamoto-san coming here today or am I going (there)?
9.		だって山本さん来ないんだもん。	It's that Yamoto-san won't be coming, you see.

#57. 国　くに　コク　ゴク　nation, country, hometown　国

1.	国(くに)	nation, country, hometown
2.	四国(しこく)	[island in Japan]
3.	国語(こくご)	Japanese (subject of study for native Japanese); national language
4.	だって、国語ってスペイン語よりむずかしいんだもん。	It's that Japanese is more difficult than Spanish.
5.	国立(こくりつ)大学	national university
6.	国立大学に行ってからメールしますね。	I will email you after I go to the national university.
7.	シンガポール国立大学	National University of Singapore

#58. 中　なか　チュウ　inside, center　中

1.	中(なか)	inside
2.	この中で	among, within [category]
3.	中国(ちゅうごく)	China
4.	中国語	Chinese (language)
5.	中国人	Chinese (person)
6.	中学校	middle school
7.	#	上中下(じょうちゅうげ)	upper, middle, lower

8.	+	中山 (なかやま)	[family name]
9.	+	山中 (やまなか)	[family name]
10.	+	川中 (かわなか)	[family name]
11.		中山先生にチェックしてからですね。	It will be after checking with Nakayama-sensei.
12.		中山さんと山中さんと川中さんの中でだれがテニスがうまいですか。	Among Nakayama-san, Yamanaka-san, and Kawanaka-san, who is good at tennis?

Now go to the Activity book for 練習 Practice.

Then do 評価 Assessment activities, including 読んでみよう Contextualized reading, 書き取り Dictation, and 書いてみよう Contextualized writing.

Note

1 See ACT 7 BTL 1.

第 10 幕
Act 10

次回、頑張ろう。

Let's do our best next time.

七転び八起き
Fall down seven times, get up eight.

◆ 話す・聞く Speaking and listening

Scene 10-1 切符買っておきますので。
Because I'll buy tickets ahead of time.

Brian invites Kawamura-senpai to a baseball game.

The script

ブライアン	川村
川村さん、野球とか好きですか。	うん、好きだよ。
よかったら、来週の週末一緒に試合見に行きませんか。	あ、いいね。ジャイアンツでしょ？行こう、行こう。
じゃ、僕、チケット買っておきますので。	いい？じゃ、よろしく。久しぶりに楽しみだなあ。

Brian	Kawamura
Kawamura-san, do you like baseball and things like that?	Yeah, I do.
If you'd like, why don't you go with me to see a game next weekend?	Oh, good (idea). The Giants, right? Let's go, let's go.
Okay then, so I'll buy tickets ahead of time.	Is that all right? Well then, please (do). It's been a while and I can't wait!

単語と表現 Vocabulary and expressions

Nouns

野球	baseball
歌舞伎	kabuki (traditional theater)

131

（お）能	noh (traditional theater)
映画	movies
試合（する）	match, contest, game
ジャイアンツ	Giants
久しぶり	a while (since the last time)

Verb

行こう	let's go

Special expressions

買っておきますので	because/so I'll buy X ahead of time
久しぶりに	for the first time in a while

Behind the Scenes

BTS 1 Verb 〜ておく

The Verb おく means 'put, place.' A 〜て form followed by おく means 'do something for later; do in advance.' Often there is no English equivalent for this, except to emphasize that the speaker is doing something with forethought. In conversation, the ておく sequence is often shortened to とく.

お客さんがいらっしゃるから、掃除しておきましょう。	A client is coming so let's clean up (ahead of time).
今使わないでしょう?あっちに片付けといて。	We're not going to use it now, right? Put it away over there for now.
ここに置いといてもいいですか?	Is it all right to put it here for later?

BTS 2 Let's Verb: Verb 〜よう・〜おう

You saw the 〜ましょう form in Act 3. The informal equivalent comes up here with Ichiro saying 行こう、行こう 'Let's go, let's go.' Here is how this is formed for the four Verb groups:

- **-RU Verbs: drop *-ru* and add *–yoo***

片付ける clean up	片付けよう
考える consider, think	考えよう
見る look	見よう

- **-U Verbs: drop *-u* and add *-oo***

k-	書く write	書こう
b-	呼ぶ call, invite	呼ぼう
m-	飲む drink	飲もう
s-	話す talk	話そう
t-	待つ wait	待とう
r-	帰る return, go home	帰ろう
g-	急ぐ hurry	急ごう
w-*	使う use	使おう

- **Irregular Verbs**

来る come	来よう
する do	しよう

- The polite –ARU Verbs do not occur in this form in modern Japanese.

The core meaning of ～よう・～おう is unchanged: 'let's' or (with か) 'shall I/we.' It may occur in final position in a Sentence as an informal equivalent of Verb ～ましょう, or be embedded with 思う or 言う.

一緒に行こうよ。	Let's go together!
もうやめようよ。	Let's stop already.
もうちょっとやろうよ。まだ時間あるから。	Let's do a little more. Since there's still time.
今日はここまでにしておこうか。	Shall we stop here for today?
何か美味しいものを食べよう。	Let's eat something delicious.
もう一度よく考えてみよう。	Let's try thinking carefully about it one more time.
みんなで頑張ろう。	Let's do our best together.
あしたもっと早く来ようか。	Why don't I come earlier tomorrow?
一緒に勉強しよう。	Let's study together.
先輩があした会おうって言っていました。	*Senpai* was saying, "Let's meet tomorrow."

a. しようと思う

This form may be used with 〜と思っている to mean 'I'm thinking of doing X.'

週末、オペラを見に行こうと思っています。 I'm thinking of going to see the opera next week.

b. しようとする

This form may also be used with 〜とする to indicate an (unsuccessful) attempt.

もっときれいに描こうとしましたが、うまくいかなかったです。	I was trying to draw it better (more prettily), but wasn't able to do it well.
自分で全部しようとしないで。	Don't try to do it all yourself.

BTS 3 Giving an explanation: Sentence ので

A Sentence followed by ので is similar to [Sentence + から]. That is, both mark the reason for, or cause of, what follows—or what is understood from context. The major difference between ので and から seems to be that から sounds more logical (the Sentence with から is a direct cause of the second Sentence), while ので is more explanatory (the Sentence with ので constitutes the basis for the conclusion). Many Japanese speakers will also say that ので also seems a bit more indirect than から.

Recall from the んです pattern that だ before の changes to な.

雨なので、行かないです。 It's raining, so I won't go.

Contrast this with だ before から which does not change:

雨だから、行かないです。 It's raining, so I won't go.

Often ので is contracted to んで when speaking informally. On formal occasions you will also hear 〜ます・です followed by ので.

まだ行ったことがないんで、是非行ってみたい。	I've never been so I want to go and see it for sure.
むずかしいので、うまくできません。	It's difficult, so I can't do it well.
自分で持っています大事なものなので。	I'm holding onto it. Because it's a valuable thing.
すごく上手いので、もう何十年も練習しているんだと思いました。すごいですね!	You're so good at it that I thought you've been practicing for decades. Amazing!

Now go to the Activity Book for 練習 Practice and 腕試し Tryout.

Scene 10-2 絶対仕上げたい論文なので。
Since it's a paper I absolutely want to finish.

Kawamura-senpai seems very busy lately.

 The script

ブライアン	川村
この頃特に忙しそうですね。	うん。
論文ですか。	そう。今週中に絶対仕上げたい論文なので。
大変ですね。	一緒にいろいろできなくて悪いね。
そんなことないですよ。勉強中にお邪魔してすみませんでした。	いやいや。再来週は何かしよう。

Brian	Kawamura
You look especially busy these days.	Yeah.
Your thesis?	Right. Since it's a paper that I absolutely want to finish within this week.
Must be tough.	Sorry I couldn't do anything with you this week.
No such thing. I'm sorry to get in your way while you're studying.	No, no. Let's do something the week after next.

135

単語と表現 Vocabulary and expressions

Nouns

論文 (ろんぶん)	thesis
絶対(に) (ぜったい)	absolutely
(ご)研究(する) (けんきゅう)	research
作文 (さくぶん)	composition, essay, formal writing
実験(する) (じっけん)	experiment
調査(する) (ちょうさ)	investigation, survey
運転(する) (うんてん)	driving (a car)
X 中 (ちゅう)	while X-ing; in the middle of X-ing; within X
一日中 (いちにちじゅう)	all day
再来週 (さらいしゅう)	week after next
再来月 (さらいげつ)	month after next
再来年 (さらいねん)	year after next

Verbs

仕上げる (-RU; 仕上げた) (しあ)	finish up, complete
済ませる (-RU; 済ませた) (す)	finish, get through
出かける (-RU; 出かけた) (で)	go out
終わらせる (-RU; 終わらせた) (お)	finish (something), close (something)

Special expressions

特に (とく)	especially
この頃 (ごろ)	lately, these days

Behind the Scenes

BTS 4 X ～ 中 (ちゅう・じゅう)

中 (ちゅう・じゅう) is attached to Nouns (including Verb stems) that refer to activities or time with one of two meanings:

a 'throughout': 今週中 'throughout this week; until the end of this week,' 今学期中 'throughout the term; until the end of the term,' 午前中 'throughout the morning; until the end of the morning,' 一日中 'throughout the day; all day,' 日本中 'throughout Japan.'

今週中はこの部屋を使ってください。	Please use this room throughout the week.
難しくて、一日中かかったんですよ。	It's so difficult that it took all day.

With the Phrase Particle に, it means by the end of that span.

今日中にこの部屋の掃除、済ませましょう。	Let's finish cleaning up this room by the end of today.
来月中に、いつかお会いしたいのですが……。	I'd like to see you some time by the end of next month, but . . .

b 'in the midst of; in the middle of.' In this meaning, it is always pronounced ちゅう. 勉強中 'in the midst of studying,' 会議中 'in the middle of a conference,' 研究中 'in the middle of research,' 調査中 'in the midst of an investigation,' テスト中 'in the middle of a test,' 買い物中 'in the midst of shopping,' 休み中 'in the middle of a break.' Verb stems that occur in this form include 考え中 'in the midst of thinking about it,' 話し中 'in the middle of a conversation; on the telephone.'

今会議中で、こちらにはおりません。	She is in (the midst of) a conference, so she isn't here.
ああ、来週はまだお休み中ですか。じゃあ、再来週連絡していただけますか。	Oh, so he's on vacation until next week? Well then, can I have him contact me some time in (within) the week after next?
ちょっと静かにしてください。今テスト中ですので。	Please be quiet. It's the middle of a test.
これ、授業中は絶対見ないでくださいね。	Please do not under any circumstances look at this during the test.

BTS 5 Apologizing

Japanese culture expects apologies more than many other cultures. When a difficult or offensive situation (usually expressed with the 〜て form) arises, explanations to justify one's own actions are generally avoided. When reasons are given, they usually follow an apology expression and are framed as a way to show concern for the other. An intention to remedy the situation in the future is often expressed, as in this Scene, where Kawamura-san promises to do something fun soon.

遅れて申し訳ありません。	I am sorry (lit. 'there is no excuse') for being late.
先週は休んですみませんでした。	I am sorry that I was absent last week.
何もできなくて悪いですね。今度からは必ずお手伝いしますから。	It's terrible that I can't do anything. So I will certainly help out next time.
テスト中にやかましくしてすみませんでした。これからはもっと静かにします。	We are sorry for being noisy during the test. We will be quieter from here on.
もっと前にご連絡しなくて、本当にすみませんでした。	I am really sorry not to have been in touch sooner.

Now go to the Activity Book for 練習 Practice and 腕試し Tryout.

Scene 10-3 お決まりでしょうか。
Have you decided?

Brian arrives at a restaurant, where he has been invited to join Kawamura-senpai and his swimming club members as a guest.

The script

店員	ブライアン
いらっしゃいませ。何名様でいらっしゃいますか。	川村で予約してあると思いますが……。
あ、はい。川村様でいらっしゃいますね。	はい。
少々お待ちください。……お待たせいたしました。はい、どうぞ。お席、こちらの方になります。	[follows host to the table]
(at the table) お食事の方は伺っておりますので、こちらお飲物のメニューです。	はい、どうも。
(a while later) お決まりでしょうか。	アルコールのない飲み物もありますか。
はい、ございますよ。こちらになります。	あ、どうも。これ、オレンジジュースですね？じゃあ、とりあえず、これで。
オレンジジュースでございますね。かしこまりました。	

Reception Desk	Brian
Welcome. How many people?	I think there is a reservation under Kawamura, but . . .
Ah, yes. You are (with the) Kawamura party, right?	Yes.
Please wait a moment.… Sorry to keep you waiting. Here you go. Your seats are this way.	[follows host to the table]

139

We have received your order (for food), so here is the drink menu.	Yes, thanks.
(a while later) Have you decided?	Are there non-alcoholic drinks?
Yes, there are. Right here.	Ah, thanks. This is orange juice? I'll try this for now.
Orange juice, right. Understood.	

単語と表現 Vocabulary and expressions

Nouns

予約(する)	reservation
(お)席	seat, seated (occasion)
(お)食事(する)	a meal
(お)肉	meat
(お)魚	fish
(お)野菜	vegetable
天ぷら	tempura
麺	noodles
焼肉	*yakiniku* (grilled meat)
和食	Japanese food
中華料理	Chinese food
料理	X cuisine
メニュー	menu
アルコール	alcohol, alcoholic beverage
オレンジジュース	orange juice
サイダー	non-cola soda
コーラ	cola
(お)酒	sake, alcohol

| デザート | dessert |
| 果物(くだもの) | fruit |

Verbs

伺う(うかが)↓ (-U; 伺った)	inquire, hear
致(いた)す・いたす↓ (-U; 致した)	do, make
待(ま)たせる (-RU; 待たせた)	make someone wait
お待(ま)たせする↓	make someone wait

Adjectives

甘(あま)い	sweet
辛(から)い	spicy
しょっぱい	salty
すっぱい	sour
苦(にが)い	bitter

Classifiers

〜名様(めいさま)	X number of people (polite)
〜名(めい)	X number of people (formal)
〜杯(はい・ぱい)	X glasses/cups full

Special expressions

いらっしゃいませ。	Welcome.
〜様(さま)	[honorific title]
Noun でいらっしゃいます↑	it's X (honorific)

Noun でございます[+]	it's X (polite)
少々 (しょうしょう)	a little (polite)
お待ちください↑。	Please wait.
お待たせいたしました↓。	Sorry to make you wait.
お食事の方 (しょくじのほう)	the food part of your order
伺って↓おります↓。 (うかがって)	We've heard. We've received.
お決まりでしょう↑か。(きまり)	Have you decided?
とりあえず	for now, first of all
これで	being this
かしこまりました↓。	Understood.

Behind the Scenes

BTS 6 More on politeness

a. Polite equivalents of [Noun です]: Noun でいらっしゃいます↑・Noun でございます (polite)

You have seen polite forms: honorifics such as いらっしゃいます↑ and おっしゃいます↑ for raising the status of those you are talking about, and humble forms such as おります↓ and 申します↓ for lowering your own or your in-group's status. In this Scene you encounter a polite form of です: でいらっしゃいます (and the negative ではいらっしゃいません). This is the honorific form of です used when referring to people.

On the other hand でございます (and the negative ではございません) is neither honorific nor humble. Rather, it is simply more polite than です. Like the Verb ございます[+] that came up in Act 5, this polite form will be marked with a + sign. This form is most typically used by service personnel (waiters, salespeople) and on very formal occasions.

Customer: これ、もっとありますか。	Customer: Are there more of these?
Salesperson: はい、こちらでございます。	Salesperson: Yes, (they're) this way.
先生(せんせい)、こちら、娘(むすめ)さんでいらっしゃいますね。	Professor, this is your daughter, isn't it?

b. Polite verbs お待ちくださいː・お決まりですːか

You saw Verb stems used as Nouns in Act 7 when Brian said that he and his mother would walk (歩きです). Verb stems can also be used as honorifics with the addition of prefix お~. [お + Verb stem + ください] is a polite directive—note that the person at the reception desk asks Brian to wait, saying, お待ちくださいː. [お + Verb stem です] is an honorific form of the Verb. The person at the reception desk then asks Brian if he has decided, saying お決まりでしょうːか。

先生、お帰りですか。	Professor, are you going home?
この会議室、どなたかお使いですか。	Is anyone using this meeting room?
お持ちのアプリをもっと上手に使いましょう。	Let's make better use of the apps that you have.
みなさんもうよくお分かりですよね。	You all (lit. 'everybody') already understand well, don't you?

c. More polite expressions

Service personnel, whether in a specialty shop, a busy restaurant, or a convenience store, tend to use formulaic expressions that are very polite. You have several examples of these expressions in this Scene. They are all in the formal ～ます・です style.

いらっしゃいませ is a typical greeting you hear when you enter a business establishment, such as shops, restaurants, commercial office reception desks, food truck counters, and counters at travel agents. Do you recognize the polite いらっしゃる 'come' in this form?

何名様ですか: If the customer wants to say how many are in the party, ～名, without the suffix ～様 would be used; 3名です, for example. (An alternative would be to use 人 (3人です.) Notice also that the person at the reception desk uses the ～様 suffix with the guest's name, 川村様.

少々お待ちくださいː: 少々 is the polite equivalent of ちょっと.

お待たせいたしましたː: You saw in Act 6 the regular humble form of Verbs, [お + Verb Stem + する], including お願いする, お話しする, and お手伝いする. いたします is the humble equivalent of します. This Verb rarely occurs in the informal form in modern Japanese.

伺っております: おります is a humble equivalent of います. It regularly occurs in the formal form in modern Japanese.

You have already seen ございます, the polite equivalent of あります.

お席, お食事, and お飲物 all feature the polite prefix お.

You also encountered in Act 4 the idea of ambiguity (曖昧) that is used as a politeness strategy. The restaurant staff uses three techniques of this ambiguity strategy: こちら

の方(ほう) (lit. 'the alternative of this way') instead of こちら, お食事(しょくじ)の方(ほう) (lit. 'the meal part') instead of お食事(しょくじ), and こちらになります (lit. 'It will be(come) these') instead of the less ambiguous こちらです.

かしこまりました↓: When the order has been placed and confirmed, the restaurant staff declares that the request has been duly received. The Verb かしこまる (written with several different kanji, depending on the context) literally means 'to fear' or 'to be afraid.' In service or business settings, it's a humble, polite way of indicating understanding of an assigned task.

BTS 7 Togetherness

It has been said that Japan is a group-oriented society. People tend to sacrifice their own interests in order to maintain a consensus among group members. In schools and at the workplace, group activities are scheduled to promote group unity. And at those gatherings, there is almost always a toast to start things off and a group photo to record the event. When you are with your Japanese friends, watch for ways in which people maintain harmony and build solidarity.

Now go to the Activity Book for 練習 Practice and 腕試し Tryout.

Scene 10-4 ……言うこともあるかもしれません。
There may even be times when I say . . .

Brian has been asked to do a self-introduction to the members of Kawamura-senpai's swimming club.

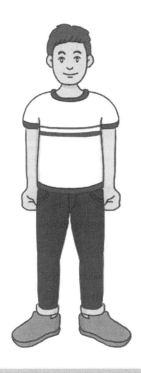

The script

ブライアン

ええと、今日は、どうもありがとうございます。クリントン大学から福沢大学に留学しているブライアン・ワンと言います。去年の9月から日本にいますが、まだしょっちゅう間違えることがあります。失礼なことを言うこともあるかもしれません。変なことを言ったときは教えてください。よろしくお願いします。

Brian	
Uhh, thank you for today. I am Brian Wang, studying abroad at Fukuzawa University from Clinton College. I've been in Japan since last September, but I still often make mistakes. There may even be times when I say things that are impolite. When I have said something strange, please tell me. It's nice to meet you.	

 ## 単語と表現 Vocabulary and expressions

Nouns

クリントン大学	Clinton University
州立大学	state or public university
県立大学	prefectural university
国立大学	national university
私立大学	private university
研修 (する)	training
インターン	intern
失礼 (な)	rude, impolite

Verbs

間違える (-RU; 間違えた)	mistake (something), make a mistake or error (on something)

Special expressions

しょっちゅう	frequently, often
あるかもしれません。	There may be. We may have.
言った時	when I have said

Behind the Scenes

BTS 8 Sentence + かもしれない

A Sentence in combination with かもしれない (or the formal equivalent かもしれません) indicates uncertainty. Possible English translations are 'may,' 'might,' 'it may/might be that.' The Sentence might be affirmative or negative, past or non-past. Notice in the following examples that だ disappears before かもしれない。

アメリカに帰るかもしれない。	She may/might return to America.
アメリカに帰ったかもしれない。	Maybe she returned to America.
アメリカに帰らないかもしれません。	She may not return to America.
アメリカに帰らなかったかもしれません。	Maybe she didn't return to America.
難しいかもしれない。	Maybe it's difficult.
難しくないかもしれません。	Maybe it isn't difficult.
課長かもしれない。	It may be the section chief.
課長じゃないかもしれません。	It may not be the section chief.
課長だったかもしれません。	It may have been the section chief.

In informal situations, かもしれない is shortened to かも.

アメリカに帰るかも。	She may/might return to America.
難しかったかも。	Maybe it was difficult.
課長じゃないかも。	It may not be the section chief.

Now compare:

連絡しないでしょう。	They probably won't be in touch.
連絡しないかもしれない。	They may not be in touch.

かもしれない is a useful expression to use when making a suggestion without sounding too knowing. Even if your opinion is in direct opposition to an opinion expressed by someone who is higher ranking than you, adding かもしれない reduces the force of your certainty and makes the speech sound more humble, allowing you to state your opinion while also maintaining a good social relationship.

こちらのほうが便利かもしれませんねえ。	This alternative may be more convenient.
このコースは来学期のほうがいいかもしれませんが……。	For this course, next term may be better, but . . .

Now go to the Activity Book for 練習 Practice and 腕試し Tryout.

Scene 10-5 分からないことが多くて……。
There are many things I don't understand . . .

The script

Sasha did some interpreting at a recent conference, but it didn't go well.

八木部長	サーシャ
モリスさん、この間の通訳、お疲れ様でした。	いえいえ。
ちょっと緊張しました？	はい。わからないことが多くて申し訳ありませんでした。
かなり専門的な内容だったから……。	でも……。
本当に、気にすることないですよ。またよろしくお願いしますね。	本当にすみませんでした。次回はもっときちんと準備しておきますから。

Division Chief Yagi	Sasha
Morris-san, good job on the interpretation the other day.	No, no.
Were you a little nervous?	Yes. I'm sorry there were so many things that I didn't understand.
The content was pretty specialized.	And yet . . .
There's really no reason to be concerned. We'll ask you again.	I'm really sorry. So I'll prepare in advance much better the next time.

単語と表現 Vocabulary and expressions

Nouns

通訳（する）	interpretation
翻訳（する）	translation

緊張（する）	tension, nervousness
専門的（な）	specialized
内容	content
次回	next time
今回	this time
前回	last time
準備（する）	preparation

Verbs

調べる (-RU; 調べた)	investigate, inquire, search
気にする	care about, be bothered, worry

Adjectives

多い	a lot, many, numerous
少ない	few, scarce

Special expressions

分からないこと	things/matters one doesn't understand
本当に	really, truly
きちんと	precisely, neatly, accurately, as it should be

Behind the Scenes

BTS 9 More on こと

You have seen こと in a number of contexts:

- Act 2 with することありますか 'is there anything for me to do';
- Act 3 with [X + のこと] 'it means X' and [Noun + のこと] 'a matter of Noun';

- Act 4 with そのこと 'that matter';
- Act 7 ということは 'that is to say';
- Act 8 with [Past Sentence + ことがある] 'have X'ed' or 'have the experience of X'; and
- Act 8 with そんなことない 'no such thing.'

こと regularly occurs with a Modifier and refers to a certain (intangible) thing, event, occurrence, or matter that is described by the Modifier. In this Scene, Sasha refers to things that she didn't understand: 分からないこと. Yagi-bucho then tells her that it isn't a matter to worry about: 気にすることないです.

そんなやかましいこと言わないでよ。	Don't say nasty things like that!
部長、大垣商会の神田健太さんのこと、ご存知ですか。	Division Chief, do you know anything about Kanda Kenta-san from Ogaki Trading Company?
オハイオ州で勉強しているということは、知らなかったです。	I didn't know that he's studying in Ohio.

BTS 10 Restoring self-image after a mishap

In this Scene, Sasha uses strategies to manage a situation that didn't go well and to recover her reputation as a responsible person. As soon as her supervisor suggests that Sasha's anxiety was apparent, Sasha offers an apology. Notice that she does not try to provide lengthy explanations about what happened and that she uses a very polite apology expression: 申し訳ありませんでした. Her immediate apology triggers Yagi-san to offer an alternative explanation, that the content of the speech was technical. To this, Sasha offers a mild protest (でも ……), taking full responsibility for what happened. At the end, and after Yagi-san provides the assurance that she wants Sasha to interpret again, Sasha concludes by offering another apology and her resolve that she will prepare better next time.

Now go to the Activity Book for 練習 Practice and 腕試し Tryout.

Scene 10-6 がっかりしないで。
Don't be disappointed.

Brian goes home to find his homestay brother, Ichiro, looking unhappy and tries to cheer him up.

The script

ブライアン	一郎
元気ないね。	別に。
悪い夢を見たとか。	ううん、そういうことじゃない。
試験の点が思ったほど良くなかったとか。	うん、国語が返ってきたんだ。
でも国語は得意だって言ってなかった？それに一生懸命やってたじゃない。	だけど、平均以下！勉強の仕方がまずかったのかも。ああ、悔しい。
残念だろうけど、そうがっかりしないで、また次、頑張ろう！	そうだね。どうも。

Brian	Ichiro
You don't have any energy, do you.	Not especially.
Did you have a bad dream or something?	Nah, nothing like that.
Your test score wasn't as good as you thought or something?	Yeah, my Japanese (test) came back.
But didn't you say that Japanese was your strong point? And you were going all out, for sure.	But I'm below average! Maybe the way I studied was bad. Ah, it's frustrating.
It's too bad, but don't be so disappointed, and try harder next time!	That's true. Thanks.

単語と表現 Vocabulary and expressions

Nouns

夢	dream
問題	problem
国語	Japanese (lit. 'national') language
外国語	foreign language
言葉・ことば	language, word(s)
得意(な)	strong point, specialty
苦手(な)	weak point, weakness
一生懸命	all out, for all one is worth
平均	average
以下	below
以上	above
しかた・仕方	way of doing
残念(な)	too bad, regrettable
がっかり(な)・(する)	feel disappointment, lose heart

Verbs

夢を見る	have (see) a dream
返ってくる	come back (inanimate)

受ける (-RU; 受けた)	receive; catch; be given
諦める (-RU; 諦めた)	be reconciled, give up
続ける (-RU; 続けた)	keep on, continue (something)

Adjectives

低い	low
高い	high, tall
悔しい	frustrating, annoying

Classifiers

1点	1 point	6点	6 points
2点	2 points	7点	7 points
3点	3 points	8点	8 points
4点	4 points	9点	9 points
5点	5 points	10点	10 points
		何点	how many points

Special expressions

元気ない	have no energy
悪い夢	nightmare
そういうこと	a thing like that; that kind of thing
思ったほど	to the extent I thought
思ったより	more (less) than I thought
X以下	below X
X以上:X以上	above X
勉強の仕方	way of studying
仕方がない・しょうがない	there is nothing to be done
Xじゃない	X, isn't it; X, for sure

Behind the Scenes

BTS 11 Sentence とか

You saw [Noun + とか] ('things like') in Act 4. Here you see とか in combination with a Sentence, meaning much the same thing.

悪い夢を見たとか。	Did you have a bad dream or something?
おいしいとかまずいとか、言わないでね。	Don't say things like 'it's delicious' or 'it's unappetizing,' okay.
金田さん、結婚したとか？	Did Kaneda-san get married or something?

BTS 12 Comparison of two activities

You encountered より, ほど, and 方 for making a comparison of two things. Recall that より is used for the point of comparison.

スペイン語より日本語が難しい。	Japanese is harder than Spanish. (Compared to Spanish, Japanese is hard.)

ほど is used in comparisons meaning 'to the extent of X' or 'as much as X.'

クラシックもいいけど、ジャズほど聴きたいとは思わないですねえ。	Classical (music) is also okay, but I never think I want to listen to it as much as jazz.
こんな色、若い人ほど似合わないと思っているかもしれませんが、そんなことありません。	Maybe you think this sort of color doesn't look as good (on you) as (it does) on younger people, but that's not the case.

And you saw 方 used (optionally) to indicate one alternative of two in making the comparison.

ここも寒いけど、北海道(の方)が大変ですよ。 It's cold here, too, but Hokkaido is worse.

より, ほど, and 方 may also follow Sentences in comparing activities. Notice that both より and ほど are preceded by a non-past form. When 方 is preceded by a past form, it sounds like a description of a specific instance; when 方 is preceded by a non-past form, it sounds like a generalization.

一人でやるより、誰かと一緒にした方が楽しいかもしれませんよ。	Compared to doing it alone, it might be more fun to do it with someone.
書くより読む方が私には易しいんです。	In fact, for me, it's easier to read than to write.
あの試験、思ったほど難しくなかった。	That test wasn't as hard as I thought.
このブログサイトの人が言うほど美味しいレストランじゃないですよ。	It's a restaurant that is not as delicious as the person in this blog site says, you know.
他の人に頼むより自分で作った方が早いかなと思いました。	I thought it would be faster to make it myself than to ask someone else.
後で全部片付けるのが簡単だと言う人もいますが、少しずつ片付ける方が楽だと言う人もいます。	There are people who say it's simpler to clean everything up afterward, but there are also those who say it's easier to clean up a little at a time.

BTS 13 Verb stem 〜方・〜かた

The phrase 仕方がない 'it can't be helped' literally means 'there is no way of doing something (or solving the problem).' 〜方 refers to a way of doing something and it works with many (though not all) Verbs. When using this form with compound Verbs that consist of [Nounする], you have [Noun + のしかた].

このロボットの使い方のわかる人、この辺にいませんか。	Is there no one around here who knows how to use this robot?
ゲームのやり方はここに説明してありますから。	The instructions for the game are written here, so . . .
人への話し方には気をつけようよね。	Be careful how you talk to people.
これ、作り方が悪かったんですよ。私の使い方には絶対問題なかったと思います。	They made this the wrong way. I think there is absolutely no problem with the way I used it.
勉強のしかたも悪かったと思うけど、いつも以上に難しかったと思います。	I think the way I studied was also bad, but I think that it was harder than usual.
掃除しなかった学生もよくないけれど、山田先生のおっしゃりかたもちょっときつかったかもしれません。	It wasn't good that students didn't clean up, but the way Yamada-sensei spoke might have been a bit harsh, too.

An alternative to 仕方がない is しょうがない.

しかたがない・しょうがない、まったく。	There's just absolutely nothing to be done about it.

BTS 14 Assertion + じゃない

In this Scene you see two distinct uses of じゃない. When Brian asks Ichiro if he had a bad dream, he responds そういうことじゃない。 'Nothing like that.' This じゃない negates what comes before it. When Brian then tells Ichiro that he's good at Japanese, he adds, それに一生懸命やってたじゃない。 'And you were going all out, for sure.' This is not a negation, but a strong assertion that what precedes じゃない, which may be a sentence, is surely true. The pitch of this second じゃない is also lower than what precedes it and does not rise at any point. Listen carefully to the Scene again.

下手?とんでもない!上手じゃない。	No good? Not at all. Surely she's good at it.
誰でもできるっておっしゃってましたけど、結構難しいじゃないですか、これ。	You said anyone could do it, but don't you think that ultimately it's really difficult.
山田さんっているじゃないですか。もう会いました?	Take Yamada-san, you know. Have you met him?

BTS 15 The こう series

You have seen そう 'that way' in a number of contexts. It is actually part of another コ・ソ・ア・ド series. The other members are こう 'this way,' ああ 'that way over there,' and どう 'what way.' They are often used followed by the Verb 言う (frequently written in kana) to describe things and people, similar in meaning to the こんな series members.

In this Scene, Ichiro rejects Brian's conjecture he had a bad dream: そういうことじゃない 'nothing like that (lit. 'not a matter of that description').'

これはね、こう使うんです。いいでしょ?	This, see, you use like this. It's nice, isn't it?
ここからはどう行くんでしょうか。	How would we go from here?
そうしましょう。	Let's do it that way.
ああいう人は珍しいんじゃないでしょうか。	Aren't people like that rare?
これ、どういうことですか?ちゃんと説明してください。	What is this? Please explain.
こういうこと、実は好きなんです。他の人は面倒だって言いますけど。	In fact I like this sort of thing. Other people say it's troublesome, but . . .

Now go to the Activity Book for 練習 Practice and 腕試し Tryout.

Then do 評価 Assessment activities.

◆ 読み書き Reading and writing

シーン 10-7R 英語(えいご)を見(み)ていただけないでしょうか。
Would you check the English?

Sasha received an email from Division Chief Yagi, with a file attached.

テキスト Text

Subject: ジャパンストアのチャンさん

モリスさん

ジャパンストアのチャンさんにメールを書いてみたのですが、今日中に英語を見ておいていただけないでしょうか。

お忙しい中すみませんが、よろしくお願いします。

八木

Subject: Chan-san from Japan Store

Morris-san,
I drafted an email to Mr. Chan of Japan Store. Would you check the English before the end of today?
Sorry to ask this of you when you are busy, but I appreciate your help.
Yagi

文字と例 Kanji with examples

#59. 書 か(く) ショ   write   書

1.   書く   write
2.   書きかた   how to write
3. # マニュアル書(しょ)   manual, booklet

157

4.	# 聖書 (せいしょ)		Bible
5.	日本語で書こうよ！		Let's write it in Japanese!
6.	日本語でも書いてみようよ。		Let's try writing it in Japanese, too.
7.	ここに書いておきますので……。		I'll have it written here in advance, so . . .

#60. 英　ひで　エイ　　England　英

1.	英語 (えい)	English (language)
2.	+ 英国 (えいこく)	England
3.	+ 英一 (えいいち)	[male given name]
4.	+ 英子 (えい・ひでこ)	[female given name]
5.	英語で書いておくので……。	I'll have it written in English, so . . .
6.	英語で書こうかな。	I wonder if I should write in English.
7.	英語で書いてみようよ。	Let's try writing it in English.
8.	もう書かないでください。	Please don't write any more.

#61. 見　み(る)　み(える)　ケン　　look, see　見

1.	見る	look, watch
2.	見える	appear, be visible
3.	# 見学(する) (けんがく)	visit (a factory, etc.), going on a field trip observe (a class, etc.)
4.	今日見ようよ。	Let's see it today.
5.	あしたも見てみようよ。	Let's try seeing it tomorrow, too.
6.	見ないでくださいね。	Please don't look at it.
7.	あそこに大学が見えるので、もうすぐですよ。	The university is over there, so we are almost there.
8.	あそこの山が見える人、いる？	Is there anyone who can see the mountain over there?
9.	今日から一週間ボランティアの先生が見えます。	A volunteer teacher is coming for a week starting today.
10.	先週ポートランド州立大学の山中さんが見えました。	Yamanaka-san from Portland State University came last week.

#62. 忙 いそが（しい）　　　　　busy　　忙
　　　ボウ (see kanji #63)

1. 忙しい — busy
2. +お忙しい中 — when you are busy
3. 忙しそう — appears to be busy
4. 忙しいけどしてみようよ。 — We are busy, but let's try it.
5. 忙しそうなので、またいつか……。 — You seem busy, so I'll (come back) someday . . .

#63. 多 おお(い)　タ　　　　　many　　多

1. 多い — a lot
2. #（ご）多忙 — busy
3. #ご多忙中 — in the midst of your being busy
4. まだ人が多いので、ちょっと……。 — There are still many people, so . . .
5. 今日も人が多そうだから、あしたまた来ようよ。 — There appear to be many people today, too, so let's come back tomorrow.

#64. 少 すく(ない)　すこ（し）ショウ　few　　少
　　　(see kanji #65)

1. 少し — a little
2. 少ない — few
3. 少なそうですね。 — It appears to be a small number/quantity.
4. 学生が少ないので、キャンセルしようと思ってます。 — There aren't many students, so I'm thinking of canceling it.

#65. 々 [symbol indicating that the preceding symbol is to be repeated]　々

1. 時々 — sometimes
2. #人々 — people
3. #日々 — days
4. 時々行こうかな。 — I'm thinking I might go some time.

#66. 待 ま（つ） タイ　　　wait　　待

1. 待つ — wait
2. 少々お待ちください。 — Please wait a moment.
3. お待ちしております。 — I'll be waiting.
4. お待たせいたしました。 — Sorry to make you wait.
5. #招待する — invite
6. もう少し待ってください。 — Please wait a little longer.
7. もう待たないでください。 — Please don't wait any longer.
8. もう少し待ってみようかな。 — I'm thinking I'll wait a little longer.
9. もう待てないので、先に行きますね。 — I can't wait any longer, so I'm going ahead.
10. まだ待ってるんですか。あの人。 — Are you still waiting for that person?

#67. 新 あたら（しい） にい シン　　　new　　新

1. 新しい — new, fresh
2. #新潟 — Niigata
3. 新しそう — appears to be new
4. 新聞 — newspaper
5. #新年 — new year
6. まだ新しいので……。 — It's still new, so . . .
7. +新田 — [family name]
8. もう新しくないから……。 — It's no longer new, so . . .
9. 新しそうなノートパソコンですね。 — Its a laptop that looks new.
10. 新しくしようよ。 — Let's make it new.
11. 新しくしてみない? — Shall we try making it new?
12. 新しくしてみようかな。 — I'm thinking I'll try making it new.

Now go to the Activity Book for 練習 Practice.

160

シーン 10-8R 昨日デパートで買ってきました。
I bought it yesterday at a department store.

Sasha found a handwritten note left on her desk by her coworker, along with a wrapped box.

テキスト Text

> サーシャさん、
> このクッキー、スイーツがお好きな
> サーシャさんへ、と思って、
> 昨日デパートで買って来ました。
> すごくおいしいですよ!
> ぜひ食べてみてください。
> 　　　　　　　　　　　中田

Sasha-san,

I bought these cookies yesterday at a department store, thinking (this should go) to you, who likes sweets.

They're really good! Please try them.

Nakata

文字と例 Kanji with examples

#68. 好　す(き)この(む)　コウ　　like, appealing　　好
5.　　好きな本　　　　　　　　　　　a book I like

161

6.	スポーツが好きです。	I like sports.
7.	大好き（な）	very likeable, favorite
8.	#好む	like
9.	#好みの人	a person who is my type
10.	#好意	affection, good feeling
11.	まだ好きかもしれませんし……。	I might still like it, so . . .
12.	もう好きじゃないかもしれませんよ。	He might not like it any more.
13.	あの人のことがまだ好きなので……。	I like her still, so . . .
14.	あの人のことがまだ好きだから……。	I still like her so . . .

#69. 思 おも(う) シ　　think　　思

6.	思う	think
7.	#意思	intention
8.	どう思いますか。	What do you think?
9.	いいと思います。	I think it's good.
10.	好きだと思います。	I think I like it.
11.	日本語で書こうと思ってます。	I'm thinking of writing it in Japanese.
12.	英語でも日本語でもいいと思うんですが……。	It is that I think it is okay either in English or Japanese . . .
13.	あそこでまだ待ってると思いますよ。	I think she is still waiting over there.
14.	ここがいいと思う人、いませんか。	Is there anyone who thinks this place is good?

#70. 昨 サク　　previous　　昨

1.	昨日	yesterday
2.	昨日だったよ。	It was yesterday.
3.	昨日だったかな。	I wonder if it was yesterday.
4.	昨日だったかもしれません。	Maybe it was yesterday.
5.	昨日だったかもしれない。	Maybe it was yesterday.
6.	昨日だったと思います。	I think it was yesterday.

#71. 買 か(う) バイ　　buy　　買

5.	買う	buy
6.	#売買	buying and selling
7.	買ってよ。	Please buy it.
8.	買おうよ。	Let's buy it.

162

9.	買ってみようよ。		Let's try buying it.
10.	買わないの？		What, are you not buying it?
11.	買わないと思います。		I think I won't buy it.
12.	買わないかもしれません。		Maybe I won't buy it.
13.	買うとは思いません。		I don't think I will buy it.
14.	買わないでください。		Please don't buy it.
15.	ノートパソコン買う人いますか。		Anyone buying a laptop?

#72. 食　た（べる）　ショク　　eat, a meal　　食

1.	食べる	eat
2.	# 少食	(person who) doesn't eat much, has a small appetite
3.	# 食前	before a meal
4.	もっと食べて。	Please eat more.
5.	もう食べないで。	Please don't eat any more.
6.	食べないかもしれないなあ。	Maybe they won't eat it.
7.	食べると思いますよ。	I think they will eat it.
8.	もう食べただろうね。	They probably ate already.
9.	前に食べたことありますか。	Have you eaten this before?

#73. 田　た・だ　デン　　rice field　　田

1.	+ 中田（なかた・だ）	[family name]
2.	+ 田中（たなか）	[family name]
3.	+ 本田（ほんだ）	[family name]
4.	山田（やまだ）	[family name]
5.	+ 村田（むらた）	[family name]
6.	+ 金田（かねだ）	[family name]
7.	+ 前田（まえだ）	[family name]
8.	+ 上田（うえだ）	[family name]
9.	+ 川田（かわた）	[family name]
10.	+ 田川（たがわ）	[family name]
11.	+ 田村（たむら）	[family name]
12.	+ 水田（みずた）	[family name]
13.	# 水田（すいでん）	paddy, (rice) field
14.	中田でございます。	I'm Nakata.
15.	田中さんでいらっしゃいますか。	Are you Tanaka-san?

次回、頑張ろう。

Additional kanji with examples

#74. 後 うし(ろ)　あと　のち　ゴ　　after, behind, later 後
(often written in hiragana: あと)

1. 後ろ — back, behind
2. クラスの後 — after class
3. + 後ほど — later
4. # 食後 — after a meal
5. # 前後 — before and after
6. 後ろにございますが……。 — It is in the back, but . . .
7. 後ろにあるかもしれないよ。 — It might be in the back.
8. 後ろでお持ちください。 — Please wait in the back.

#75. 午 ゴ　　noon 午

1. 午前 — a.m., morning
2. 午後 — p.m., afternoon
3. 午前中 — throughout the morning; until the end of the morning
4. 午前でも午後でもいいですよ。 — Either a.m. or p.m. is fine.
5. まだ午前中なので、もう少し待ってみましょう。 — It is still in the morning, so let's try waiting a little longer.

#76. 去 さ(る)　キョ　　leave, previous 去

1. # 去る — leave
2. 去年 — last year
3. 去年だったと思いますよ。 — I think it was last year.
4. 去年からしているんですよ。 — It is that I've been doing it since last year.
5. 去年まで大学に行ってた人はだれかいますか。 — Is there anyone who was going to college until last year?

#77. 明 あか(るい)　あ(ける)　メイ　ミョウ　bright 明

1. 明日 — tomorrow
2. ¥ 明治 — Meiji Era
3. 明後日 — day after tomorrow
4. 明るい — bright, cheerful
5. + 明けましておめでとうございます。 — Happy New Year.

6.	明日書こうと思ってます。	I'm thinking of writing it tomorrow.
7.	田中さんは明るいですね。	Tanaka-san is cheerful.
8.	まだ明るいので、もう少し待ってもいいと思いますよ。	It is still bright, so I think it's okay to wait a little longer.

Review: relative time expressions

	-2	-1	now/this	+1	+2
day	一昨日 （おととい・ イッサクジツ）	昨日 （きのう・ サクジツ）	今日 （きょう）	明日 （あした・ ミョウニチ）	明後日 （あさって・ ミョウゴニチ）
week	先々週 （センセンシュウ）	先週 （センシュウ）	今週 （コンシュウ）	来週 （ライシュウ）	再来週 （サライシュウ）
month	先々月 （センセンゲツ）	先月 （センゲツ）	今月 （コンゲツ）	来月 （ライゲツ）	再来月 （サライゲツ）
year	一昨年 （おととし・ イッサクネン）	去年 （キョネン）	今年 （ことし）	来年 （ライネン）	再来年 （サライネン）

#78. 飲　の(む)　イン　　　　drink　飲

1. 飲む — drink
2. # 飲食 — eating and drinking
3. ビールは飲みません。 — I don't drink beer.
4. ジュースは飲まないと思いますよ。 — I don't think he drinks juice.
5. 飲みに行きませんか。 — Would you like to go drinking?
6. みんなで飲みに行こうよ。 — Let's go drinking with everyone.
7. 3人で飲みに行こうと思っています。 — We're thinking of going out to drink, the three of us.
8. どうぞお飲みください。 — Please drink it.
9. 今日飲みに行く人は何人いますか。 — How many people are going out to drink today?

Now go to the Activity Book for 練習 Practice.

シーン 10-9R 会社のほうに TEL ください。
Call me at work.

Kawamura-san and his acquaintance, Yamamoto-san, are making plans.

 テキスト Text

Kawamura-san, I'm thinking of eating out today (since it's been a while) after work. If you'd like, won't you go with me?

                   That sounds good.

I'll be in the office until about 6:00 so please call me at work.

                         Okay!

Behind the lines

BTL 1 Punctuation in long sentences

Punctuation, especially the comma, is a relatively new concept in Japanese writing. If you look at writing from pre-Meiji Japan you will see very little punctuation. But along with many other language conventions that entered Japan from the West in the 19th century, breaking up long sentences with commas became a concern. In fact, there are no strict rules for commas in Japanese. Some places that you can expect to see commas are: in lists, after Particles (especially は), when the Sentence Modifier is extremely long (a comma follows the modified Noun's Particle), after a 〜て form, after phrases ending in が or けど, and to break up consecutive *hiragana* or *kanji* sequences. Essentially, wherever a speaker might take a breath, you are apt to see a comma.

After Particles, listing Nouns

明日のクラスは、田中さん、村上さん、金子さんでお願いします。	For tomorrow's class, Tanaka-san, Murakami-san, Kaneko-san, please (be ready).

Long Sentence Modifier

先週の火曜日に電話をかけてきた大学生の安田さんが、明日のクラスを教えることになった。	It has been decided that Yasuda-san, who called last Tuesday, will teach class tomorrow.

After a 〜て form

神田さんは明日で、サーシャさんは明後日です。	Kanda-san will be tomorrow, and Sasha-san will be the day after tomorrow.
昨日はショッピングをして、前から読みたかった本を買った	Yesterday I went shopping and bought a book that I wanted to read for some time.

After phrases ending in が or けど,

ドリンクですが、コーヒー、オレンジジュース、お茶、水はあります。	As for the drinks we have coffee, orange juice, tea, and water.

Consecutive hiragana and kanji sequences

ざるそばと、かけうどんを買いました。	I bought *zaru-soba* and *kake-udon*.
あの試験、緊張しました。	I was nervous about that test.

文字と例 Kanji with examples

#79. 仕 シ (see kanji #80) serve 仕

#80. 事 こと ジ thing, matter 事

1. 仕事 — job, work
2. 仕事中 — in the middle of working
3. # 火事 — a fire
4. 食事 — meal
5. 食事中 — in the middle of having a meal
6. 仕事に行くことが多くて……。 — It's that I frequently go to work . . .
7. 午前中だから仕事中だろうね。 — It is in the morning, so (he is) probably working.
8. みんなで食事するとかってどうですか。 — How about we go out to eat?
9. もう食事中かもしれませんよ。 — They might be eating already.

#81. 外 そと ガイ outside 外

1. ビルの外 — outside the building
2. 外食 — dining meal
3. 外人 — foreigner
4. 外国 — foreign country
5. 外国人 — foreigner
6. 外には行かないと思うよ。 — I don't think she will go out.
7. 思ったほど外人が多くないね。 — There aren't as many foreigners as expected.
8. 思ったより外に人がいないかもしれないね。 — There may be more people outside than expected.

#82. 会 あ(う) カイ meet, get-together 会

1. 会う — meet
2. + 日本語学生会 — Japanese Language Student Organization
3. # 女子会 — girls' meeting, girls' (night) out
4. # 飲み会 — drinking party
5. + 会田 — [family name]
6. 先生に会いに行こうよ。 — Let's go see (our) teacher.
7. もう会わないと思う。 — I think I won't see him any more.
8. 思ったより学生が多いですね、日本語学生会。 — There are more students than expected in the Japanese Language Student Organization.

168

#83. 社　シャ　　　　company　　　社

1.	会社 (かいしゃ)	company
2.	タクシー会社 (がい)	taxi company
3.	社会	society, social studies
4.	社会学	sociology
5.	+ 社会人 (しゃかいじん)	a (working) member of society, an employed adult
6.	思ったほど会社に人がいない。	There aren't as many people at the company as expected.
7.	会社に来ないことが多くて……。	There are many times she doesn't come to the work.
8.	今日は会社に来ないかもしれないよ。	They might not come to the company today.

Now go to the Activity Book for 練習 Practice.

Then do 評価 Assessment activities, including 読んでみよう Contextualized reading, 書き取り Dictation, and 書いてみよう Contextualized writing.

第11幕
Act 11

どうしたらいい？

What shall I do?

目(め)は口(くち)ほどに物(もの)を言(い)う
Eyes say as much as words.

◆ 話す・聞く　Speaking and listening

Scene 11-1 必要でしたらおっしゃってください。
If you need it, please say so.

Sasha takes a call at the office. You hear only her side of the conversation. Can you guess who's calling? And what the caller must be saying?

The script

サーシャ	白井
はい、大垣商会、企画部、サーシャ・モリスです。	あ、モリスさん、吉田運送の白井です。いつもお世話になっております。
あ、白井さん。いつもお世話になっております。	この間はありがとうございました。
いえいえ、ご丁寧にありがとうございます。	いや、本当に助かりました。
もしまた必要でしたら、いつでもおっしゃってください。	モリスさんと神田さんのお陰で、社長も喜んでいます。
あの、神田と代わりましょうか。	いえいえ、お忙しいでしょうから結構です。どうぞよろしくお伝えください。
承知いたしました。申し伝えます。	では、またこれからもよろしくお願いいたします。
はい、こちらこそ、よろしくお願いいたします。	どうも失礼いたしました。
では、失礼いたします。	どうも、失礼いたします。

Sasha	Shirai
Hello, Ogaki Trading, Planning Division; this is Sasha Morris.	Ah, Morris-san. It's Shirai from Yoshida Transport. We always appreciate your business.
Ah, Shirai-san. We are grateful to you.	Thank you for the other day.
No, no, you're very polite (to say so).	No, it really helped.
If you need it again, then please say so any time.	Thanks to you and Kanda-san, our president is very happy.
Um, shall I switch you over to Kanda-san?	No, no, he must be busy so it's fine. Please pass along our regards.
Understood. I will tell him.	Well, then, we look forward to (working with you) again.
Yes. Not at all. We look forward (to working with you).	Well then, sorry to bother you.
So then, excuse me.	Excuse me.

単語と表現 Vocabulary and expressions

Nouns

企画部 (きかくぶ)	planning division
開発部 (かいはつぶ)	development division
営業部 (えいぎょうぶ)	operations division
(ご)丁寧(な) (ていねい)	polite, careful, meticulous
(ご)必要(な) (ひつよう)	necessary
(ご)承知(する) (しょうち)	acceptance, consent

Verbs

申し伝える↓ (もうつた) (-RU; 申し伝えた)	convey a message
申し上げる↓ (もうあ) (-RU; 申し上げた)	say, tell
伝える (つた) (-RU; 伝えた)	convey a message
Xと代わる (か) (-U; 代わった)	switch over to X (on the telephone)

Special expressions

もし	if, supposing
必要(ひつよう)でしたら	if (it's) needed

拡張 Expansion

Have you ever had an injury, such as a broken bone, a sprain, a burn, or a cut? Find out from Japanese associates/friends how they would describe the injury.

Behind the Scenes

BTS 1 Conditional 〜たら + non-past Sentence

All Core Sentences (Verbs, Adjectives, Noun です) have a Conditional or 〜たら form, a combination of the 〜た form plus ら. Verbs and [Noun です] may be formal (行(い)きましたら, 必要(ひつよう)でしたら) or informal (e.g., 行(い)ったら, 必要(ひつよう)だったら); there is only one form for Adjectives (高(たか)かったら).

The basic meaning of the 〜たら form is 'given X, then Y.' This has a number of English equivalents that come up in this Act. In this Scene, Sasha tells Kanda-san また必要(ひつよう)でしたら、いつでもおっしゃってください. 'If you need it again, then please just say so any time.' Thus a 〜たら form in combination with a non-past Sentence may mean 'if' or it may mean 'when' in English, depending on the context. Consider the examples below.

わかったら、是非(ぜひ)教(おし)えてください。	When you find out, please be sure to tell me.
使(つか)い終(お)わったら捨(す)ててください。	When you finish using it, please throw it away.
来学期(らいがっき)だったらもっと時間(じかん)があるので、アルバイトもかなりできると思(おも)うんですが……。	When it's next semester I'll have more time, so I think I'll be able to do a part time job.
高(たか)かったら、買(か)わないでね。	If it's expensive, don't buy it, okay?

BTS 2 Business phone conversations

Business calls on the telephone follow a predictable pattern. In fact, new recruits are often drilled on this when they enter a company. In practice, employees are even instructed on small details such as "Hold the telephone in your left hand and take a message with your right" (assuming that one is right-handed). The sequencing often goes like this: 1. Identify yourself and verify who is calling; 2. Use a ritual expression that acknowledges the relationship (here Sasha says いつもお世話になっております); 3. Find out the reason for the call; 4. Confirm important details, especially dates, times, and intended follow-up; 5. Acknowledge the relationship again (here Sasha uses よろしくお願いいたします); 6. End the call (here Sasha uses 失礼いたします). Note that telephone calls tend to be more formal and more polite than face-to-face interactions. This explains the use of ritual expressions, as well as polite forms such as お世話になっております↓ and 申し伝えます↓. Note the frequent substitution of いたします↓ in phrases that might take します (承知いたしました↓, お願いいたします↓, 失礼いたします↓). There are also set expressions that acknowledge the other person's attention to your situation; Sasha uses ご丁寧に 'you are very polite,' but she might also use ご親切に 'you are very kind.'

BTS 3 Xと・に代わる

The Verb 代わる means 'switch to' (on the telephone) or 'take the place of; substitute for' depending on the [Noun + Particle] that precedes it. Look closely at the Particles in the following examples.

神田さんと代わりますので、少々お待ちください。	I will switch to Kanda-san so please wait a moment.
明日のバイトを先輩に代わっていただきたいんですが。	It's that I would like to take the place of my *senpai* at work tomorrow.
坂本先生に代わって、今日は私がこの授業を教えます。	I will teach this class today, substituting for Prof. Sakamoto.

Now go to the Activity Book for 練習 Practice and 腕試し Tryout.

Scene 11-2 それにしたら？ If you do that?

Sasha is trying on an outfit at home and realizes there is a slight issue.

The Script

サーシャ	恵理
この服、面接に着ようと思ってるんだけど、どうかな。	なかなかいいんじゃない？色もよく似合ってる。
フォーマル過ぎない？	いや、全然。考え過ぎだよ。
じゃあ、やっぱりこれ着ていくか。	いいんじゃない？それにしたら？

Sasha	Eri
I'm thinking of wearing this outfit to my interview, but I wonder.	Isn't it pretty nice? The color looks good on you.
Isn't it too formal?	No, not at all. You're overthinking it.
Well then, I guess I'll wear it after all.	Won't it be okay? If you do that?

単語と表現 Vocabulary and expressions

Nouns

服	clothing, outfit
ワイシャツ	dress shirt (for men)
ブラウス	blouse
スカート	skirt
パンツ	slacks, pants
スーツ	suit
ドレス	dress

指輪(する)	ring
イアリング(する)	earring
インタビュー(する)	interview (television, media, also job)
フォーマル	formal
カジュアル	casual
学会	academic conference
考え過ぎ	thinking too much
食べ過ぎ	eating too much
飲み過ぎ	drinking too much
面接(する)	interview (for a job)
全然	not at all, never

Verbs

着る (-RU; 着た)	put on, wear (on the top of the body, such as shirts, blouses)
履く(-U; 履いた)	put on, pull on, wear (on the legs, such as slacks)
過ぎる (-RU; 過ぎた)	exceed, go beyond
脱ぐ (-U; 脱いだ)	take off (clothing)
(XがYに)似合う(-U; 似合った)	X looks good on Y

Adjectives

濃い	dark (color), thick, strong (flavor, possibility)
薄い	light (color), thin, diluted, weak (taste, probability)

Special expressions

〜過ぎ(る)	over- (overeat, overdo, etc.)
面接に着る	wear to an interview
なかなか + affirmative	rather, more than expected
それにしたら?	If you did that (how would it be)?

Behind the Scenes

BTS 4 Clothing and Verbs for wearing

In English, the Verbs 'wear' and 'put on' can be used for almost any item of clothing. In Japanese, the Verb is different depending on the part of the body and the action that is required to put something on. The Verb 履く is used when you pull something (such as slacks, hose, socks, or shoes) onto your feet or legs. The Verb 着る is used for items of clothing (shirts, blouses, coats, sweaters, etc.) that go on the top of your body. Other Verbs will appear in later Acts.

BTS 5 Giving/seeking suggestions それにしたら?

Because ～たら expresses something as a condition ('given X, then Y'), it can also be used for making and seeking suggestions. It is often followed by どうですか。to mean 'How about if you do X?' and with (or without) a question word plus いいですか to seek advice.

諦めないで一生懸命やってみたらどうですか。	How about if you didn't give up but instead tried your best?
ああ、だめだ。どうしたらいいでしょうか。	Oh, this won't work. What shall we do? (lit. 'What would it be good to do?')
私よりよく知っている人に相談してみたらどうでしょうか。	How would it be if you consulted with a person who knows more than I do?
しばらく休んだらよくなるよ。	If you rest for a while, it will get better, you know.

BTS 6 Excess: ～過ぎ（る）

The Verb 過ぎる attaches to the stem of a Verb to form a compound that means you have overdone the Verb. It may also attach to Adjective stems and な-Nouns to indicate excessiveness. As is the case with many compound words, the second portion (過ぎる) is sometimes written in hiragana. The stem of the compound (過ぎ) is often used as a Noun.

食べ過ぎ、飲み過ぎのお薬です。	It's a medicine for overeating and overdrinking.
考えすぎですよ、それは。	That is overthinking it, you know.
多過ぎたら申し訳ありません。	If it was too many, I'm really sorry.
大変過ぎたらそう言ってください。お手伝いしますから。	If it's too tough, please say so. Because we'll help you.

In the negative, use of 過ぎる indicates negative excess or inadequacy.

娘はお野菜を食べなさ過ぎです。	My daughter doesn't eat enough vegetables.
そのスーツ着るの？ちょっとフォーマルじゃなさ過ぎると思うけど。	You are going to wear that suit? I think it's not formal enough, but. . . .
弟の話って、あまり面白くなさ過ぎて、泣きたくなっちゃいますよ。	My brother's story is so uninteresting I want to cry.

Recall from Act 8 that for negative Verbs in ～そう 'appearance' さ is usually optional. Thus both 食べなさそう and 食べなそう are acceptable, while する is always しなさそう. The same is true for negative verbs in すぎる. Both 食べなさすぎ(る) and 食べなすぎ(る) are acceptable while する is always しなさすぎ(る).

Now go to the Activity Book for 練習 Practice and 腕試し Tryout.

Scene 11-3 10月になったら長袖
Long sleeves as soon as it's October

Ichiro notices that Brian is always wearing T-shirts, even in winter.

The script

一郎	ブライアン
ブライアンは冬でも半袖で寒くないの?	Tシャツが好きなんで。
日本の方が、季節によって着るものがはっきり変わるのかもしれないね。僕は10月になったら長袖。	僕はいつもTシャツで、寒かったらその上にセーターとかオーバーとか重ねることにしてるから。
それも実用的かもね。	うん、それに、楽だよ、Tシャツは。

Ichiro	Brian
Brian, isn't it cold wearing short sleeves even in winter?	It's that I like T-shirts.
Maybe it's because in Japan, depending on the season, what we wear changes completely. I wear long-sleeves as soon as it becomes October.	I always wear T-shirts, and if it's cold, I usually put a sweater or coat on top of that, so...
That may also be practical.	Yeah, and they're comfortable—T-shirts.

単語と表現 Vocabulary and expressions

Nouns

季節	season
半袖	short sleeves
長袖	long sleeves
シャツ	shirt
セーター	sweater
ジャケット	jacket
オーバー	coat
実用的(な)	practical

Verbs

重ねる(-RU; 重ねた)	layer, put on top
変わる(-U; 変わった)	change, switch

Special expressions

季節によって	depending on the season
重ねることにして(い)る	usually layer (habit)

Behind the Scenes

BTS 7 〜ことにする

You have seen こと in a number of contexts. Remember that こと regularly occurs with a Modifier and refers to a certain (intangible) thing, event, occurrence, or matter that is described by the Modifier. Here we will discuss three combinations that involve 〜ことにする, all of which have to do with some kind of decision.

a. Verb 〜ことにする for decision to do X

A Sentence plus 〜ことにする in non-past or past form indicates a decision. 〜ことにしませんか is a suggestion for a decision.

雨なので、今日は行かないことにしました。	Since it's raining, we decided not to go today.
あの有名なレストランで食べることにしました。	We decided to eat at that famous restaurant.
みんなで集まることにしませんか。	Shall we have everyone gather together?

b. 〜ことにしている for routine action

We find Brian using a 〜ことにしている in this Scene to express his personal routine.

その上にセーターとかオーバーとか重ねることにしてる。	I usually put a sweater or coat on top of that.
土曜日は一日遊ぶことにしています。	It's my routine to take it easy all day on Saturday.

c. 〜ということにする to indicate an assumption

こと can also be used to indicate an assumption in the pattern 〜ということにする.

昨日、病気だということにして休んだけど、本当は病気じゃなかったんだ。	I took a day off yesterday, claiming I was sick, but in fact I wasn't sick.
まだみんな来てないけど、集まったということにしましょう。	Not everyone is here yet, but let's just say that they are.
これからプレゼンをするということにして、ちょっと練習してみましょうか。	Let's assume that we're going to have a presentation and do a little practice.

Now go to the Activity Book for 練習 Practice and 腕試し Tryout.

Scene 11-4 知っていたら持ってきたんですけど……。
If I had known I would have brought it, but . . .

Sasha sees Kanda-san wearing a brightly colored tie.

The script

サーシャ	神田
あ、素敵なネクタイですね。	どうも。実は昨日誕生日でね、妻からのプレゼントです。
わあ、奥様から?さすが、神田さんのイメージにピッタリです。	どういう意味かな。僕こんなに明るいですか。
明るいですよ。明るくて積極的。その上同僚思い。	それはどうも。
あ、お誕生日、おめでとうございます!知っていたらお祝い持ってきたんですけど……。	いやいや、いいですよ。

Sasha	Kanda
Oh, that's a nice necktie, isn't it.	Thanks. Actually, yesterday was my birthday, see, and it's a present from my wife.
Wow, from your wife? Wouldn't you know, it fits your image perfectly.	What do you mean? Am I this colorful?
You are colorful! Colorful and active. Plus, thoughtful about your co-workers.	Thanks for (saying) that.
Oh, happy birthday! If I had known I would have brought a present, but. . .	No, no, that's okay.

単語と表現 Vocabulary and expressions

Nouns

素敵(な)	sharp, nice, good-looking
おしゃれ(な)	stylish
ネクタイ	necktie
靴	shoes
アクセサリー	accessory
帽子	hat
手袋	gloves
メガネ	eyeglasses
ヘアスタイル	hairstyle
もの	thing (tangible)
パートナー	(romantic) partner
親戚	relative, family (in-group)
祖母	grandmother (in-group)
祖父	grandfather (in-group)
伯父・叔父 [1]	uncle (in-group)
伯母・叔母	aunt (in-group)
いとこ	cousin (in-group)
奥様	wife (polite)
ご主人(様)	husband (polite)
ご親戚	relative, family (polite)
おじさん・叔父様	uncle (polite)
おばさん・叔母様	aunt (polite)
おいとこさん	cousin (polite)
彼	he, boyfriend
彼女	she, girlfriend

1. The kanji for terms referring to 'uncle' and 'aunt' reflect an earlier distinction made between those who are older (伯父, 伯母) or younger (叔父, 叔母) than one's parents. This distinction is far less salient in modern Japan, and in casual settings, people often use hiragana.

185

イメージ	image
ピッタリ・ピッタシ	perfectly, exactly
赤ちゃん	baby, infant
意味	meaning
積極的(な)	active, positive, optimistic
消極的(な)	passive, unmotivated, pessimistic
社会的(な)	social
歴史的(な)	historical
文学的(な)	literary
自分的(な)	like oneself
私・僕的(な)	like me
お祝い	congratulations, celebration, gift

Verbs

合う (-U; 合った)	match; goes together
被る (-U; 被った)	wear, put on (one's head, such as a hat)
締める (-RU; 締めた)	wear, put on, fasten (a necktie) (lit. 'tie, tighten')
掛ける (-RU; 掛けた)	wear, put on (glasses, buttons) (lit. 'hang, suspend')
付ける (-RU; 付けた)	wear, put on (jewelry, accessories, make-up) (lit. 'attach, apply')
する	wear, put on (jewelry, accessories, make-up)

Adjectives

カッコいい	good-looking, stylish, cool

Special expressions

その上	what's more, in addition, plus
PERSON + 思い	thoughtful about PERSON
どういう意味	what do you mean? what does that mean?

Behind the Scenes

BTS 8 More compliments

Giving and responding to compliments in Japan depends in large part on your relationship to the other person. It is fine to tell your friends that you like something new they are wearing by describing the item in a positive manner (きれい！, かわいい！, よく似合ってる). The word 好き is not commonly used for complimenting as it sounds too evaluative, too intimate, or as if you want the item! Refrain from making evaluations of your superiors' abilities ("that was a great lecture," "you did a good job at the meeting"). If you appreciate your teacher's class, an appropriate comment is 勉強になりました。 'I learned a lot.' Don't be surprised if the other person turns your compliment aside, in which case you can be somewhat persistent.

BTS 9 Conditional ～たら + past Sentence 知っていたら 'if I had known'

A ～たら form in combination with a past Sentence has two possible English equivalents. The one we see in this Scene is ～たら used to express an "imagined" condition that never happened. In English, we would say 'If X had happened, Y would have happened.' Here Sasha tells Kanda-san, 知っていたらお祝い持ってきたんです 'If I had known (it was your birthday), I'd have brought you a present.' In the next Scene, you will see the second possible English equivalent.

もっと早く話していたら、こんなに大きなことにはならなかったと思います。	I think if you had spoken up sooner, it wouldn't have gotten to be such a big problem.
昨日の晩、あのケーキ食べていたら、今日は大変だったよね。よかった！	If we had eaten that cake last night, we would have felt awful today. Good thing!
山田さんが来なかったら、プロジェクトはキャンセルになっていたかもしれませんよ。	If Yamada-san hadn't come, we may have had to cancel the project.

BTS 10 X ～的 X-like

The suffix ～的 attaches to Nouns to form a な Noun that means 'X-like,' or 'from X's perspective,' e.g. 日本人的 'like a Japanese person,' 歴史的 'like history' or 'from the perspective of history.' 日本人的な見方 means 'a Japanese-like way of looking at things.'

The elements 積極 (せっきょく) and 消極 (しょうきょく) do not occur by themselves; they are always combined with another element such as 〜的 (てき). Note also in the examples below that 〜的 (てき) combines with に to express manner.

明(あか)るくて積極的(せっきょくてき)で、友達思(ともだちおも)いの本当(ほんとう)にいい人(ひと)です。	He is cheerful and optimistic, a good person who is considerate of his friends.
ちょっと消極的(しょうきょくてき)なほうかもしれませんが、頭(あたま)はいいし、仕事(しごと)は速(はや)いですし、悪(わる)いイメージは全然(ぜんぜん)ありません。	He may be pessimistic, but he's smart, he works fast, and there's nothing negative about his image.
これは、歴史的(れきしてき)に大変(たいへん)なことです。	From a historical perspective that is a very bad thing.
すぐ「すみません」と言(い)うのは日本人的(にほんじんてき)でしょうか。	Wouldn't it be just like a Japanese person to say "*Sumimasen*"?
これ、数学的(すうがくてき)に説明(せつめい)してくださいませんか。	Would you explain this to me from a mathematical perspective?

Its use has been expanded to personal reference when describing the identified person's opinion. This is an informal use and should only be used in a casual setting.

自分的(じぶんてき)にはあまり明(あか)るいと思(おも)ってないんですけど。	In my opinion, I don't think he's so cheerful, but...
この店(みせ)、どう思(おも)いますか、一郎君的(いちろうくんてき)には。	What do you think of this store—in your (Ichiro's) opinion?

BTS 11 Extended family and terms of address and reference

In Act 7 you encountered the terms for members of the nuclear family. Here you see the terms for the extended family. Again, note that there are humble and polite alternatives for most of these.

Although 彼(かれ) and 彼女(かのじょ) mean 'he' and 'she,' either can also mean 'significant other.' Since Japanese Sentences don't require a subject, overusing these terms is almost always interpreted to indicate a romantic relationship. Also the term パートナー, as in English, can simply mean a collaborator in something as well as a significant other, especially of the same gender.

So-called "step" relations (stepmother, stepfather, stepsister, etc.) as well as "in-laws" are most commonly referred to using the simple kin term (母(はは), 父(ちち), 姉(あね), etc.). There are technical terms for these relationships but they are not ordinarily used.

Many of these kin terms are also used generically to refer to (but not necessarily to address) people whose identity you do not know. おじいさん and おばあさん can refer to "older" people, but many people do not like being addressed with these terms so be cautious. Otherwise, an adult of indiscriminate age whose identity you do not know may be referred to as おじさん or おばさん. A younger person may be referred to as おねえさん or おにいさん and a very young person as お嬢(じょう)さん or 坊(ぼっ)ちゃん.

Now go to the Activity Book for 練習 Practice and 腕試し Tryout.

Scene 11-5 休んだらよくなりました。
When I rested it got better.

Brian earlier had to leave his class with Professor Sakamoto. He is now in her office to explain and apologize for missing the class.

ブライアン	坂本先生
先生、先ほどはすみませんでした。	いえいえ、ちゃんと連絡頂いてましたから。それより、大丈夫?
はい、急に頭がズキズキ痛くなって、あんまり痛いので保健室に行ったんです。	そう。
でも、しばらく横になって休んだら良くなりました。	お薬は?
一応もらっておきました。	そう。無理しないでね。
ご心配おかけして、すみませんでした。	いえいえ。

Brian	Professor Sakamoto
Professor, I'm sorry for a while ago.	No, no. I got your message, so... More importantly, were you all right?
Yes. Suddenly my head started to throb, and it was so painful, I went to the clinic.	I see.
But after I lay down and rested for a while it got better.	How about medicine?
I got some just in case.	I see. Don't overdo it.
I'm sorry to make you worry.	No, no.

単語と表現 Vocabulary and expressions

Nouns

先ほど	a while ago, just now
急(な)	sudden
ズキズキ(する・痛む)	throbbing
シクシク(する・痛む)	dull continuous pain
ヒリヒリ(する・痛む)	prickling pain; stinging
カサカサ(する・になる)	dry
フラフラ(する)	dizzy
ムカムカ(する)	nauseated, queasy
痛み	pain
しばらく	a while, a moment
保健室	infirmary, clinic
クリニック	clinic
頭	head
首	neck
肩	shoulder
腰	(lower) back
手	hand
腕	arm
指	finger
足・脚	feet/legs
背中	back
胸	chest
(お)尻	buttocks, behind
顔	face
目	eye
耳	ear
鼻	nose
口	mouth

歯 (は)	tooth
舌 (した)	tongue
横 (よこ)	side, horizontal
縦 (たて)	vertical
斜め (なな め)	diagonal
(ご)心配(しんぱい)(な)・(する)	worry

Verbs

こる (-RU; こった)	become stiff
痛む (いた) (-U; 痛んだ)	become painful
もらう (-U; もらった)	get, receive
のむ・呑む (の) (-U; 呑んだ)	ingest, swallow
無理(むり)する	try/work too hard, overdo
洗う (あら) (-U; 洗った)	wash
掻く (か) (-U; 掻いた)	scratch

Adjectives

痛い (いた)	painful
痒い (かゆ)	itchy

Special expressions

急(きゅう)に	suddenly
あまり・あんまり + affirmative	so, to such an extent
気持(きも)ちが悪(わる)い	feel unwell; sickening, unpleasant, revolting
横(よこ)になる	lie down
心配(しんぱい)をかける	make (someone) worry

Behind the Scenes

BTS 12 Sentence 〜たら + past sentence: 休（やす）んだら良（よ）くなりました when I rested it got better

The second English equivalent for [〜たら + Past Sentence] is 'when' (not 'if'). But the second (past) Sentence must be something outside the speaker's control: 'When I did X, Y happened.'

やってみたらそんなに難（むずか）しくなかったです。	When I tried it, it wasn't that hard.
駅（えき）から出（で）てきたら、そこに祖母（そぼ）がいました。	When I came out of the station my grandmother was waiting there.
今回（こんかい）はあまり勉強（べんきょう）できなかったので半分（はんぶん）諦（あきら）めていたんだけどね、帰（かえ）って来（き）たテストを見（み）たら結構高（けっこうたか）い点（てん）だったんだ。よかった！	I wasn't able to study this time so I had half given up hope, you know, but when I looked at the test that came back it had a pretty high score. Nice!
駅（えき）を出（で）たら、ちょうどそこにコンビニがあったのでそこで必要（ひつよう）なものを買（か）いました。	When we came out of the station, there was a convenience store right there, so we bought what we needed.
5時（じ）ごろは誰（だれ）もいなかったけど、ちょっと待（ま）っていたら8人（にん）ぐらい来（き）て、5時半（じはん）には15人（にん）になりました。	At about 5:00 no one was there, but when I waited a while about eight people came, and at 5:30 that had become 15 people.

BTS 13 あまり・あんまり + Affirmative Sentence

Earlier you saw あまり in combination with a negative meaning 'not very' (あまり面白くない 'it's not very interesting'). あまり can also combine with affirmative Sentences meaning 'so' in the sense of extent (あんまり痛（いた）いので 'It was so painful that (I went to the hospital).'

あまりびっくりして、声（こえ）が大（おお）きくなりました。	I was so surprised, my voice got loud.
あまり難（むずか）しかったら、無理（むり）して仕上（しあ）げなくていいですよ。	If it's so difficult, it's fine not to overdo it finishing up.

BTS 14 Onomatopoeia

Onomatopoeia or "sound symbolism" refers to words that either (a) sound like what they are (such as animal noises like arf arf or meow) or (b) are evocative by convention (such as pow or zoom). In Japanese, dogs say ワンワン and cats say ニャン. Onomatopoetic words can make your Japanese sound vivid and animated.

There are not separate words for 'ache,' 'pain,' 'throb,' 'hurt,' etc. in Japanese. But there are onomatopoetic words that accompany the Verb 痛む or Adjective 痛い to clarify the kind of discomfort someone is suffering. In this Scene, Brian explains that his head started to throb with 頭がズキズキ痛くなった. Although there is no distinction between aches and pains, you will often hear Japanese people say that their shoulders hurt with 肩がこった (lit. 'my shoulders are stiff'). Notice also that many of these onomatopoetic elements combine with both 痛む and する, and that they are usually written in katakana.

ちょっと冷たいもの食べ過ぎたのかもしれません。さっきからお腹がシクシク痛んで勉強ができないんです。	Maybe I ate too much of something that was cold. My stomach has been aching since a little while ago and I can't study.
さっき紙で指を切って、そこがヒリヒリしてます。	I cut my finger on a piece of paper a while ago and it stings like anything.
ここ、赤くなってるでしょう？新しい靴を履いていたから。ヒリヒリ痛くて……。バンドエイド、ありますか。	This is getting red, isn't it? Because I'm wearing new shoes. It smarts... Do you have a band-aid?

Now go to the Activity Book for 練習 Practice and 腕試し Tryout.

Scene 11-6 そう言ったら笑ってた。
When I said that they laughed.

Amy recently had an interview for an internship program in Japan. Takashi is curious about how it went.

The script

孝	エイミー
面接、どうだった?	まあまあかな。
それで、難しかった?	ん〜それほど。
(相槌を打つ)	「日本のどこで働きたいですか」って聞くから、「日本だったらどこでも行きます!」って言ったら、笑ってた。
ふうん、結果はいつ分かるの。	来月だって。

Takashi	Amy
How was the interview?	So-so maybe.
So was it hard?	Not so much.
(nodding and commenting)	They ask, "Where do you want to work in Japan?" so when I say, "If it's Japan I'll go anywhere!" they laugh.
Huh, so when will you know the result?	They say next month.

単語と表現 Vocabulary and expressions

Nouns

| 結果 | result |

Verbs

働く (-U; 働いた)	work
打つ (-U; 打った)	hit, strike
答える	answer, respond

Special expressions

それで、	then, following that
相槌を打つ	provide nods, interjections, etc.

Behind the Scenes

BTS 15 Storytelling

In this Scene you see the first of several ways to recount an incident or tell a story. Here, you learn a basic structure of connecting quotes.

Use non-past Sentence plus ので (or から) to introduce what someone else said/did that caused your response. Imagine that you are telling a friend about a trick that your roommate played on you. She brought home a textbook that you also have to use in class, and quite seriously told you it was ¥50,000.

「5万円です」って言うのでびっくりした。	I was stunned when she said, "It's ¥50,000."

Alternatively, imagine that someone is collecting signatures for an environmental campaign.

「お願いします」って言うから名前を書こうと思ってペンを持ったんです。	They said, "Please," so I picked up a pen thinking I would sign my name.

The use of the non-past to describe the preliminary speech/action of others has the effect of bringing the listener into the Scene, similar to the use of the present tense in English story telling.

Use the 〜たら form to describe what you said or did, followed by the outcome.

びっくりして「えええぇ？」って言ったら「冗談」だって。	I was stunned and when I said, "Whaaaat?" she said, "It's a joke."
名前を書こうと思ってペンを持ったら、一緒にいた友達が「だめだめ」って。	I picked up a pen thinking I would sign my name. Then my friend who was with me said, "No. That's not a good idea."

Use a past Sentence at the end of the story. Frequently, you add a comment—often evaluative—about your take on what happened. Let's put together the parts of the two stories together.

「５万円です」って言うので、びっくりして「えええぇ？」って言ったら、「冗談です」だって。本当にびっくりした。	She said, "It's ¥50,000," so I was stunned and said, "Whaaaat?" Then she said, "It's a joke." I was really shocked.
「お願いします」って言うから、名前を書こうと思ってペンを持ったら、一緒にいた友達が「だめだめ」って。それでまずいって気がついたんです。	Since they said, "Please," I picked up a pen thinking I would sign my name. Then my friend who was with me said, "No. That's not a good idea." And I realized that that was not a good move.

As a listener, you are expected to respond to others' narration. You have already learned many 相槌 expressions: そうですか。はい、へえ、ふうん、そうなんだ, and silent nodding of the head, for example. Nodding is a typical non-verbal gesture to indicate that you are following; it does not necessarily mean that you are agreeing with what the speaker is saying.

While another person is telling a story, you as the listener need to provide 相槌 continually and at the right moments, often overlapping with what the speaker is saying, but you should not be so loud or assertive as to create an interruption.

Now go to the Activity Book for 練習 Practice and 腕試し Tryout.

Then do 評価 Assessment activities.

◆ 読み書き Reading and writing

シーン 11-7R お世話になっております。
Thank you for your support.

Sasha was copied on a message from Division Chief Yagi to Nakamura-san of Japan Travel.

テキスト Text

Subject: ゴルフコンペのスライドショー

ジャパン・トラベル

中村様

いつもお世話になっております。

先日のゴルフコンペ、お疲れさまでした。

Slidegram を使ってスライドショーを作ってみました。

こちらからダウンロードできます。

www.box.co.jo/public/4nayrn72jru

よろしくお願いいたします。

八木

Subject: Slideshow from golf competition

Japan Travel

Mr. Nakamura,

We are grateful for your continued support, as always.

Thank you for participating in the golf competition the other day.

I made a slideshow using Slidegram.

You can download it here:

www.box.co.jo/public/4nayrn72jru

Thank you,

Yagi

BTL 1 Business emails: お世話になっております、お疲れ様です、よろしくお願いいたします

When you have to send email messages in a work context, using the right phrases to structure your content can make a big difference to how others view you as a representative of your company. Phrases that you learned in speaking (よろしくお願いします、お疲れ様です、お世話になっています) are only the beginning of language that puts people at ease. And even though you may be quite informal with colleagues face-to-face, in written business communication you probaby want to use at least 〜ます・です. In this Act you will see a number of other important expressions along with examples for how they are used.

文字と例 Kanji with examples

#84. 様　さま　ヨウ　　manner, ways, appearance; Mr./Mrs./Ms.　　様

1. 中村様　　　　　　　　　　　　　　Mr/s. Nakamura
2. #様子　　　　　　　　　　　　　　　appearance
3. 山田様でしたらあちらです。　　　　　Mr/s. Yamada is over there.
4. ワン様でしたらもういらっしゃらないですよ。　Mr/s. Wang is no longer here.

#85. 話　はな(す)　ワ　　Talk　　話

1. 話す　　　　　　　talk
2. （お）話　　　　　a talk, story
3. 会話　　　　　　　conversation, dialogue

1　There is no 送り仮名 in 話 as a noun.

4.	# 英会話(えいかいわ)		English conversation (class)
5.	話してください。		Please speak.
6.	話したら？		How about you talk (to them)?
7.	話しに行かない？		Shall we go and talk?
8.	川上さんに話してみたら？		How would it be if you talk to Kawakami-san?
9.	まだでしたら話してください。		If you haven't spoken yet, please do.
10.	お話でしたらスミスさんにおっしゃってください。		Please speak to Smith-san if you have something to say.

#86. 世　よ　セ　セイ　　world, society, generation　　世

1.	# 世(よ)の中(なか)	world, in the world
2.	世話(せわ)	looking after, help, assistance, support
3.	+ お世話様(せわさま)	your kindness
4.	お世話様です	thank you for your kindness
5.	# 一世紀(いっせいき)	first or one century
6.	お世話になります	I will be in your debt
7.	お世話になっております	I am in your debt
8.	お世話になりました	I was helped

#87. 疲　つか(れる)　ヒ　　tired　　疲

1.	疲(つか)れる	get tired
2.	疲れ	fatigue, tired feeling
3.	# 疲労(ひろう)	fatigue, tired feeling
4.	疲れなかったら	if you are not tired
5.	お疲れ様(さま)です	good job, thanks for your work (様 is often written in hiragana: さま)
6.	お疲れ様でした	good job, thanks for your work
7.	もう疲れたの？	You are already tired?
8.	まだ疲れてないの？	You are not tired yet?
9.	疲れてたら来なくてもいいですよ。	If you are tired, you don't need to come.
10.	疲れてなかったら来てくださいね。	If you are not tired, please come.

#88. 使　つか(う)　シ　　use　　使

1.	使(つか)う	use
2.	# 大使(たいし)	(diplomatic) ambassador

200

3.	使ってください。	Please use it.
4.	もう使わないでください。	Please don't use it any more.
5.	何か使ったら？	How would it be if you used something?
6.	使いすぎはよくないですよ。	It is not good to use too much.
7.	使ってみたらいいと思いますよ。	I think it's good if you try using it.
8.	使わなかったらどうしましょう。	What shall we do if they don't use it.
9.	使ってないのでいいですよ。	It's okay since I'm not using it.

#89. 作　つく(る)　サク　　make, create　　作

1.	作る	make, create
2.	作文	essay
3.	作りすぎた。	I made too much.
4.	何か作ってみたら？	How about you try making something?
5.	まだ作らないでくださいね。	Please don't make it yet.
6.	どこかで作ってから来てください。	Please come after you make this somewhere else.
7.	川村さんが来たら作りましょう。	Let's make it after Kawamura-san comes.
8.	先生に聞いてから作ったら？	Why don't you try making it after you ask the teacher.

Additional kanji with examples

#90. 言　い(う)　こと　ゲン　ゴン　　say, be called　　言

1.	言う	say
2.	言語	language
3.	言語学	linguistics
4.	#伝言	message
5.	#言葉	word
6.	だれかに言ってください。	Please tell someone.
7.	何も言わないでください。	Please don't say anything.
8.	もう言ったら？	Say it already.
9.	もう言ってもいいでしょう？	Is it okay if I tell already?
10.	言わなくてもいいですか？	Is it alright if I don't say anything?
11.	ちょっと言いすぎじゃない？	Maybe you are saying too much.
12.	言ったら分かると思いますよ。	I think he'll understand if you tell.

#91. 読　よ(む)　ドク　　　　　read　　　　　　読

1. 読む　　　　　　　　　　　　　　　　read
2. 読書　　　　　　　　　　　　　　　　reading books
3. マンガの読みすぎはだめですよ。　　　It is not good to read too many manga.
4. 読んでから行こう。　　　　　　　　　Let's go after reading it.
5. 読んだから行こう。　　　　　　　　　We read it so let's go.
6. もう少し読んだら？　　　　　　　　　How would it be if you read a little more?
7. この本も読んでみたらどうでしょう。　How about you try reading this book, too?
8. 読まなかったら分かりませんよ。　　　If you don't read it, you won't understand it.
9. 読書でしたらあちらでどうぞ。　　　　If you are reading books, please do it over there.

#92. 電　デン　　　　　　　　electricity　　　　電

1. 電話　　　　　　　　　　　　　　　　telephone
2. 電話だった。　　　　　　　　　　　　There was a phone call.
3. 電話してみたら？　　　　　　　　　　How would it be if you tried making a phone call?
4. だれからの電話？　　　　　　　　　　A phone call from who?
5. 電話でしたらここにありますよ。　　　The phone is here.
6. もう電話しないでください。　　　　　Please don't call any more.
7. 電話してから来てくださいね。　　　　Please come after you call.

Now go to the Activity Book for 練習 Practice.

シーン 11-8R 東京駅（とうきょうえき）から電話（でんわ）します。
I'll call from Tokyo Station.

Sasha is responding to a text message from Yagi-bucho, who is on her way back to Tokyo.

テキスト Text

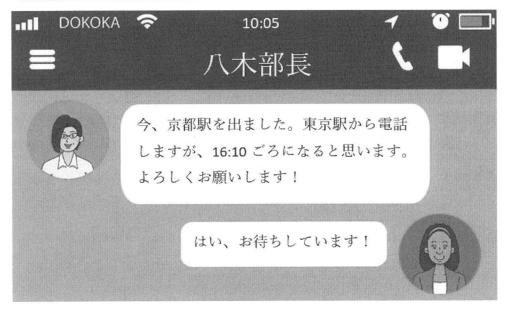

Yagi-bucho

I have just left Kyoto Station. I'll call you from Tokyo Station. I think it will probably be around 16:10. Thanks!

                                                      Got it. I'll be waiting.

BTL 2 Expressions with multiple meanings: 出る

Just as expressions like すみません having different meanings and functions, many vocabulary have more than one meaning. For instance, the word 出る changes its meaning depending on what Nouns and Particles occur with it.

会議に出る	attend a meeting
電話に出る	answer the phone
外に出る	go outside
テレビに出る	appear on TV
部屋を出る	exit a room
大学を出る	graduate from college
疲れが出る	get tired (lit. tiredness emerges/surfaces)
痛みが出る	experience pain (lit. pain emerges/surfaces)

Watch for these variations in English equivalents for Japanese words, and do not expect one-to-one mappings for vocabulary in two languages.

文字と例 Kanji with examples

#93. 京 キョウ ケイ   imperial capital   京

1. 京子 — [female given name]
2. #京急 — Keikyu Line
3. 京子様でしたらいらっしゃいませんでした。 — Kyoko didn't come.
4. 京子さんと話したらどうかな。 — How would it be if you talked with Kyoko-san?

#94. 都 みやこ ト   capital, metropolis   都

1. 京都 — Kyoto
2. 京都外国語大学 — Kyoto University of Foreign Studies
3. 京都女子大学 — Kyoto Women's University
4. #都立 — metropolitan
5. #都立大学 — Metropolitan University
6. #都会 — urban area, city
7. #大都会 — big city
8. #都 — capital

204

9.	# 住めば都		"Home is where you make it." (*kotowaza*)
10.	京都だったと思うけど……。		I think it was Kyoto.
11.	京都に行ってからまた電話しようと思ってます。		I'm thinking of calling again after I get to Kyoto.
12.	京都でしたらもう行ってきましたよ。		I've already gone and come back from Kyoto.

#95. 駅　エキ　　　　　　　　　　(train) station　　　駅
1. 駅 — station
2. + 駅前 — in front of the station
3. 京都駅 — Kyoto Station
4. 駅のキオスク — a kiosk in the station
5. 駅だったらあそこです。 — The station is over there.
6. 京都駅にもういらっしゃると思いますよ。 — I think he is already at Kyoto Station.

#96. 出　だ(す)　で(る)　　go out, leave, depart, attend, submit, send out, take out　　出
　　　シュツ

1. 出る — leave, attend
2. 出す — take out
3. 思い出す — remember
4. # 思い出 — memory
5. 出かける — go out, leave
6. # 外出(する) — go out
7. # 外出中 — out (of the office), away (from home)
8. # 出社(する) — go/come to the office
9. ここから出ないでください。 — Please don't leave from here.
10. もう少し出てみようかな、このセミナー。 — I wonder if I should attend this seminar a little longer.
11. ケーキはまだ出さないんですか? — Are you not putting out the cake yet?
12. お金、もう少し出したらどう? — How about you take out a little more money?

#97. 東　ひがし　トウ　　　　　east　　　東
1. # 東 — east; [family name]
2. 東京 — Tokyo
3. 東京都 — Tokyo (metropolis)
4. 東京駅 — Tokyo Station

5.	+	東大 (とうだい)	University of Tokyo
6.		東京大学	University of Tokyo
7.	#	東京都立大学 (とうきょうとりつだいがく)	Tokyo Metropolitan University
8.	#	東京外国語大学 (とうきょうがいこくごだいがく)	Tokyo University of Foreign Studies
9.		東京からの人	a person from Tokyo
10.		東京に行ってみたい。	I'd like to try going to Tokyo.
11.		東京駅から出てみたら？	How would it be if you left from Tokyo Station?

Additional kanji with examples

#98.　口　くち　コウ　　　　mouth　　　　口

1.	#	口 (くち)	mouth
2.		出口 (でぐち)	exit
3.	+	田口 (たぐち)	[family name]
4.	+	川口 (かわぐち)	[family name]
5.		山口 (やまぐち)	[family name]
6.	#	人口 (じんこう)	population
7.		出口はどこですか。	Where is the exit?
8.		出口でしたらあっちです。	The exit is over there.
9.		あそこは出口じゃないかもしれませんよ。	That may not be the exit.

#99.　入　はい(る)　い(れる)　ニュウ　enter, go in; put in　　　入

1.		入り口、入口 (いりぐち)	entrance
2.		人が入る (はいる)	people enter, go in
3.		水を入れる (いれる)	put water in
4.	#	入学(する) (にゅうがく)	get into a school, start school, get admitted to school
5.	#	入社(する) (にゅうしゃ)	enter a company, get employed at a company
6.		入り口から来てください。	Please go in through the entrance.
7.		大学に入ったらどう？	How about you go to the university?
8.		東大に入ることにしました。 (とうだい)	I decided to enter Tokyo University.
9.		ここから入れてみたら？	How about you put it in from here?

#100. 車　くるま　シャ　　　　　　car　　　　　車

1. 車 — car
2. 電車 — train
3. #新車 — new car
4. 電車で来てください。— Please come by train.
5. 電車にしたら？— How about the train?
6. 京都からの電車 — a train from Kyoto
7. 車では来ないでください。— Please don't come by car.
8. 車で行くことにしようと思ってます。— I'm thinking of deciding to go by car.
9. 先生の車でしたらあちらのグレーのですよ。— The teacher's car is the grey one over there.

Now go to the Activity Book for 練習 Practice.

シーン 11-9R 駅から歩いて5分です。
About a five-minute walk from the station.

Kanda-san is reading an email from Yagi-bucho regarding a reception next week.

テキスト Text

Subject: レセプション

神田さん

お疲れさまです。

来週の火曜日（２３日）のレセプションは５時からですが、少し早く来てください（４時半ごろ）。去年と同じホテル（立川プリンスホテル）です。立川駅を出て、東のほうに歩いて５分ぐらいです。ホテルの入口を入って右のほうにロビーがありますから、そこで待っていてください。私も４時半までには行きます。

よろしくお願いします。

八木

Subject: Reception

Kanda-san,

Thank you for your hard work.

The reception next Tuesday (23rd) starts at 5:00, but please come a little early (around 4:30). It's the same hotel as last year (Tachikawa Prince Hotel). Exit Tachikawa Station, and it's about a five-minute walk to the east. There is a lobby to the right side of the entrance, so please wait for me there. I'll be there by 4:30 as well.

Thank you,
Yagi

文字と例 Kanji with examples

#101. 早　はや(い)　ソウ　　　　early　　　　早
1. 早い — early
2. # 早々(そうそう) — as soon as
3. 早く作ったら？ — Why don't you make it quickly?
4. 早く書こう。 — Let's write it fast.
5. 早く話したら分からないよ。 — I can't understand you if you speak fast.

#102. 同　おな(じ)　ドウ　　　　same　　　　同
1. 同じ(おな) — same
2. 同じ日 — the same day
3. # 同一(どういつ) — same
4. # 同時(どうじ) — at the same time
5. 同じ車 — the same car
6. 同じだったらよかったね。 — It would have been good if it had been the same.
7. 同じ電車で行ってみたら？ — How about you try going by the same train?
8. 田口さんのと同じです。 — It is the same one as Taguchi-san's.

#103. 歩　ある(く)　ホ　　　　walk　　　　歩
1. 歩く(ある) — walk
2. 歩いて5分 — five-minute walk
3. 歩き — on foot
4. # 歩行(ほこう) — walking
5. # 一歩(いっぽ) — one step
6. 歩いていこう。 — Let's go on foot.
7. そこはまだ歩かないで。 — Please don't walk there yet.
8. 歩いたらよくなりました。 — I got better after I walked.
9. きのうは歩きすぎて疲れました。 — I got tired, having walked too much yesterday.

#104. 右　みぎ　ウ　ユウ　　　　right (as opposed to left)　　　　右
1. 右(みぎ) — right (direction)
2. # 右手(みぎて) — right hand
3. + 右京(うきょう) — [family name]

	4.	右に行ったら同じでした。	It was the same when I went right.
	5.	右でも同じですか。	Going right is the same?
	6.	右に行きすぎですよ。	You are going too far to the right.

#105. 私　わたし　わたくし　シ　　　I, myself, private

1. 私 — I, I (formal)
2. 私立 — private (as opposed to public)
3. 私立大学 — private university
4. 私の電話 — my phone
5. 車でしたら私のを出しましょうか。 — Shall I drive (lit. take out) mine (if we are going by car)?
6. 私からのメールってもう見ましたか。 — Have you already seen the email from me?

Additional kanji with examples

#106. 左　ひだり　サ　　　left

1. 左 — left
2. # 左手 — left hand
3. # 左右 — left and right
4. + 左京 — [family name]
5. 左からの車 — car from the left
6. 左に行ったらまよいました。 — I got lost when I went left.
7. ここは右でも左でもいいかもしれないよ。 — Here it might be okay (to go) either right or left.

#107. 遅　おく(れる)　おそ(い)　チ　　late, slow

1. 遅い — late
2. 遅くなってすみません — sorry for being late
3. 遅れる — become late
4. 時間に遅れる — be late for
5. # 遅刻(する) — be late, tardy
6. 遅すぎですよ。 — You are too slow.
7. ちょっと遅すぎじゃないですか。 — Aren't you a little too slow?
8. ちょっと遅かったので先に来ました。 — You were a little late, so I came early.
9. 電車が遅くてこまりました。 — I was inconvenienced because the train was late.
10. 遅くなったらどうしよう。 — What shall we do if we are going to be late?

11.	遅れてすみません。	Sorry for being late.
12.	遅れたら先に行きますよ。	I'll go ahead if you are late.

#108. 帰　かえ(る)　キ　　return, go home　帰

1.	帰る	return, go home
2.	帰り	on the way back
3.	# 日帰り	a day trip, one-day trip
4.	# 帰国(する)	go back to one's country
5.	早く帰ることにします。	I'm going to decide to leave early.
6.	早く帰ろうよ。	Let's go home early.
7.	まだ帰らないでください。	Please don't leave yet.
8.	帰りは電車で帰ろうかな。	I wonder if I should go home by train.
9.	もう帰ったらどう？	Why don't you leave already?
10.	少し遅く帰ったらどう？	How about you leave a little late?

Now go to the Activity Book for 練習 Practice.

Then do 評価 Assessment activities, including 読んでみよう Contextualized reading, 書き取り Dictation, and 書いてみよう Contextualized writing.

第 12 幕
Act 12

母が送ってくれたんだけど……。
My mom sent it to me…

可愛い子には旅をさせよ。
If you love your child, send them
out into the world.

◆ 話す・聞く Speaking and listening

Scene 12-1 くれるの？ You'll give it to me?

Amy is working with Takashi on a project and needs to write down something quickly. She notices that Takashi has a pen with a design of a cute character.

The script

エイミー	孝
このかわいいキャラのペン、借りていい？	あ、それ、使ってて。僕、まだ２本あるから。
え？くれるっていうこと？	うん。
でも……。	いいから、いいから。エイミーが使ってくれたら嬉しいよ。
そう？じゃあ。もらうね。わーい！	

Amy	Takashi
Is it okay to borrow this character pen?	That one, use it. I still have two.
What? You'll give it to me?	Yeah.
But…	It's okay, it's okay. It will make me happy if you use it.
Really? Well then. I'll take it. Wow!	

単語と表現 Vocabulary and expressions

Nouns

キャラ(クター)	(fictional) character
文房具(ぶんぼうぐ)	office supplies
漫画(まんが)	comics, *manga*
机(つくえ)	desk
椅子(いす)	chair
棚(たな)	shelf
いっぱい	a lot, much

Verbs

貸(か)す (-U; 貸(か)した)	lend, rent (to someone)
くれる (-RU; くれた)	give (to うち)
くださる↑ (-ARU; くださった)	give (to うち) (honorific)

Special expressions

使(つか)ってくれたら	if you would use it (for me)
わーい	wow! (surprise)

拡張 Expansion

Ask your Japanese friends/associates what local characters besides *kumamon* they know of and talk about those characters (e.g., where they are from, how well known they are).

Behind the Scenes

BTS 1 Verbs of giving (from そと to うち): くれる・くださる↑ and 〜てくれる・くださる

Japanese people are keenly aware of the ways in which they benefit from the good will of others. The word 恩(おん) 'benevolence, favor' refers to social indebtedness that you incur when someone does even a minor favor for you. It is matched by 義理(ぎり) 'obligation,' which refers to duties and social obligations that derive from social relationships. For example, teachers are expected to nurture their students; this is their obligation.

This sense of indebtedness is evident everywhere in the language. You have seen requests in the form 〜てください. In Act 5 you also saw 〜てくださってありがとうございます (いろいろ教(おし)えてくださって、ありがとうございました。 'Thank you for explaining everything to me.'). ください and くださって come from the honorific Verb くださる, which means '(someone) gives to me/us/うち.' The plain equivalent of くださる is くれる。Both of these are used when any kind of giving occurs from someone in the out-group (そと) to the in-group (うち). In this case, the ultimate in-group is oneself, so these Verbs are used to describe giving from family members and friends.

In English, we might say that someone did something "for me/us," but even that is optional. Japanese does not use such phrases (you have seen how rarely pronouns appear in Japanese); instead, the benefit is acknowledged through the Verb. The giving might involve an object: ティッシュ（を）くれました。 'They (street vendors) gave me tissues.' Or it might involve an action in the 〜て form: 待(ま)ってくれました。 'They waited for me.' When the giver is higher-ranking or when the favor is somehow special, it is acknowledged through the honorific Verb くださいます。Imagine a situation where one of your colleagues does you a favor: (a) ¥100 貸(か)してくれました。 'He lent me a hundred yen.' and (b) 大事(だいじ)なカメラを貸(か)してくださいました。 'He lent me his expensive camera.'

駅(えき)の前(まえ)を歩(ある)いていたら、ティッシュくれました。	When I was walking in front of the station they gave me (a pack of) tissues.
え？これ、全部(ぜんぶ)くださるんですか。いや、それは多(おお)すぎます。	What? You are giving me all of these? No, that's too many.
¥50貸(か)してくれない？	Would you lend me fifty yen?
あ、ここは見(み)なくていいですよ。あとで八木(やぎ)さんが見(み)てくださるから。	Oh, you don't need to look at this part. Yagi-san will look at it (for us) later, so . . .
先(さき)に初(はじ)めてくださらない？	Please, start ahead of me. (lit. 'Won't you start ahead of me?')

BTS 2 Sentence って・ということ

You saw ということは in Act 7 at the beginning of a Sentence that summarized what the speaker heard or understood.

ということは全部(ぜんぶ)で4人(にん)ですね。	In other words, there are four people in all, right?

A similar meaning can be expressed with a Sentence preceding って・ということ:

全部(ぜんぶ)で4人(にん)だということですね。	There are four people in all then, right?

って is a bit less formal; と is more likely in writing. っていうこと can also be shortened to the more casual ってこと.

お電話がありました。明日はキャンセルということです。	There was a phone call. To the effect that (the plan for) tomorrow is canceled.
ええと、では、お二人様で今晩 7 時半からということですね。	Ummm, well then, that means there will be two people this evening at 7:30, correct?
え？明日、来ないってこと？本当？	What? You mean to say you're not coming tomorrow? Really?

BTS 3 Local promotional characters

Outsiders are often struck by the proliferation of mascots and promotional characters that are associated with everything from consumer products to media companies to prefectural offices in Japan. These promotional characters foster a sense of brand loyalty and civic pride. There is even a competition among prefectures for best character; see http://www.yurugp.jp/ranking/?year=2016 for the best of characters of 2016. This textbook provides two examples of such characters: ゴー君 and ニャウちゃん.

Now go to the Activity Book for 練習 Practice and 腕試し Tryout.

Scene 12-2 ちゃんと食べて（い）るかどうか心配なんだね。
She's worried about whether you're eating right or not.

At a project meeting, Takashi brings sweets that his mother sent him from Japan.

The script

孝	エイミー
これ、日本から母が送ってくれたんだけど、よかったら食べて。	ありがとう。でも、こんなにもらっちゃっていいの？
うん。いつもいっぱい送ってくるから。	ちゃんと食べてるかどうか心配なんだね、きっと。
まあ、離れているからね。	

Takashi	Amy
My mother sent these to me from Japan, but if you'd like, have some.	Thanks. But is it okay to take this much?
Yeah. She sends me lots all the time.	Surely she worries whether you're eating right.
Well, it's because we're apart, y'know.	

単語と表現 Vocabulary and expressions

Verbs

送る (-U; 送った)	send
受け取る (-U; 受け取った)	take, accept
しまう (-U; しまった)	put away
Xから・と離れる (-RU; 離れた)	be away, separate from

219

Special expressions

もらっちゃって	take, get
食(た)べてるかどうか	whether you're eating or not
きっと	surely, undoubtedly

Behind the Scenes

BTS 4 Embedded yes/no questions

When you don't know, have forgotten, don't remember, or otherwise want to comment on a yes/no question, the question can be embedded into a longer Sentence. For example, in the case of うちにいますか 'Are they at home?' the original question in informal style with か (うちにいるか) combines with an alternative (such as どうか) and is followed by the rest of the Sentence: うちにいるかどうかわかりません。 'I don't know if they are at home or not.' The second question may be どうか, the negative of the first (うちにいるかいないかわかりません。), or some other alternative that makes sense in the context (うちにいるか、クラスに行っているかわかりません。 'I don't know if they're home or if they've gone to class.'). Notice that if the embedded question is a [Noun だ] sentence, だ is dropped. Notice also that は does not occur in embedded questions.

料理(りょうり)できない娘(むすめ)が、一人(ひとり)でちゃんと食(た)べてるかどうか心配(しんぱい)です。	I'm worried about my daughter who can't cook—whether, living alone, she is eating right or not.
うまくできるかどうかわからなかったけど、やってみたら結構(けっこう)すぐできました。	I didn't know whether it would go well or not, but when I gave it a try I was able to do it fairly quickly.
似合(にあ)うかどうか店(みせ)の人(ひと)に聞(き)いてから、買(か)うか買(か)わないか決(き)めました。	After I asked the person at the store whether it looked good on me or not, I decided whether or not to buy it.
好(す)きか好(す)きじゃないか、人(ひと)によって違(ちが)うでしょうから聞(き)いてみましょう。	Since it probably depends on the person, let's ask whether they like it or not.

As you can see from the above examples, these embedded yes/no questions are typically followed by Verbs that pertain to cognition or perception, such as 分(わ)かる、聞(き)く、連絡(れんらく)する、質問(しつもん)する, and 覚(おぼ)える.

It is also possible for the embedded question to be followed by は when there are other questions that might have been asked within the context.

納豆が好きか好きじゃないかは、聞いていないけど、ロシア人だから、危ないんじゃない？	I haven't asked her if she likes *natto* or not, but she's Russian so don't you think it would be risky?

BTS 5 Verb 〜てしまう・ちゃう

The Verb しまう by itself means 'put away.' In combination with a 〜て form, it means 'end up doing' or 'finish doing.' This 〜てしまう is often contracted to 〜ちゃう (忘れてしまう＞忘れちゃう) while 〜でしまう is often contracted to 〜じゃう (飲んでしまう＞飲んじゃう).

置いておいたら悪くなってしまいました。	When I left it there it ended up going bad.
もう少しでできますから、頑張ってやってしまいましょう。	We can do it with a little more (effort/time), so let's hang in there and finish it up.
バス、行っちゃいましたよ。次のは３０分あとです。	The bus has gone. The next one is in thirty minutes.
美味しいから食べ過ぎちゃいました。	It was so good that I ended up overeating.
前よりかなり消極的になっちゃって、心配ですね。	Compared to before you've gotten quite pessimistic, so I'm worried.

Now go to the Activity Book for 練習 Practice and 腕試し Tryout.

Note

1 納豆 is a traditional food made from fermented soybeans. It is highly nutritious but something of an acquired taste since it has a strong smell and slimy texture.

Scene 12-3 誰か知らないんだけど……。
I don't know who that is, but . . .

At another project meeting, Amy begins to talk about a person Takashi doesn't know.

 The script

エイミー	孝
ジェシカがね、	ジェシカ？ジェシカって？誰か知らないんだけど。
あのすごく静かで、おとなしい人。	いや、あのさ、見てわかる説明してくれる？髪の色とか、背が高いとか低いとか。
ああ、そういう意味。茶色の目をしていて、髪も茶色で肩ぐらいの長さ。背は私よりちょっと低いくらいかな。	女性だね。メガネは？
かけてない。	誰だろう。で、そのジェシカが？

Amy	Takashi
Jessica, you know…	Jessica? You said Jessica? I don't know who that is, but…
That really quiet, laidback person.	No, look, explain for me how I could know her if I saw her? Things like the color of her hair, whether she's tall or short.
Ah, you mean that. She has brown eyes, brown hair about as long as her shoulders. Maybe a little shorter than me.	A woman, right. How about glasses?
She doesn't wear them.	Who could it be? So that Jessica did what?

単語と表現 Vocabulary and expressions

Nouns

頑固(な)	stubborn
髪	hair
毛	fur
長さ	length
体	body
女性	woman, girl
男性	man, boy
ペット	pet
犬	dog
猫	cat

Verb

| 飼う (-U; 飼った) | keep (a pet or other animal) |

Adjectives

おとなしい	laidback, quiet, docile
賢い	clever, smart
頭が・のいい	intelligent

Classifiers

| 〜匹 | classifier for counting small animals |
| 〜羽 | classifier for counting bids and rabbits |

Particle

| さ | [Informal particle checking on whether the other person is following] |

Special expressions

誰(だれ)か知(し)らない	don't know who that is
茶色(ちゃいろ)の目(め)をしている	has brown eyes
痩(や)せている	is thin
太(ふと)っている	is heavy
で、	so then; so
それで、	and; because of that

Behind the Scenes

BTS 6 Embedded information questions

You saw in Scene 1 that embedded yes/no questions involve offering two alternatives: 行(い)くか行(い)かないか 'are they going or not.' Information questions (those using *who, what, where, when, why, how*), in contrast, require only changing all formal forms to informal. Thus 何時(なんじ)に行(い)きますか becomes 何時(なんじ)に行(い)くか. As with embedded yes/no questions, embedded information questions are typically followed by Verbs that express concern, understanding, or doubt such as 分(わ)かる, 聞(き)く, 連絡(れんらく)する, 質問(しつもん)する, and 覚(おぼ)える.

ジェシカって誰(だれ)かわかる？	Do you know who Jessica is?
いくつ必要(ひつよう)か聞(き)いています。	I'm asking how many will be necessary.
何人(なんにん)か、もう分(わ)かっていますか。	Do you know yet how many people there are?
悪(わる)いけど、会議(かいぎ)が何時(なんじ)からか聞(き)いてきてくれますか。	It's terrible (of me to ask), but would you go and ask what time the conference starts?
その車(くるま)、どんな色(いろ)だったか、覚(おぼ)えていますか。	Do you remember what color that car was?
何(なん)という名前(なまえ)か、思(おも)い出(だ)したらご連絡(れんらく)します。	If I remember what her name is, I'll you contact you.
なぜこの調査(ちょうさ)をすることにしたか、今(いま)もわかりません。	Even now I don't know why they decided to do this survey.
どのぐらいの速(はや)さで運転(うんてん)していたか、調(しら)べてみましょう。	Let's try finding out how fast they were driving.
誰(だれ)がわかるかと言(い)っています。	They are saying, "who knows?"

Notice that the above examples do not use Phrase Particle と, except in the last example, in which the question is quoted directly.

BTS 7 Sentence Particle さ

The informal Sentence Particle さ is used in two ways: 1. at the end of a phrase it can be used to bring up a topic; 2. at the end of a Sentence it sounds assertive (similar to よ). Some speakers, especially those in the Tokyo region, consider this to be dialectal and prefer instead to use ね in the first instance or よ in the second.

これさ、いつ受け取ったの？どうしてもっと早く教えてくれなかったの？	This, y'know, when did you get it? Why didn't you tell me sooner?
ま、いいさ。気にしないで。	Come on, it's fine! Don't worry about it.
「ありがとう」ってちゃんと言ったさ。お父さん、聞いてなかったの？	I said "thanks" just as I was supposed to! Didn't you hear me, Dad?

BTS 8 で at the beginning of a Sentence

You will often hear Japanese speakers begin their utterances with で 'so then, so.' This use of で links what follows to what came before. As a question, it presses for a response to the situation.

で、何時からって言いました？	So then, what time did they say it starts?
そうでしたか。で？これからどうするんですか？	Is that the way it was? So then? What are you going to do next?

In this Scene, Takashi interrupted Amy when she started to say something about Jessica. After discussing who Jessica is, he prompts Amy to return to the subject.

Now go to the Activity Book for 練習 Practice and 腕試し Tryout.

Scene 12-4　2時を過ぎると……
When it gets past 2:00 . . .

Yagi-bucho comes to pick up Sasha to go play tennis together. Sasha makes a point of acknowledging her indebtedness to Yagi-bucho for going out of her way.

The script

サーシャ	八木
わざわざ迎えに来てくださってありがとうございます。	いえいえ、
朝早くに来ていただいて、申し訳ありません。	とんでもない。私 ね、朝には強いの。サーシャさんは夜型？
いえ、私 もどちらかと言うと朝型です。2時を過ぎると眠くなってしまって……。	ハハ、それはただ寝不足なんじゃないの？
確かに、そうかもしれませんね。	

Sasha	Yagi
Thank you for taking the trouble to come and meet me.	No, no.
I'm sorry that I had you come so early in the morning.	Not at all. You know, I'm a morning person. Are you a night person?
No, if I say which it would have to be, I'm a morning person. I end up feeling sleepy when it gets past 2:00.	Ha ha. That's just because you haven't had enough sleep, isn't it?
That may certainly be true.	

単語と表現 Vocabulary and expressions

Nouns

迎え	greeting, welcome
早く	early
遅く	late
夜型	night person
朝型	morning person
ただ	simply; free of charge
寝不足	lack of sleep
勉強不足	lack of study
練習不足	lack of practice
不足(する)	insufficiency

Verbs

迎える (-RU; 迎えた)	go to meet; welcome
回る (-U; 回った)	go around; visit several places; revolve
足りる (-RU; 足りない)	be enough, suffice

Adjective

眠い	sleepy

Special expressions

来てくださってありがとうございます。	Thank you for coming.
来てくれてありがとう(ございます)。	Thanks for coming.
来ていただいて申し訳ない	getting you to come / I'm very sorry
朝に強い	morning type (lit. 'strong in the morning')
どちらかと言うと	if I have to say which

Behind the Scenes

BTS 9 Verbs of receiving: もらう・いただく↓ and 〜てもらう・いただく↓

You encountered the Verb もらう 'get, receive' in Act 11. The subject is the person who receives (うち). The person from whom you get something (そと) is marked by particle に or から.

このセーター、姉からもらった。	I got this sweater from my older sister.
先生にもらった本、どこにおいておいたか忘れちゃった!	I forgot where I put the book that I got from the teacher!

もらう and its humble equivalent いただく combine with Verb 〜て forms to indicate that you or your in-group (うち) got or had someone (from そと) do something. Alternatively, in the 〜たい form, they indicate that you want to get or have someone do something.

昨日橋本先生に宿題をチェックしていただいて、とても助かりました。	I had Hashimoto-sensei check my homework yesterday and it was a big help.
これ、神田先輩に説明してもらいたいと思っているんです。	You know, I think I'd like to get Kanda-senpai to explain this to us.
上田さんへのメールは、日本人に手伝ってもらったから、大丈夫だと思います。	I got a Japanese person to help me with my email to Ueda-san, so I think it will be all right.
兄が調べてくれるって言うから調べてもらいました。助かりました。	My older brother offered to research it for me so I accepted (the offer). It was a big help.

Compare (a) and (b) below.

(a) サーシャが貸してくれました。	Sasha lent it to me.
(b) サーシャに貸してもらいました。	I got Sasha to lend it to me.

Both of these might be used to describe the same situation, but they differ in viewpoint. In the first, Sasha is the subject and she did something for me. In the second, I am the subject and I got Sasha to do something. The first sounds more polite than the second because くれる acknowledges that Sasha's action helped me.

In this Scene, Sasha uses the 〜てもらう pattern in an apology for making Yagi-san go out of her way to pick her up. You can specify what you are apologizing for with the てもらって・いただいて sequence.

来ていただいて申し訳ないです。	I'm sorry for having you come to get me.
お忙しい課長にいらしていただいて申し訳ございません。	We're sorry for having you (the section chief) come when you are busy.
こんなにたくさん考えてもらって悪いね。	It's terrible of me to have you think about it this much.
ごめん、ごめん！全部やってもらっちゃって。	Sorry, sorry! To get you to do it all.

These apologies are actually expressions of appreciation. Japanese people often use apologies in situations where other cultures would say "Thank you." But increasingly the 〜てもらって・いただいて form is also used with gratitude expressions.

今日はいらしていただいて、本当にありがとうございます。	We are really grateful that we got you to come today.
素晴らしいアイデアをいっぱい考えてもらって、どうもありがとう。	Thanks for thinking of so many great ideas.

BTS 10 Adjective 〜く forms as Nouns

You have seen the Adjective 〜く form in the negative of the Adjective (強くないです 'I'm not strong') and combined with the Verb なる 'become' (強くなった 'I got stronger'). Some 〜く forms can also function as Nouns (you already saw 近く 'nearby' in Act 6), as in this Scene when Sasha thanks Yagi-bucho for coming to get her: 朝早くに、来ていただいて申し訳ありません。' I'm sorry that I had you come so early in the morning.'

駅の近くで集まりましょうって上野先輩が言っていました。	Ueno-senpai was saying that we should meet in the vicinity of the station.
仕事はいつもおそくまでやっているから、奥さんが心配している。	He's always working till late, so his wife is worried.

Not all Adjectives will do this, so only use those that you have heard from native speakers.

BTS 11 ただ + Sentence

ただ by itself means 'free, no charge.' There is a saying in Japanese: ただほど高いものはない meaning 'There is nothing as expensive as free' (perhaps comparable to the English expression, 'There is no such thing as a free lunch.').

At the beginning of a Sentence ただ means 'just, only.' ただ食べる 'just eat' implies that one eats without savoring the flavor or considering the caloric intake. In this Scene, Yagi-bucho suggests that Sasha gets sleepy in the afternoon because she hasn't had enough sleep: ただ寝不足なんじゃないの？ 'Isn't it just because you haven't had enough sleep?'

練習する時は、ただリピートするだけじゃなく、意味を考えてください。	When you practice it isn't just repeating—please also think about the meaning.
どうしてかはわかりません。ただ行きたくないんです。すみません。	I don't know why. I just don't want to go. I'm sorry.

BTS 12 朝に強い・弱い

The phrase [X + に強い/弱い] is used to describe things that you are good or bad at. Often there is a special English phrase that is equivalent to this, as when we say 'I'm a morning person' while Japanese say 朝に強い.

数学に強い人はいいですよね。僕は数学に弱いので、いろいろ困ることが多いです。	People who are good at math are lucky. I'm bad at math, so I have a lot of problems.
私ね、あの課長に弱いんです。いい人だと思うんですけど、なぜか一緒に仕事しにくいんですよ。	Me, I don't get along with that section chief. I think he's a good person, but he's somehow hard to work with.

BTS 13 Affirmative non-past Sentence₁ と Sentence₂

You have already seen と expressing the idea of 'with' in [Noun と Noun]. In [Affirmative Non-past Sentence₁ と Sentence₂], Sentence₂ happens simultaneously with Sentence₁. Sentence₁ is always in the non-past form. と suggests a tight relationship between the two Sentences. Contrast this with the idea of the 〜たら structure, in which Sentence₁ indicates a condition and Sentence₂, an unanticipated outcome.

Remember: [Verb と Verb] cannot be used to list sequences of activities. As you know, that is done with the [〜て + Verb] sequences.

どんなに美味しくても食べ過ぎると体に悪いですよ。	No matter how delicious it is, when you eat too much it's bad for your body.
子供が小さいと心配なことが多いですか。	When children are small are there a lot of things to worry about?
歩くと２０分ぐらいかかりましたが、車だと５分でした。	When I walked it took about twenty minutes, but in a car it was about five.
ロックも好きですが、どちらかというと日本の演歌の方が好きです。	I like rock too, but if I have to say which, I like Japanese *enka* better.
寝不足が続くと仕事が遅くなると聞きました。	I heard that your work slows down if you don't get enough sleep.
ちょっとでも雨が降ると道が悪くなります。道が悪くなると歩きにくいです。歩きにくいと外に出たくなくなります。外に出たくなくなると、学生は学校に来ません。学生が来ないと授業ができません。	The roads get bad when there's even a little rain. When the roads get bad, it's hard to walk. When it's hard to walk, no one wants to go out. When no one wants to go out, the students don't come to school. When the students don't come to school, we can't have class.

Notice in the last example how a sequence of Sentences may provide a long-winded explanation of the connection between the initial condition (it's raining) and the final outcome (students don't show up for class) that may seem unfathomable without the middle portions.

The second Sentence in many connected sequences may be dropped when its content is obvious from the context. For example, in the earlier Scene, in which Takashi receives a care package from his mother, Amy conjectures that his mother is worried about him and Takashi responds with a reason: 離れているからね 'Because we're apart.' He could have also said 離れているとね 'When we're apart, you know?'

BTS 14 Successive んです: 寝不足なんじゃないの？

You have encountered んです used for reasons.

遅れてしまって、すみません。バスが来なかったんです。	I'm sorry to be late. The bus didn't come.

Sometimes these reasons are reinforced by repeating the pattern. In this Scene, Yagi-bucho suggests that Sasha gets sleepy in the afternoon because she hasn't had enough sleep:

寝不足なんじゃないの？ 'That's just because you haven't had enough sleep, isn't it?' The first 寝不足なんじゃない？ 'because you haven't had enough sleep' is a reason for getting sleepy. The second の is a confirmation seeker.

上手になりたいんじゃないんですか。そうだったら練習、練習！	It's the case that you want to get better, right? If that's so, practice, practice!
ここのところね、この言い方だと弱いいんじゃないの？	This place here, you know? It's because this way of saying it is too weak, isn't it?
わからないよ、全然。日本語じゃないんじゃないの？	I don't understand, not a bit. It's because this isn't Japanese, isn't it?

Now go to the Activity Book for 練習 Practice and 腕試し Tryout.

Scene 12-5 並んでいると似てるかな？
Maybe when we're standing side by side we look alike?

In the car, Sasha notices a photo of Yagi-bucho and a man on Yagi-bucho's smartphone.

The script

サーシャ	八木
あの、こちらは……。	それ？息子。
こんなに大きな息子さんがいらっしゃるんですね！	小さいときは可愛かったのよ。このままでいてほしいと思ったけど、こんなに大きくなっちゃった。
顔が八木部長にそっくりですね。あ、ひげ以外。	そう？並んでいると似てるかな。
一人っ子ですか。	じゃなくて、これは3人兄弟の一番上でね。

Sasha	Yagi-san
Ummm, this would be…	That? My son.
You have a son this old (lit. 'big')!	He was cute when he was young. I thought, 'I wish he could be like this (forever),' but he got to be this big.
He looks just like you. Ah, aside from the beard.	Really? When we stand next to each other maybe we look alike.
You have one child?	No, he is the oldest of three.

233

単語と表現 Vocabulary and expressions

Nouns

大きな	large, big (alternative of 大きい)
小さな	small, little (alternative of 小さい)
立派(な)	splendid, elegant
教授	professor (academic rank)
まま	as is, condition
そっくり	exactly like, completely
ひげ	beard
X以外	outside of X; besides X
一人っ子	only child
姉妹	sisters
X人兄弟	X number of siblings (including oneself)
X人姉妹	X number of sisters (including oneself)
X人家族	X number in a family (including oneself)
双子	twins
(お)一人	one (person); alone; single
独身	single; unmarried

Verbs

生やす(-U; 生やした)	grow (a beard)
Xと・に並ぶ(-U; 並んだ)	stand alongside; line up
Xと・に似る (-RU; 似た)	look like X; resemble X

Adjective

若い	young

Special expressions

このまま	like this, without change
〜てほしい	want (someone) to X; want X to happen
Xにそっくり	look exactly like X

ひげを生やす	grow a beard
並んでいると似てる	look alike standing next to each other

Behind the Scenes

BTS 15 More on families: birth order

You have encountered many terms to describe a nuclear family so far. How do you describe your place in terms of birth order? In the case where there are at least three children, the oldest is described as 一番上, the youngest as 一番下. For example, 三人兄弟の一番上は一郎です。 'Ichiro is the oldest of three siblings.' When you have two older brothers or two older sisters, the older is described as 上の兄 or 上の姉, while the younger is described as 下の兄 or 下の姉. In the case of two younger brothers or two younger sisters, the older is 上の弟 or 上の妹 while the younger is 下の弟 or 下の妹.

BTS 16 Description + まま

The word まま means 'as it is' or 'condition.' It is always preceded by a Modifier—either one of the この series or a Sentence Modifier.

このまま置いておきましょう。	Let's leave it as it is ('in this state').
そのまましばらくそこにいてくれますか。	Would you stay where you are for a little while?
ここが大きいままだと似合わないので、ここだけちょっと小さくしてもらいたいんですが。	When it's big like this, it won't look good on me, so I'd like to have you make just this part a little smaller, but…
静かなままだといいんですが、もうすぐやかましくなりますよ。	It's fine when they're quiet, but they'll soon get noisy!

BTS 17 Verb ～てほしい

The Adjective ほしい means 'want.' You can specify items that you want using Particle が.

この犬、欲しい！	I want this dog!
新しいオーバーが欲しくてデパートへ行った。	Wanting a new overcoat, I went to the department store.

欲しいものと必要なものとは同じじゃない。　　Things you want and things you need are not the same.

In addition, a Verb〜て form plus ほしい describes what you want done or what you want to happen. If you are reporting what someone else wants, it should be made clear with って（言っていた）.

開発部の人に代わって欲しかったんですが、ちょうど誰もいないということで、残念でした。　　I wanted it communicated to the Development Division, but it was just when no one was there, so it was too bad.

東京に行ったら是非上野公園に行って欲しい。　　When you go to Tokyo we want you to go to Ueno Park for sure.

もう少し親切に、丁寧に教えて欲しいって。　　She said she wants me to explain it a little more kindly and politely.

〜てほしい overlaps with 〜てもらいたい in some cases. Either of the examples above could substitute もらいたい for ほしい. But there is often a difference between the two. ほしい describes general desires, not necessarily linked to any person. In the case of もらいたい, you must want someone to do something. For this reason, もらいたい sounds warmer and more personal than ほしい. Thus コーチに覚えてもらいたくて大きな声で名前を言いました 'Wanting to get the coach to remember me, I said my name really loud' sounds much more personal than the same Sentence with ほしくて. Compare お母さんにたまにはゆっくり休んでもらいたい 'I want to get my mom to take it easy sometimes (so she doesn't get sick)' and お母さんにたまにはゆっくり休んで欲しい 'I want to get my mom to take it easy sometimes (so that I don't have to deal with her complaining about being busy all the time).'

Remember: 買いたい 'I want to buy it' tells what I want to do while 買ってほしい 'I want you to buy it' tells what I want someone else to do.

Now go to the Activity Book for 練習 Practice and 腕試し Tryout.

Scene 12-6 喜んで案内してあげるよ。
I would be happy to show you around.

Amy gets the results of her application for an internship program in Japan.

The script

エイミー	孝
来年日本に行くことになりました！	決まったんだ。おめでとう！日本のどこ？
まだどこになるかわからないけど、もしかしたら京都かもしれない。	京都？どうしてそう思うの？
いや、ただ何となく。	何となくねえ。まあ、東京に来ることがあったら連絡して。
案内してくれる？	もちろん！喜んで案内してあげるよ。こっちですっかりお世話になっているもん。

Amy	Takashi
It's been decided that I'll go to Japan next year!	So you're set. Congratulations! Where in Japan?
I don't know where it will be yet, but maybe by some chance Kyoto.	Kyoto? Why do you think so?
Nah, just somehow or other.	So it's somehow or other. Well, if you have a chance to come to Tokyo, get in touch.
Will you show me around?	Of course! I'll happily do a tour for you. I owe you big time. (lit. 'I am completely in your debt.')

単語と表現 Vocabulary and expressions

Nouns

(ご)案内(する)	show around
すっかり	completely

Verbs

(お)世話する(IRR)	look after (someone)
あげる・上げる (-RU; あげた)	give (to out-group)
差し上げる↓ (-RU; 差し上げた)	give (to out-group) (humble)
やる (-U; やった)	give (to in-group)

Special expressions

行くことになりました。	It has been decided I will go.
なんとなく	somehow or other
もしかしたら	by some chance; maybe
もしかすると	by some chance; maybe
喜んで	happily, with pleasure
案内してあげる	I'll do you the favor of showing you around

Behind the Scenes

BTS 18 Verbs of giving (from うち to そと): あげる・差し上げる↓ and 〜てあげる・差し上げる↓

Earlier in this Act you saw the Verbs くれる and くださる↑ for giving from そと to うち. The counterparts for giving from in-group to out-group are あげる is 差し上げる↓. Again, the ultimate うち is oneself, so these Verbs are used when you give something to family members and friends.

このセーター、友達の誕生日にあげようと思って買いました。	I bought this sweater thinking I would give it to my friend for his birthday.
先学期描いた絵、先生が「いい、いい」っておっしゃってくださってるんでしょう?先生に差し上げちゃったら?	Your teacher was saying how good the picture you drew last term was, right? Why not give it to your teacher?

Another Verb of giving is やる which is sometimes used to describe giving to pets, plants, or subordinates. But today, やる has been replaced by あげる in most situations.

庭の野菜に水をやりましょうか。	Shall I water the vegetables in the garden?
庭の野菜に水をあげましょうか。	

These Verbs can be used when reporting what you have done for a member of そと. But a word of caution is in order. When you use these Verbs in describing what you did for someone, you are drawing attention to your own good will—which can sound pretentious, especially to a superior. Thus when you want to do something for another person, the 〜ましょう form of the Verb is more appropriate. For example, to volunteer to research something for your teacher/supervisor, say 調べましょう 'Shall I research it?' and not 調べて差し上げます 'I'll research it for your benefit.'

A: 作ってくれる? B: いいよ。今すぐ作ってあげる。 A: サンキュー!	A: Would you make it for me? B: Sure! I'll make it for you right away. A: Thanks!
A: だめだ。無理! B: 助けてあげようか? A: いいよ、一人でやるから。	A: It's no use. I can't do it! B: Shall I bail you out? A: It's all right. I'll do it alone.

BTS 19 Sentence + ことになる

You have already seen [Sentence + ことにする] for intentional actions or decisions—almost always on the part of the speaker. [Sentence + ことになる] is used when an action or decision comes about outside of the speaker's resolve. Even if you know who made a decision or caused something to happen, you should use ことになる. ことになる also often refers to customs and conventions. Consider these three email messages:

おめでとうございます！あなたのご研究を今年の学会で発表していただくことになりました。	Congratulations! It has been decided that your research will be presented at this year's conference.
この会社では、週末は２日休むことになっています。	At this company it has been decided that the weekend will be two days off.
申し訳ございません。送っていただいた作文はお返しできないことになっておりますので……。	I am terribly sorry. (As a matter of policy) we cannot return the essay that you sent us…

BTS 20 もしかしたら・もしかすると

Like よかったら, もしかしたら 'maybe, perhaps' is a common expression that includes the 〜たら form. It is often, but not always, used with かもしれない.

すみません。もしかしたら、具合が悪いんじゃありませんか。	I'm sorry. Maybe it's that you're not feeling well?
あ、もしかしたら今会議中でしたか？どうも気が付かなくて、失礼しました。	Ah, maybe she was in the middle of a meeting? I'm sorry, I didn't notice.
山田君はもしかしたら双子のお兄さんがいるのかもしれないね。山田君にそっくりの人と九州で会ったよ。	Maybe it's possible Yamada-kun has a twin brother. I met someone who looks just like him in Kyushu.

Now go to the Activity Book for 練習 Practice and 腕試し Tryout.

Then do 評価 Assessment activities.

◆ 読み書き Reading and writing

シーン 12-7R 漢字を勉強してください。
Please study kanji

Brian found a notice from his teacher at the bottom of a handout.

テキスト Text

お知らせ

来週月曜日（8日）の漢字の小テストはいつもの日本語の教室ではなく、そのとなりの小さい教室を使います。レッスン１５の漢字を勉強しておいてください。

Announcement

For the kanji quiz next Monday (the 8th), we will use the small classroom next door, not the usual Japanese language classroom. Please study kanji in Lesson 15 (to prepare).

BTL 1 Joining Sentences in written style

In spoken Japanese you have seen the 〜て form of each of the Core Sentences used to connect Sentences as follows:

Verb: もう古くなって、ダメです。 It's already gotten old and is spoiled.

Adjective: おとなしくて、いい学生です。He is a good, quiet student
Noun です: 病気で、学校に行けなくなりました。I got sick and was unable to go to school.

In written Japanese, however, other forms can also be used to connect two sentences. In this Scene you see 日本語の教室ではなく 'not the Japanese language classroom' without the 〜て form. Note the different forms that are used in spoken and written style to join two sentences.

Core sentence			Linking form: spoken	Linking form: written
Verb	Affirmative	なる	なって	なり
	Negative	ならない	ならなくて	ならなく
Adjective	Affirmative	おとなしい	おとなしくて	おとなしく
	Negative	おとなしくない	おとなしくなくて	おとなしくなく
Noun です	Affirmative	病気だ	病気で	病気であり
	Negative	病気じゃない	病気じゃなくて	病気じゃなく
		病気ではない	病気ではなくて	病気ではなく

Note that the [Noun です] sentences are constructed from the full form of です: であります (informal form: である).

Spoken
電車じゃなくて車で来ました。
メールじゃなくて電話です。
アメリカからじゃなくてカナダからなんですか。
右じゃなくて左に行ったんです。

Written
電車ではなく車で来ました。
メールではなく電話です。
アメリカからではなくカナダからなのですか。
右ではなく左に行ったのです。

文字と例 Kanji with examples

#109.	知	し(る) チ		get to know	知
1.		知っている		know	
2.		知る		find out	
3.		知らない		don't know	
4.	+	お知らせ		announcement, notice (lit. 'letting know')	
5.	#	知人		acquaintance	
6.	#	知識		knowledge	

7.	知ってるだろう。		They probably know.
8.	電車で行くかどうか知ってる？		Do you know whether we are going by train or not?
9.	右か左か知らない？		Do you know whether it's right or left?
10.	同じか同じじゃないか知らないの？		Don't you know if it's the same or not?
11.	あの人のこと知ってる人はいませんか。		Isn't there anyone who knows that person?
12.	３年前のことを知ってしまった。		I found out about three years ago.
13.	ちょっと知りすぎてしまったね。		You found out too much about it.

#110. 漢　カン (see kanji #111)　China　漢

#111. 字　ジ　letter, character　字

1.		字	letter, character
2.		漢字	kanji
3.	+	ローマ字	romanization
4.		字がきれいだね。	Your handwriting is pretty.
5.		これが漢字かどうか知ってる？	Do you know whether this is kanji or not?
6.		字がもっときれいだったらよかったな。	I wish my handwriting were prettier.
7.		漢字で書いてくれる？	Will you write in kanji?

#112. 小　ちい(さい)　ちい(さな)　こ　お　ショウ　small　小

1.		小さい	small
2.		小さな子	small child
3.	+	小テスト	small test, quiz
4.		小学校	elementary school
5.	+	小学生	elementary school student
6.	#	大小	big and small, sizes
7.	+	小山	[family name]
8.	+	小川	creek, [family name]

12-7R　母が送ってくれたんだけど……。

9.	+	小田 (お だ)		[family name]
10.		思ったほど小さくないね。		It is not as small as expected.
11.		ちょっと小さすぎですね。		It is a little too small.
12.		小さくなってしまったよ。		It became small.
13.		小さなことでも知りたいから……。		Because I want to know even the small details (lit. things)…

#113. 教　おし(える)　キョウ　teaching　教

1.		教える (おし)	teach
2.	+	教会 (きょうかい)	church
3.	#	キリスト教 (きょう)	Christianity
4.	#	イスラム教 (きょう)	Islam
5.		教えてくれる?	Will you tell me?
6.		だれに教えたらいい?	Who shall I tell?
7.		日曜日は教会に行ったらどう?	How about you go to church on Sunday?
8.		村山さんが教会に来てるかどうか分からない。	I'm not sure whether Murayama-san is at church or not.

#114. 室　むろ　シツ　room, dwelling　室

1.		教室 (きょうしつ)	classroom
2.		コピー室	copy room
3.	#	小室 (こ むろ)	[family name]
4.		日本語の教室	Japanese language class
5.		教室で読むかどうか知ってる?	Do you know whether we are reading it in the classroom or not?
6.		この教室で書いたらどう?	How about we write it in this classroom?

#115. 勉　ベン (see kanji #116)　endeavor, make an effort　勉

#116. 強　つよ(い)　キョウ　ゴウ　strong　強

1.		強い (つよ)	strong
2.		勉強する (べんきょう)	study

244

3.	勉強ができる	can study, is good at studying
4.	プレッシャーに強い	good at handling pressure
5.	強すぎ！	It's too strong!
6.	強かったら教えて。	Please tell me if it's strong.
7.	強くなってしまったよ。	It became strong.
8.	この教室で勉強してから帰ろうと思っています。	I'm thinking of going home after I study in this classroom.
9.	ちゃんと勉強してくださいますか。	Please study hard.

Additional kanji with examples

#117. 弱   よわ(い) ジャク   weak   弱

1.	弱い	weak
2.	プレッシャーに弱い	bad at handling pressure
3.	強弱	strengths and weaknesses, stress
4.	弱くなっちゃった。	It became weak.
5.	日本人の弱さ	Japanese people's weakness
6.	ちょっとパソコンに弱いので……。	I'm not good at computers, so…

Now go to the Activity Book for 練習 Practice.

シーン 12-8R ハイキングに行きませんか。
Won't you go hiking?

Hiroshi is reading an email message sent by Oda-san from the International Center at Fukuzawa University.

テキスト Text

Subject: ハイキング

川村さん
あさって（土曜日）は天気がよさそうなので、留学生センターのみんなと山へハイキングに行くんですが、川村さんもいっしょに行きませんか。
ここから電車で日帰りで、2時間ぐらいの短いコースです。
https://yamap.co.jp/activity/1590704
いかがでしょうか。
小田

Subject: Hiking

Kawamura-san,

It looks like it's going to be good weather the day after tomorrow (Sat), so I'm going hiking in the mountains with everyone from the International Student Center. Won't you go, too?
It's going to be a day trip by train, and the trail (lit. hiking course) is short, about 2 hours.

What do you think (lit. how would it be)?
Oda

文字と例 Kanji with examples

#118. 天　テン　　　　　　　　　sky, heaven　天
 1.　　天ぷら　　　　　　　　　tempura
 2.　　天ぷらを食べすぎてしまった。　I ate too much tempura.

246

3.		この天ぷらだれが作ったか知ってる？	Do you know who made this tempura?
4.		田中さんに天ぷら作ってもらったよ。	I had Tanaka-san make me some tempura.

#119. 気　キ　　spirit, mind, mood

1.		天気 (てんき)	weather
2.		いい天気ですね。	Nice weather, isn't it.
3.		気分	mood, personal condition
4.		気分がいい	feels good, in a good mood
5.		人に気がつく	notice people
6.		人を気にする	care about, be bothered by, worry about people
7.	+	電気 (でんき)	electricity, light
8.		天気がよかったら行こうよ。	Let's go if the weather is good.
9.		天気がいいと気分もいいですね。	When the weather is good, don't we feel good, too?
10.		休(やす)んだら気分がよくなったよ。	I'm feeling better since I took a break.
11.		天気がよくなかったら歩いてきてもらいたくないんですが……。	It's that I don't want to have you walk (here) if the weather is not good.
12.		あのことに気がついてしまったの？	Have you noticed that?
13.		私のこと気にしてくれてるの？	Are you worried about me?

#120. 留　と(める)　と(まる)　リュウ　　keep, remain

1.		留学(りゅうがく)(する)	study abroad
2.		留学生	international student
3.	#	気に留(と)まる	(something) stays in mind
4.	#	気に留(と)める	keep in mind
5.		いつまで留学するか知ってる？	Do you know how long she is going to study abroad?
6.		だれが留学生か知らない？	Do you know who the international students are?
7.		だれか留学生知らない？	Do you know any international students?

247

#121. 短　みじか(い)　タン　　　　　short　　　短

1. 短い — short
2. # 気が短い — short-tempered
3. # 短気(な) — short-tempered
4. 短かったら教えてください。 — Please tell me if it's short.
5. 短くなってしまったよ。 — It became short.
6. 来年の休みは短いだろうね。 — Next year's break will probably be short.

Additional kanji with examples

#122. 元　もと　ガン　ゲン　　　origin, basis　元

1. 元気(な) — healthy, energetic
2. 元気がない — have no energy
3. 元気じゃない — not well, not healthy
4. 元年 — first year (of a new era)
5. # 火の元 — origin of a fire
6. # 元々 — originally
7. あの子、元気すぎだよ。 — That child is too energetic.
8. 休んだら元気になりました。 — I got better after I took a break.
9. 早く元気になってくれる? — Will you get better soon?

#123. 雨　あめ　ウ　　　　　　　rain　　　雨

1. 雨 — rain
2. + 大雨 — heavy rain
3. # 小雨 — light rain
4. # 雨天 — rainy weather
5. # 五月雨 — raining on and off
6. まだ雨なの? — Is it still raining?
7. 雨になるかどうか分からない。 — I'm not sure if it's going to be raining or not.
8. あーあ、雨になっちゃったよ。 — Oh no, it's raining.
9. 雨だったら帰ろう。 — If it's rainy, let's go home.
10. 雨の時に使ってもらいたいんだけど……。 — It's that I'd like to have you use it when it rains.

#124. 雪　ゆき　セツ　　　　　　　snow　　　雪

1. 雪 — snow
2. + 大雪 — heavy snow
3. + 雪子 — [given name]
4. # 新雪 — new snow
5. 雪になってしまうよ。 — It will snow.
6. 雪だったらどうしよう。 — What shall we do if it snows?
7. 外が雪だといやだなあ。 — It will be unpleasant if it's snowing outside.
8. 雪だったら車出してもらいたいんですけど……。 — If it's snowing, I'd like to have you drive the car.
9. 雪なので電車で帰ります。 — Because it is snowing, I'm going home by train.
10. 雪だったら遅くなるかもしれないよ。 — If it's snowing, then I might be late.

#125. 部　ブ　　　　　　　　　　part, division　　部

1. 全部 — all
2. # 一部 — (one) part
3. # 部分 — part
4. # 部下 — subordinate
5. + テニス部 — tennis club
6. # 本部 — headquarters
7. # 部会 — sectional meeting
8. 全部知ってしまったよ。 — I found out everything.
9. テニス部に入ってもらいたいんだけど……。 — It's that I'd like you to have you join the tennis club, but…

#126. 長　なが(い)　チョウ　　　long; chief　　長

1. 長い — long
2. # 気が長い — patient, have a long fuse, deliberate
3. 部長 — division chief
4. 社長 — company president
5. 学長 — school (university/college) president
6. # 校長 — school principal

7.	#	村長(そんちょう)	village mayor
8.		長いか短いか分かる？	Do you know whether it's long or short?
9.		学長に聞いてもらいたいんだけど……。	It's that I'd like to have you ask the school president, but…
10.		社長になるといそがしくなるよ。	When you become the company president, you will be busy.

Now go to the Activity Book for 練習 Practice.

シーン 12-9R 晩ご飯、いっしょにどう？
How about dinner together?

Sasha is reading a text message from Eri.

テキスト Text

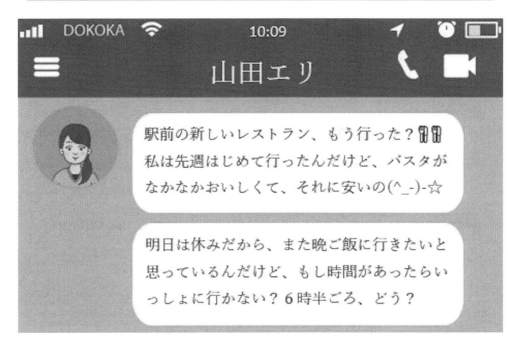

Have you been to the new restaurant in front of the station yet?

I went there for the first time last week. The pasta was quite good, and besides, it's inexpensive ☺

I'm thinking of going there again for dinner since I have the day off tomorrow. If you have time, won't you go with me? How about around 6:30?

文字と例 Kanji with examples

#127. 安　やす(い)　アン　　　　　cheap, tranquility　　安

1. 安い　　　　　　　　　　　　　cheap, inexpensive
2. + 安田　　　　　　　　　　　　[family name]
3. + 安子　　　　　　　　　　　　[given name]
4. # 平安(な)　　　　　　　　　　peaceful
5. 安かったら買います。　　　　　I'll buy it if it's cheap.
6. 安田さんに書いてほしいな。　　I want Yasuda-san to write it.

#128. 休　やす(み)　やす(む)　キュウ　　rest, be absent　　休

1. 休む　　　　　　　　　　　　　walk
2. お休みなさい。[1]　　　　　　　Good night.
3. (お)休み　　　　　　　　　　　absent, a day off, holiday
4. # 休日　　　　　　　　　　　　a day off, holiday
5. 学校を休みすぎると分からなくなりますよ。　You'll fall behind if you take too many days off from school.
6. 少しは休まないと……。　　　　You should take a little break or else…
7. もっと休んでもらいたいんだけど……。　So I'd like to have you rest more…

#129. 晩　バン　　　　　　　　　　evening　　晩

1. 晩　　　　　　　　　　　　　　evening
2. 今晩　　　　　　　　　　　　　this evening
3. 今晩は[2]　　　　　　　　　　 good evening
4. 今晩中にやってほしいです。　　I want you to do it by tonight.
5. 今晩はだれにも来ないでもらいたい。　I don't want to have anyone visit tonight.

#130. 飯　めし　ハン　　　　　　　cooked rice, meal　　飯

1. ご飯　　　　　　　　　　　　　cooked rice, meal
2. 晩ご飯　　　　　　　　　　　　dinner (lit. evening meal)
3. # 晩飯　　　　　　　　　　　　dinner

252

4. ご飯にしましょう。 Let's have a meal.
5. 山田さんが晩ご飯を作ってくれた。 Yamada-san made dinner for me.
6. 山田さんに晩御飯を作ってもらった。 I had Yamada-san make dinner.

Additional kanji with examples

#131. 朝　あさ　チョウ　　morning　　朝

1. 朝 — morning
2. # 朝日 — morning sun, Asahi (Newspaper)
3. 朝ご飯 — breakfast
4. 今朝 — this morning
5. # 朝食 — breakfast
6. # 早朝 — early morning
7. 朝までに読んでほしい。 I want you to read it by the morning.
8. 朝ごはんを作ってあげようか。 Shall I make breakfast for you?
9. もしかしたら今朝は来ないかもしれないよ。 He may not come this morning.

#132. 昼　ひる　チュウ　　noon　　昼

1. 昼 — morning
2. （お）昼ご飯 — lunch
3. + 昼休み — lunch break
4. # 昼食 — lunch
5. 昼になると学生が多くなる。 More students are here at noon time.
6. 昼休みに来てほしいところがあるんだけど……。 So there is a place that I'd like to have you come at lunch.
7. よかったらお昼作ってさしあげましょうか。 If you'd like, shall I make lunch for you?
8. お昼ちょっと食べすぎちゃったなあ。 I ate too much lunch.
9. 昼休みに教室に行くことになりました。 It was decided that we go to class during lunch.

#133. 毎　マイ　　every　　毎

1. 毎日 — every day, Mainichi (Newspaper)
2. 毎週 — every week

253

3.	毎週(の)火曜日	every Tuesday
4.	毎月 (つき・げつ)	every month
5.	毎年 (とし・ねん)	every year
6.	毎朝 (あさ)	every morning
7.	毎晩 (ばん)	every evening
8.	毎日やることになりました。	It was decided that we do it everyday.
9.	毎週来てほしいと思っています。	I'm thinking that I'd like to have you come every week.
10.	もしかしたら毎年あるかもしれませんよ。	Maybe it occurs every year.

Now go to the Activity Book for 練習 Practice.

Then do 評価 Assessment activities, including 読んでみよう Contextualized reading, 書き取り Dictation, and 書いてみよう Contextualized writing.

Notes

1 Often written in hiragana as well.
2 Often written in hiragana as well.

Appendix A: Japanese-English glossary in *Gojuuon* order

List of abbreviations

N = Noun
V = Verb
Adj = Adjective
Sp. Exp. = Special Expressions

	あ、	あ、	Sp. Exp.	Oh	1	10
	ああ	ああ	Sp. Exp.	ahh, oh	2	7
	あいきどう	合気道	N	aikido (martial art)	6	1
+	あいだ	会田	N	[family name]	10	9R
	あいだ	Amount of time 〜間	Sp. Exp.	number of hours, days, weeks, years	6	2
	あいだ	間	N	interval, space between	7	6
	あいだ	XとYの間	Sp. Exp.	between X and Y	7	6
	あいだ	間	N	during; between	8	6
	あいづち	相槌	N	back-channeling (nods, interjections and the like that indicate one is paying attention)	11	6
+	あいづちをうつ	相槌を打つ	Sp. Exp.	provide back-channel comments and nods	11	6
+	あいてぃー	IT	N	IT	9	3
+	あいまい	曖昧(な)	N	ambiguity (BTS 12)	4	2
+	あう	会う(-U; 会った)	V	see, meet	3	4
+	あお	青	N	blue, green	6	3
+	あおい	青い	Adj	blue	3	5
+	アオイしゅっぱん	アオイ出版	N	Aoi Publishing	3	1
+	あか	赤	N	red	6	3
	あかい	赤い	Adj	red	3	5
	あかいの	赤いの	Sp. Exp.	the red one	3	5

255

+	あかちゃん	赤ちゃん	N	baby	7	2
	あがる	上がる (-U; 上がった)	V	rise, go up, enter a house	8	3
+	あかるい	明るい	Adj	light, bright	7	1
+	あき	秋	N	autumn, fall	8	6
+	あきらめる	諦める (-RU; 諦めた)	V	be reconciled, give up	10	6
	あく	空く・あく (-U; 空いた)	V	become free, empty	6	5
+	アクセサリー	アクセサリー	N	accessory	11	4
	あけてみる	開けてみる	Sp. Exp.	try opening and see	8	1
+	あけましておめでとうございます	明けましておめでとうございます	Sp. Exp.	Happy New Year	10	8R
	あける	開ける (-RU; 開けた)	V	open (something)	8	1
	あげる	あげる/上げる (-RU; あげた)	V	give (to out-group)	12	6
+	あさ	朝	N	morning	3	4
	あさがた	朝型	N	morning person	12	4
+	あさごはん	朝ごはん	N	breakfast	2	3
	あさって	あさって	N	day after tomorrow	3	4
	あさにつよい	朝に強い	Sp. Exp.	morning type (lit. 'strong in the morning')	12	4
+	あし	足/脚	N	feet/ leg	11	5
+	あした	あした・明日	N	tomorrow	2	2
	あす	あす	N	tomorrow (slightly more formal than あした)	5	1
	あすのひゃくよりきょうのごじゅう	明日の百より今日の五十	Kotowaza	A bird in the hand is worth two in the bush.	6	0
+	あそこ	あそこ	N	over there, there (away from both of us), that place (that we both know about)	2	7
	あそび	遊び	N	play, fun	9	3
	あそぶ	遊ぶ (-RU; 遊んだ)	V	play	9	3
	あたたかい	暖かい・温かい	Adj	warm (climate, personality)	7	1
	あたたかくてきもちがいい	暖かくて気持ちがいい	Sp. Exp.	warm and good feeling	7	1
	あたま	頭	N	head	11	5
+	あたまが・のいい	頭が・のいい	Adj	intelligent	12	3
+	あたらしい	新しい	Adj	news	4	1
	あたり	当たり!	Sp. Exp.	right (on target)!; you got it!	8	1
	あたる	当たる (-U: 当たった)	V	hit on target	8	1

+	あちら	あちら	N	there (away from both of us), that thing (away from both of us), in that direction (away from both of us), that alternative (of two away from both of us), that place (that we both know about), that person over there (polite)	2	4
+	あつい	暑い	Adj	hot (weather, climate)	7	1
+	あつい	熱い	Adj	hot (non-weather, non-climate)	7	1
+	あっち	あっち	N	there (away from both of us), in that direction (away from both of us), that alternative (of two away from both of us), that place (that we both know about)	2	7
	あつまる	集まる (-U; 集まった)	V	get together, assemble	7	5
	あと	あと	Sp. Exp.	lastly, remaining, and then	4	2
	あと	あと・後	N	time after	5	6
	あとで	あとで	Sp. Exp.	later	2	2
	あとで	Xのあとで	Sp. Exp.	later, N のあとで = 'after N'	5	6
+	アドバイス	アドバイス	N	advice	5	6
+	アドレス	アドレス	N	(email) address	6	4
+	あなた	あなた	N	you	1	7
+	あに	兄↓	N	older brother (humble)	7	2
+	あね	姉↓	N	older sister (humble)	7	2
+	あの	あの+N	Sp. Exp.	that N over there	3	5
	あのう	あのう	Sp. Exp.	umm (hesitation noise),	2	2
+	アパート	アパート	N	apartment	2	5
+	あびる	浴びる (-RU; 浴びた)	V	take (a shower) (lit. 'bathe in' or 'be covered in')	9	5
+	あぶない	危ない	Adj	dangerous	7	6
+	アプリ	アプリ	N	app, application	3	3
+	アフリカ	アフリカ	N	Africa	8	4
+	アポ	アポ	N	appointment	6	5
	あまい	甘い	Adj	sweet	10	3
+	あまり・あんまり	あまり・あんまり+ negative	Sp. Exp.	not very much	4	2
	あまり・あんまり+ affirmative	あまり・あんまり+ affirmative	Sp. Exp.	so, to such an extent	11	5
	あめ	雨	N	rain	3	6
	アメリカ	アメリカ	N	America	6	1

+	アメリカじん	アメリカ人	N	American (person)	3	1
	あやまる	謝る(-U; 謝った)	V	apologize	9	1
+	あらう	洗う(-U; 洗った)	V	wash	9	1
+	ありがたい	ありがたい	Adj	grateful, thankful	7	1
+	ありがとう。	ありがとう。	Sp. Exp.	Thank you. (non-past or past, informal)	1	2
	ありがとうございました。	ありがとうございました。	Day1 Phrase	Thank you. (past, formal)	0	0
	ありがとうございます。	ありがとうございます。	Sp. Exp.	Thank you. (non-past, formal)	1	2
	ある	ある(-U; あった; ない)	V	exist (inanimate)	2	8
	あるいて	歩いて	Sp. Exp.	on foot	5	4
	あるかもしれません。	あるかもしれません。	Sp. Exp.	There may be.	10	4
	あるき	歩き	N	walk	7	5
	あるく	歩く(-U; 歩いた)	V	walk	5	4
	あるくひと	歩く人	Sp. Exp.	people who (will) walk	7	5
	アルコール	アルコール	N	alcohol, alcoholic beverage	10	3
+	アルバイト	アルバイト(する)	N	part-time work, part-timer	9	3
+	あれ	あれ	N	that (thing over there)	2	1
	あれ？	あれ？	Sp. Exp.	What? Huh?	7	6
	あんない	(ご)案内(する)	N	show around	12	6
	あんないしてあげる	案内してあげる	Sp. Exp.	I'll do you the favor of showing you around	12	6
+	いい	いい	Adj	good	2	1
+	いいえ	いいえ	Sp. Exp.	no	2	1
	いう	いう・言う(-U; 言った)	V	is called, say	3	1
+	いえ	いえ	Sp. Exp.	no	2	1
+	いえ	いえ・家	N	house, home	2	5
	いえいえ	いえいえ	Sp. Exp.	no, no	2	1
	いか	以下	N	below	10	6
	へいきんいか・いじょう	X以下・以上	Sp. Exp.	below / above X	10	6
	いがい	X以外	N	outside of X; besides X	12	5
	いかが	いかが	Sp. Exp.	how (polite)	6	5
	いきますよ。	行きますよ。	Sp. Exp.	Here we go!	6	3
+	イギリス	イギリス	N	England, U.K.	6	1
+	いく	行く(-U; 行った)	V	go; Scene 9-2 cover (as in a task)	2	2
	いくことになりました。	行くことになりました。	Sp. Exp.	It has been decided I will go.	12	6
	いくつ	(お)いくつ	Classifier	how many things/items	5	3

	いくら	いくら	N	how much	3	5
	いくんだ。	行くんだ。	Sp. Exp.	The fact is, I'm going.	7	2
	いこう	行こう	V	let's go	10	1
+	いしゃ	医者	N	(medical) doctor	6	2
+	いじょう	以上	N	above	10	6
+	いす	椅子	N	chair	12	1
	いそがしい	(お)忙しい	Adj	busy	2	4
	いそがばまわれ	急がば回れ	Kotowaza	More haste, less speed. (lit. 'If you are in a hurry, go the long way.')	3	0
+	いそぐ	急ぐ(-U; 急いだ)	V	hurry	5	1
	いたい	痛い	Adj	painful	11	5
+	いたす	いたす(-U; いたした)	V	do (humble)	6	5
	いただきます。	いただきます。	Sp. Exp.	I humbly receive. (eating ritual)	1	6
	いただく	いただく↓(-U; いただいた)	V	eat; receive (humble)	2	3
	いただける	いただける (-RU; いただけた)	V	can/may have someone do X	5	3
+	いたむ	痛む (-U; 痛んだ)	V	become painful	11	5
	いち	一・1	Numbers	1	3	2
	いち、に、さん!	いち、に、さん!	Sp. Exp.	One, two three!		
	いちおう	一応	N	for the time being, tentatively, more or less	5	3
	いちごいちえ	一期一会	Kotowaza	'Once in a lifetime' or 'carpe diem' (seize the day).	1	0
+	いちにちじゅう	一日中	N	all day	10	2
+	いちばん	一番	Sp. Exp.	most, best	4	5
	いちばん	[Category]の中で一番行ってみたいの	Sp. Exp.	within/among [category] the one I want to go to most	9	4
	いちろう	一郎	N	[given name]	1	7
	いちろうくん	一郎君	Sp. Exp.	Ichiro (addressing or referring to)	1	7
	いつ	いつ	N	when?	4	3
	いつか	いつか	Sp. Exp.	sometime	6	5
	いっかいも	一回も number+ も+ neg	Sp. Exp.	not a single time	8	6
	いっしょ	一緒	N	together	3	4
	いっしょうけんめい	一生懸命	N	all out, for all one is worth	10	6
	いったとき	言った時	Sp. Exp.	when I have said	10	4
	いっていらっしゃい。	行って(い)らっしゃい。	Sp. Exp.	See you later. (lit. 'Go and come back.')	1	8
	いってきます。	行ってきます。	Sp. Exp.	See you later. (lit. 'I'll go and come back.')	1	8

	いってください。	言ってください。	Inst. Exp	Please say it.	0	0
	いってください。	PERSON に言ってください。	Inst. Exp	Please say it to PERSON.	2	0
+	いっぱい	いっぱい	N	a lot, much, full	12	1
	いつも	いつも	N	always, usual(ly)	4	4
	いつもおせわになっております↓。	いつもお世話になっております↓。	Sp. Exp.	I/we are always in your debt.	6	4
	いつもの N	いつもの N	Sp. Exp.	the usual N (e.g., *basho* 場所 place, *jikan* 時間 time, *tokoro* ところ place,	4	4
+	いとう	伊藤	N	[family name]	3	9R
+	いとこ	いとこ	N	cousin (in-group)	11	4
+	いぬ	犬	N	dog	12	3
+	いのうえ	井上	N	[family name]	3	9R
+	イベント	イベント	N	event	4	4
	いま	今	N	now	2	2
	いみ	意味	N	meaning	11	4
	イメージ	イメージ	N	image	11	4
+	いもうと	妹↓	N	younger sister (humble)	7	2
+	いもうとさん	妹さん	N	younger brother	7	2
	いや	いや	Sp. Exp.	no (informal); uhh (hesitation noise)	2	4
	いや	嫌（な）	N	disagreeable, unpleasant	8	2
+	イヤリング	イヤリング	N	ear ring	11	2
	いらしたこと	いらしたこと	Sp. Exp.	have gone; the experience of having gone	8	4
	いらっしゃいませ。	いらっしゃいませ。	Sp. Exp.	Welcome.	10	3
+	いらっしゃる	いらっしゃる↑ (-ARU; いらっしゃった)	V	be (honorif form of います 'be')	6	4
	いらっしゃる↑	いらっしゃる↑／いらっしゃって↑ or いらして↑(-ARU; いらっしゃった or いらした)	V	go, come (honorific)	5	5
+	いりぐち	入り口／入口	N	entrance	6	3
+	いる	いる(-RU; いた)	V	be, exist (animate)	2	2
+	いる	いる(-U; いった)	V	need	4	6
	いれる	入れる/いれる (-RU; いれた)	V	put (something) in; brew or infuse (tea)	8	4
	いれる	淹れる/いれる (-RU; いれた)	V	brew or infuse (tea)	8	4
+	いろ	色	N	color	6	3
	いろいろ	いろいろ(な)	Sp. Exp.	various	8	1
+	いわい	（お）祝い	N	congratulations, celebration	8	4
+	インターン	インターン	N	intern	10	4
+	インタビュー(する)	インタビュー(する)	N	interview (television, media, also job)	11	2

+	インドネシアご	インドネシア語	N	Indonesian (language)	8	8R
	う～ん	う～ん	Sp. Exp.	well (hesitation)	2	7
	う～ん	う～ん	Sp. Exp.	u-m-m	9	4
+	ウーロンちゃ	ウーロン茶	N	oolong tea	2	3
	ううん	ううん	Sp. Exp.	no (informal)	7	1
+	うえ	上	N	top, over	6	2
+	うえだ	上田	N	[family name]	10	8R
+	うえやま	上山	N	[family name]	9	9R
	うかがう	伺う↓(-U; 伺った)	V	visit (humble); Scene 10-3 inquire, hear	5	5
	うかがって↓おります↓。	伺って↓おります↓。	Sp. Exp.	We've heard. We've received.	10	3
+	うきょう	右京	N	[family name]	11	9R
+	うけとる	受け取る (-U; 受け取った)	V	take, accept	12	2
+	うける	受ける (-RU; 受けた)	V	receive; catch; be given	10	6
	うしろ	後ろ	N	back, behind	6	3
+	うすい	薄い	Adj	light colored, thin, diluted, weak (taste, probability)	11	2
	うそ	嘘	N	lie	8	2
	うた	歌	N	song	9	5
	うたう	歌う (-U; 歌った)	V	sing	9	5
+	うち	うち	N	house, home; Scene 5-5 our company	2	5
	うち	うちのX	Sp. Exp.	our company's X	5	5
	うちで	X, Y, Zのうちで	Sp. Exp.	among X, Y, and Z	9	4
	みっつのうちで	三つのうちで	Sp. Exp.	among three	9	4
+	うつ	打つ (-U; 打った)	V	hit, insert	11	6
+	うで	腕	N	arm	11	5
+	うどん	うどん	N	udon (wheat noodles)	2	3
	うまい	上手い・美味い・旨い・うまい	Adj	delicious, skillful	9	6
+	うみのひ	海の日	N	Marine Day (BTS 18)	4	4
	うるさい	うるさい	Adj	annoying, loud, noisy, tiresome	8	5
+	うれしい	うれしい / 嬉しい	Adj	happy, glad	7	1
	うん	うん	Sp. Exp.	yes (informal)	7	1
+	うんてん	運転(する)	N	driving (a car)	10	2
+	え	絵	N	drawing, picture	9	5
	え?	え?	Sp. Exp.	what?	2	3
+	えいいち	英一	N	[male given name]	10	7R
+	えいが	映画	N	movies	10	1
	えいがかん	映画館	N	movie theater	7	6
	えいぎょうぶ	営業部	N	operations division	11	1
+	えいこ・ひでこ	英子	N	[female given name]	10	7R

261

+	えいご	英語	N	English (language)	3	1
+	えいこく	英国	N	England	10	7R
+	エイティーエム	ATM	N	ATM	7	1
+	ええ	ええ	Sp. Exp.	yes (suggesting agreement or indicating understanding; less formal than *hai*)	1	1
	ええと	ええと	Sp. Exp.	uhh (hesitation noise),	2	2
+	えき	駅	N	train station	2	5
+	えきまえ	駅前	Sp. Exp.	in front of the station	11	8R
+	えらい	偉い	Adj	excellent, distinguished, admirable	9	6
	えり	恵理	N	Eri [female given name] (Eri is Sasha's house mate)	1	13
	えん	〜円	Classifier	yen (Japanese currency)	3	5
	えんか	演歌	N	*enka* (a popular ballad style of singing)	9	5
+	エンジニア	エンジニア	N	engineer	9	3
+	えんぴつ	鉛筆	N	pencil	3	3
	えんりょ	(ご)遠慮(する)	N	restraint	8	3
+	おおゆき	大雪	N	heavy snow	12	8R
	おいしい	おいしい	Adj	delicious	2	3
	おいしそう	おいしそう	N	look(s) delicious	2	3
+	おいそがしいなか	お忙しい中	Sp. Exp.	when you are busy	10	7R
+	おいとこさん	おいとこさん	N	cousin (polite)	11	4
	おいわい	お祝い	N	congratulations, celebration, gift	11	4
+	おおあめ	大雨	N	heavy rain	12	8R
	おおい	多い	Adj	a lot, many, numerous	10	5
+	おおがきしょうかい	大垣商会	N	Ogaki Trading Company, Ltd.	3	1
+	おおきい	大きい	Adj	big	2	7
	おおきな	大きな	N	large, big	12	5
+	おおさか	大阪	N	Osaka	9	4
+	オーストラリア	オーストラリア	N	Australia	8	4
	オーバー	オーバー	N	coat	11	3
	おかえりなさい。	おかえりなさい。	Sp. Exp.	Welcome back.	1	13
	おかげさまで	おかげさまで	Sp. Exp.	thanks to you	7	4
	おかしい	おかしい	Adj	funny, weird, odd, strange	7	6
+	おかね	お金	N	money	9	7R
	おかまいなく	お構いなく	Sp. Exp.	don't go to any bother	8	4
+	おがわ	小川	N	[family name]	12	7R
+	おきなわ	沖縄	N	Okinawa	9	4
	おきまりでしょうか。	お決まりでしょうか。	Sp. Exp.	Have you decided?	10	3
	おきる	起きる(-RU; 起きた)	V	wake up, rise	8	1
+	おく	億	Numbers	hundred millions (BTS 4)	4	1

	おく	置く (-U: 置いた)	V	put, place, position	9	1
	おくさま	奥様	N	wife (polite)	11	4
+	おくさん	奥さん	N	wife	7	2
	おくる	送る (-U; 送った)	V	send	12	2
	おくれる	遅れる (-RU; 遅れた)	V	become late, run late	7	3
+	おさきに	お先に	Sp. Exp.	I'll be x-ing (ahead of you)	1	12
+	おさきにしつれいします。	お先に失礼します。	Sp. Exp.	I'll be leaving (ahead of you).	1	12
+	おじ	伯父/叔父	N	uncle (in-group)	11	4
+	おじいさん・おじいさま	おじいさん/お祖父様	N	uncle (polite)	11	4
+	おしえる	教える (-RU; 教えた)	V	tell, teach	5	5
	おじかん	お時間	N	your time	5	6
+	おしゃれ	おしゃれな (な)	N	stylish	11	4
	おしょくじのほう	お食事の方	Sp. Exp.	the food part of your order	10	3
+	おしらせ	お知らせ	N	announcement, notice (lit. 'letting know')	12	7R
+	おせわさま	お世話様	Sp. Exp.	your kindness	11	7R
+	おそい	遅い	Adj	late	3	4
+	おそく	遅く	N	far	12	4
+	おだ	小田	N	[family name]	12	7R
	おだいじに	お大事に	Sp. Exp.	take care	7	4
+	おたく	お宅	N	home (polite)	2	5
	おたんじょうびおめでとう(ございます)。	お誕生日おめでとう (ございます)。	Sp. Exp.	Happy birthday. (lit. 'Congratulations on your birthday.')	8	1
+	おちゃ	お茶	N	tea	2	3
	おちゃをいれる	お茶を淹れる	Sp. Exp.	brew or infuse tea	8	4
	オッケー	オッケー	Sp. Exp.	okay	3	4
+	おっしゃる	おっしゃる↑(-ARU; おっしゃった)	V	say (honorific)	6	2
+	おっと	夫↓	N	husband	7	2
	おつかれさま。	お疲れ様。	Sp. Exp.	Good work. Hello. (informal)	1	11
	おつかれさまでした。	お疲れ様でした。	Sp. Exp.	Good work.	1	12
	おつかれさまです。	お疲れ様です。	Sp. Exp.	Good work. Hello.	1	11
+	おと	音	N	sound	8	1
+	おとうと	弟↓	N	younger brother (humble)	7	2
	おとうとさん	弟さん	N	younger sister	7	2
+	おとこのこ	男の子	N	boy	7	2
+	おとこのひと	男の人	N	man	6	3
+	おととい	おととい	N	the day before yesterday	4	3
+	おとな	おとな・大人	N	adult	7	2
	おとなしい	おとなしい	Adj	laidback, quiet, docile	12	3

263

+	おなか	お腹	N	abdomen, stomach	8	4
+	おなかがすく	お腹が空く	Sp. Exp.	get hungry	8	4
+	おなじ	同じ	N	same	3	6
	おなじ	同じX	Sp. Exp.	the same X	7	5
	おねがいします。	お願いします。	Sp. Exp.	please help me with this	1	3
	おねがいできますか?	お願いできますか?	Sp. Exp.	Can I ask a favor of you?	5	3
	おねがいできる	お願いできる (-RU)	V	can request	5	3
+	おば	伯母/叔母	N	aunt (in-group)	11	4
+	おばあさん/おばあさま	おばあさん/お祖母様	N	aunt (polite)	11	4
	おはなしする↓	お話しする↓	V	talk (humble)	6	5
	おはよう。	おはよう。	Day1 Phrase	Good morning. (informal)	1	6
	おはようございます。	おはようございます。	Day1 Phrase	Good morning. (formal)	0	0
	おひる	お昼	N	noon, lunch time	9	2
	オフィス	オフィス	N	office	4	5
+	おぼえる	覚える (-RU; 覚えた)	V	remember, memorize	8	2
	おまたせいたしました↓。	お待たせいたしました↓。	Sp. Exp.	Sorry to make you wait. (humble)	10	3
	おまたせしました。	お待たせしました。	Sp. Exp.	Sorry to make you wait.	6	6
	おまたせする	お待たせする↓	V	make someone wait	10	3
	おまちください。	お待ちください。	Sp. Exp.	Please wait.	10	3
	おみや	お土産・おみやげ	N	souvenir, gift	8	4
	おもい	[person]+ 思い	Sp. Exp.	thoughtful about [person]	11	4
+	おもいだす	思い出す (-U; 思い出した)	V	remember	9	5
	おもいやり	思いやり	N	onsideration	3	4
	おもう	思う (-U; 思った)	V	think	7	4
	おもしろい	おもしろい	Adj	interesting	2	3
+	おもしろそう	おもしろそう	N	look(s) interesting	2	3
	おや	親	N	parent	8	5
	おやこうこう	親孝行	N	filial piety (a Confucian virtue); dedication to parents	8	6
	おやすみなさい。	おやすみなさい。	Sp. Exp.	Good night.	1	14
+	おやふこう	親不孝	N	lack of filial piety	8	6
+	おやま	小山	N	[family name]	12	7R
	およぐ	泳ぐ(-U; 泳いだ)	V	swim	7	2
	おる	おる↓(-U; おった)	V	be (humble form of います 'be') The 〜て form is rarely used today.	6	4

+	おれ	俺	N	I (masculine, informal) (BTS 15)	1	7
	オレゴンしゅう	オレゴン州	N	Oregon	6	1
	オレンジジュース	オレンジジュース	N	orange juice	10	3
+	おわらせる	終わらせる (-RU; 終わらせた)	V	finish (something), close (something)	10	2
	おわり	終わり	N	the end	9	2
	おわります。	終わります。	Inst. Exp	That's all for today (used at the end of a class).	0	0
+	おわる	終わる(-U; 終わった)	V	end	2	2
+	おわる	Verb Stem+ おわる (-U; おわった)	V	finish X-ing	9	2
+	おん	恩	N	benevolence, favor (BTS 1)	12	BTS 1
	おんがく	音楽	N	music	9	5
	おんせん	温泉	N	hot spring	9	4
+	おんなのこ	女の子	N	girl	7	2
+	おんなのひと	女の人	N	woman	6	3
	おんよみ	音読み	N	Chinese-based readings of kanji	1	BTL 2
	か？	〜か？	S. Particle	[question particle]	2	1
+	が	〜が	S. Particle	but, and	2	4
	が	〜が	Particle	[subject particle]	4	3
+	かあさん	（お）母さん	N	mother	7	2
+	かい	〜会	N	organization, club, association, group	3	1
	かい	〜階	Classifier	naming and counting floors	4	5
	かい	〜回	Classifier	times, instances	8	6
+	かいぎ	会議(する)	N	meeting	3	2
	かいぎしつ	会議室	N	meeting room	4	4
+	がいこくご	外国語	N	foreign language	10	6
+	がいこくじん	外国人	N	foreigner	3	1
	かいしゃ	会社	N	office, company	2	5
	かいしゃいん	会社員	N	company employee	9	3
+	がいじん	外人	N	foreigner (can be derogatory)	3	1
	かいてください。	書いてください。	Inst. Exp	Please write it.	0	0
+	かいはつ	開発(する)	N	development	6	2
+	かいはつぶ	開発部	N	development division	11	1
+	かいもの	買い物	N	shopping	5	4
	がいらいご	外来語	N	loan words (BTS 14)	3	3
	かいわ	会話	N	conversation	5	6
+	かう	買う(-U; 買った)	V	buy	4	1
+	かう	飼う(飼った)	V	keep (a pet or other animal)	12	3

	かえってくる	返ってくる	V	come back (inanimate)	10	6
+	かえる	帰る(-U; 帰った)	V	return [home]	3	2
	かえる	変える(-RU; 変えた)	V	change (something)	8	2
+	かお	顔	N	face	11	5
	かかる	かかる(-U; かかった)	V	take (time/money)	4	6
+	かかん・にちかん・にち	〜日間	Classifier	classifier for counting days	6	2
+	かき	書き	N	writing	5	6
+	かきとり	書き取り	N	dictation	5	6
+	かく	描く(-U; 描いた)	V	draw, paint, sketch	9	5
	がくせい	学生	N	student	3	1
+	かく	書く(-U; 書いた)	V	write	2	2
+	がくちょう	学長	N	school president	6	5
+	がくぶ	学部	N	academic division, college	6	1
+	かげつ	〜ヶ月・〜カ月	Classifier	classifier for counting months	4	6
	かける	かける・掛ける (-RU; かけた・掛けた)	V	cause (lit. 'hang (something)'); Scene 11-4 suspend, wear (glasses, buttons) (lit. 'hang, suspend')	7	4
	かげん	(お)加減	N	personal condition	7	4
	かさ	傘	N	umbrella	3	6
+	カサカサ	カサカサ(する・になる)	N	dry	11	5
	かさねる	重ねる(-RU; 重ねた)	V	put on top	11	3
	かさねることにして(い)る	重ねることにして(い)る	Sp. Exp.	usually layer (habit)	11	3
	かし	(お)菓子	N	sweets, candy	8	4
+	かしこい	賢い	Adj	clever, smart	12	3
	かしこまりました↓。	かしこまりました↓。	Sp. Exp.	Understood.	10	3
+	カジュアル	カジュアル	N	casual	11	2
+	かす	貸す(-U; 貸した)	V	lend, rent (to someone)	12	1
+	かぞく	(ご)家族	N	family	7	2
+	かぞく	X人家族	N	X number in a family (including oneself)	12	5
	かた	方(かた)	N	person (honorific)	6	3
+	かた	肩	N	shoulder	11	5
	カタカナ	片仮名・カタカナ	N	katakana syllabary	1	BTL 1
	かたづく	片付く(-U; 片付いた)	V	be in order; be finished; be taken care of	9	2
+	かたづける	片付ける(-RU; 片付けた)	V	clean (something) up, tidy up	9	1
	かちょう	課長	N	section chief	6	5

	がつ	~月（がつ）	Classifier	classifier for naming the months of the year	4	4
+	がっかい	学会	N	academic conference	11	2
+	がっかり	がっかり（な）・（する）	N	feel disappointment, lose hear	10	6
+	がっき	~学期	Classifier	school /term	4	6
+	カッコいい	カッコいい	Adj	good-looking, stylish, cool	11	4
+	がっこう	学校	N	school	2	5
	かっておきますので	買っておきますので	Sp. Exp.	because/so I'll buy X ahead of time	10	1
+	かど	角	N	corner	7	6
+	かとう	加藤	N	[family name]	3	9R
	かな	かな	N	syllabary	1	BTL 1
	かなあ	~かなあ	S. Particle	[sentence particle indicating a shared question]	2	6
+	かなざわ	金沢	N	Kanazawa	9	4
+	かなしい	悲しい	Adj	sad	7	1
+	カナダ	カナダ	N	Canada	6	1
	かならず	必ず	Sp. Exp.	without fail, always, without exception	8	6
	かなり	かなり	Sp. Exp.	quite, considerably	7	3
+	かねだ	金田	N	[family name]	10	8R
+	かのじょ	彼女	N	she, girlfriend	11	4
+	かばん	かばん	N	bag, briefcase	3	6
+	カフェ	カフェ	N	café	4	4
+	カフェテリア	カフェテリア	N	cafeteria	7	1
+	かぶき	歌舞伎	N	kabuki (traditional theater)	10	1
+	かぶる	被る (U; 被った)	V	wear, put on (one's head, such as a hat)	11	4
	かまう	構う (-U; 構った)	V	mind, care, be concerned about (most commonly occurs in the negative)	5	1
+	かみ	紙	N	paper	3	6
	かみ	髪	N	hair	12	3
+	かみむら・うえむら	上村	N	[family name]	9	9R
+	かゆい	痒い	Adj	itchy	11	5
+	かよう	通う(-u; 通った)	V	commute	7	1
+	かよう（び）	火曜(日)	N	Tuesday	4	6
	から	~から	Particle	from (starting point)	4	4
	から	REASON ~から	S. Particle	because of REASON X	5	5
+	からい	辛い	Adj	spicy	10	3
+	カラオケ	カラオケ	N	karaoke	7	2
+	からだ	体・身体・からだ	N	body	12	3
+	かりる	借りる (-RU; 借りた)	V	borrow	5	3
+	かれ	彼	N	he, boyfriend	11	4

	ほとんど	ほとんど	N	almost; barely (plus negative)	4	6
	カレーかきょうのランチか	カレーか今日のランチか	Sp. Exp.	curry or today's lunch special	6	6
+	カレーライス	カレーライス	N	curry rice	2	3
	かわいい	かわいい	Adj	cute	3	5
	かわいいこにはたびをさせよ	可愛い子には旅をさせよ	Kotowaza	If you love your child, send them out into the world.	12	0
+	かわかみ	川上	N	[family name]	9	8R
	かわく	渇く/乾く (-U; かわいた)	V	become dry	8	4
+	かわぐち	川口	N	[family name]	11	8R
+	かわた	川田	N	[family name]	10	8R
+	かわなか	川中	N	[family name]	9	9R
	かわる	Xと・に代わる (-U; 代わった)	V	switch over to X (on the telephone)	11	1
	かわる	変わる(-U; 変わった)	V	change, switch	11	3
	かんがえすぎ	考え過ぎ	N	think too much	11	2
+	かんがえる	考える (-RU; 考えた)	V	think about, consider	4	3
	かんけい	関係(する)	N	relationship	9	3
	かんけいの	X関係のY	Sp. Exp.	Y related to X	9	3
	がんこ	頑固(な)	N	stubborn	12	3
+	かんこく	韓国	N	Korea	6	1
+	かんこくご	韓国語	N	Korean (language)	3	1
+	かんこくじん	韓国人	N	Korean (person)	3	1
	かんじ	漢字	N	kanji	1	BTL 1
+	がんじつ	元日	N	New Year's Day (BTS 18)	4	4
+	かんだ	神田	Name	Mr/s. Kanda	1	1
	かんださんですか?	神田さんですか?	Sp. Exp.	Are you Mr./Ms. Kanda?	1	10
+	かんとんしょう	広東省	N	Guangdong Province	6	1
+	がんねん	元年	N	first year (of a new era) (BTS 18)	4	4
	かんぱい	乾杯(する)	N	toast	9	3
	かんぱい!	乾杯!	Sp. Exp.	Cheers!	9	3
	がんばりましょう。	頑張りましょう。	Inst. Exp	Do your best.	2	0
	がんばる	頑張る (-U; 頑張った)	V	will do my best	2	1
+	き	木	N	wood, tree	9	7R
	きいてください。	聞いてください。	Inst. Exp	Please listen.	0	0
	きいてください。	PERSONに聞いてください。	Inst. Exp	Please ask PERSON.	2	0
+	きいろ	黄色	N	yellow	6	3
	きかく	企画(する)	N	plan, project, design	6	2
	きかくぶ	企画部	N	planning division	11	1
	きがつく	Xに気がつく(-U; 気がついた)	V	notice X	9	5
+	ききとり	聞き取り	N	listening	5	6

	きく	聞く (-U; 聞いた)	V	hear; listen	4	4
+	きく	Xに聞く	Sp. Exp.	ask X	6	6
	きくのせんもん	聞くの専門	Sp. Exp.	listening is my specialty	9	5
	きくはいっときのはじ、きかぬはいっしょうのはじ	聞くは一時の恥、聞かぬは一生の恥	Kotowaza	To ask may lead to shame for a moment, but not to ask leads to shame for a lifetime.	5	0
+	きこえる	聞こえる (-RU; 聞こえた)	V	be audible	8	1
	きせつ	季節	N	season	11	3
	きせつによって	季節によって	Sp. Exp.	depending on the season	11	3
	きちんと	きちんと	Sp. Exp.	precisely, neatly, accurately, as it should be	10	5
	きつい	きつい	Adj	severe, intense	7	1
	きっと	きっと	Sp. Exp.	surely, undoubtedly	12	2
	きっぷ	切符	N	ticket(s)	8	2
	きていただいて	来ていただいて	Sp. Exp.	getting you to come	12	4
	きてくださってありがとうございます。	来てくださってありがとうございます。	Sp. Exp.	Thank you for coming.	12	4
+	きてくれてありがとう(ございます)。	来てくれてありがとう(ございます)。	Sp. Exp.	Thanks for coming.	12	4
	きにする	気にする	V	care about, be bothered, worry	10	5
+	きのう	きのう	N	yesterday	4	3
+	きのした	木下	N	[family name]	9	8R
	きびしい	厳しい	Adj	strict, severe, intense	7	3
+	きむら	木村	N	[family name]	3	9R
	きめる	決める (-RU; 決めた)	V	decide (something)	5	1
	きもち	気持ち	N	feeling, sensation	7	1
	きもちがいい	気持ちがいい	Adj	good feeling	7	1
+	きもちがわるい	気持ちが悪い	Sp. Exp.	feel unwell; sickening, unpleasant, revolting	11	5
	きゃく	(お)客(様)	N	guest, customer, client	8	5
+	キャラクター	キャラ(クター)	N	(fictional) character	12	1
	キャンパス	キャンパス	N	campus	7	1
	きゅう	急(な)	N	sudden	11	5
	きゅう	急に	Sp. Exp.	suddenly	11	5
	きゅう・く	九・9	Numbers	9	3	2
+	きゅうか	休暇	N	break, holiday	8	6
+	きゅうしゅう	九州	N	Kyushu	9	4
+	きょう	きょう・今日	N	today	2	2
+	きょういく	教育(する)	N	education	9	3
+	きょうかい	教会	N	church	12	7R
+	きょうかしょ	教科書	N	textbook	2	2
+	きょうこ	今日子	N	[female given name]	9	7R

269

	きょうし	教師	N	instructor, teacher	6	2
+	きょうしつ	教室	N	classroom	4	4
+	きょうじゅ	教授	N	professor (academic rank)	12	5
+	きょうだい	(ご)兄弟	N	brothers, siblings	7	2
	きょうだい	X人兄弟	N	X number of siblings (including oneself)	12	5
	きょうまでだったでしょう?	今日までだったでしょう?	Sp. Exp.	It was until today, wasn't it?	5	2
	きょうみ	興味	N	interest	9	3
	きょうみがある	X に興味がある	Sp. Exp.	have an interest in X	9	3
+	きょねん	去年	N	last year	4	3
+	ぎり	義理	N	obligation (BTS 1)	12	BTS 1
	きる	着る (-RU; 着た)	V	wear, put on	11	3
+	きれい	きれい(な)	N	pretty, clean	2	3
	ぎんこう	銀行	N	bank	5	4
	きんちょう	緊張(する)	N	tension, nervousness	10	5
+	きんよう(び)	金曜(日)	N	Friday	4	6
+	きんろうかんしゃのひ	勤労感謝の日	N	Labor/Thanksgiving Day (BTS 18)	4	4
+	ぐあい	具合	N	condition	7	4
+	ぐあいがいい・わるい	具合がいい・悪い	Adj	be in a good/bad condition	7	4
+	くすり	(お)薬	N	medicine	2	3
	くださってありがとう(ございます)。	Xくださって↑ありがとう(ございます)。	Sp. Exp.	Thank you for doing X.	5	5
+	くださる	くださる↑(-ARU; くださった)	V	give (to in-group) (honorific)	12	1
+	くだもの	果物	N	fruit	10	3
+	くだる	下る(-U; 下った)	V	come/go down from	7	2
+	くち	口	N	mouth	11	5
+	くつ	靴	N	shoes	11	4
	クッキー	クッキー	N	cookie	2	3
	くてん	句点	N	phrase point, comma	2	BTL 2
	くとうてん	句読点	N	punctuation	2	BTL 2
+	くに	国	N	the nation	9	4
+	くび	首	N	neck	11	5
+	くもる	曇る (-U; 曇った)	V	get cloudy	8	2
	くやしい	悔しい	Adj	frustrating, annoying	10	6
	くらい	暗い	Adj	dark	7	1
	ぐらい・くらい	X ぐらい・くらい	Sp. Exp.	about X	4	1
+	クラシック	クラシック	N	classical (music)	9	5
+	クラスメート	クラスメート	N	classmate	3	6
	クラブ	クラブ	N	club	3	1
	クリニック	クリニック	N	clinic	11	5
	クリントンだいがく	クリントン大学	N	Clinton University	10	4

270

+	くる	来る (IRR; 来た)	V	come	2	1
	くるま	車	N	car	5	4
	グルメ	グルメ	N	gourmet, connoisseur	6	6
+	グレー	グレー	N	gray	6	3
	くれる	くれる (-RU; くれた)	V	give (to in-group)	12	1
+	くろ	黒	N	black	6	3
+	くろい	黒い	Adj	black	3	5
	くん	NAME 〜君	Sp. Exp.	[informal title]	6	1
	くんよみ	訓読み	N	Japanese-based readings of kanji	1	BTL 2
+	け	毛	N	fur	12	3
+	ケーキ	ケーキ	N	cake	2	3
+	ゲーム	ゲーム	N	game(s)	9	5
	けさ	今朝	N	this morning	4	4
+	けいご	敬語	N	politeness, polite language (BTS 10)	5	5
+	けいざい（がく）	経済（学）	N	economics	4	2
+	けいたい	携帯/ケータイ	N	cell phone, mobile phone	2	2
	けいたいをみないでください。	携帯を見ないでください。	Inst. Exp	Please don't look at your phone.	0	0
	けいろうのひ	敬老の日	N	Respect for the Aged Day (BTS 18)	4	4
+	けしゴム	消しゴム	N	(pencil) eraser	3	6
	けっか	結果	N	result	11	6
	けっこう	けっこう	Sp. Exp.	a fair amount	4	2
	けっこう	結構（な）	N	nice, wonderful, quite, enough, sufficient (often by implication 'no thank you')	8	5
+	けっこん	（ご）結婚（する）	N	wedding, marriage	8	1
+	げつよう（び）	月曜（日）	N	Monday	4	6
	けど	〜けど	S. Particle	but	2	4
+	ケニア	ケニア	N	Kenya	6	1
+	けれど（も）	〜け（れ）ど（も）	S. Particle	but	2	4
+	げんかん	玄関	N	entry way	9	5
+	げんき	元気（な）	N	healthy, energetic	8	5
+	げんきそう	元気そう（な）	N	looks healthy, energetic	8	5
	げんきない	元気ない	Sp. Exp.	have no energy	10	6
+	けんきゅう	研究（する）	N	research	10	2
+	けんきゅうしょ	研究所	N	research institute	9	3
	げんこうようし	原稿用紙	N	Japanese writing paper	1	BTL 5
+	げんごがく	言語学	N	linguistics	4	2
+	けんこくきねんび	建国記念日	N	Foundation Day (BTS 18)	4	4
+	けんしゅう	研修（する）	N	training	10	4
+	けんじょうご	謙譲語	N	humble language (BTS 10)	5	5
	げんち	現地	N	the place, destination	3	4

271

+	けんちく	建築	N	architecture	9	3
+	けんどう	剣道	N	kendo	9	5
+	けんぽうきねんび	憲法記念日	N	Constitution Day (BTS 18)	4	4
+	けんりつだいがく	県立大学	N	prefectural university	10	4
+	こ	〜個	Classifier	classifier for counting small objects	3	5
	ご	五・5	Numbers	5	3	2
+	こい	濃い	Adj	dark colored, thick, strong (flavor, possibility)	11	2
+	ごい	語彙	N	vocabulary	5	6
+	こうえん	公園	N	park	4	4
+	こうがく	工学	N	engineering	4	2
	こうかん	交換	N	exchange	6	4
+	こうこう	高校	N	high school	3	1
+	こうこうせい	高校生	N		9	8R
	こうさてん	交差点	N	intersection	7	6
+	ごうしつ	〜号室	Classifier	classifier for naming room numbers	4	5
+	こうじょう	工場	N	factory, workshop	5	4
+	こうちゃ	紅茶	N	black tea	2	3
+	こうはい	後輩	N	junior (BTS 30)	2	8
+	こうばん	交番	N	police box	7	6
+	こうむいん	公務員	N	public servant, government worker	9	3
	こえ	声	N	voice	8	1
	ごえんりょなく	ご遠慮なく	Sp. Exp.	without reservation	8	3
+	コーヒー	コーヒー	N	coffee	2	3
+	コーラ	コーラ	N	cola	10	3
	こくご	国語	N	Japanese (lit. 'national') language	10	6
+	こくりつだいがく	国立大学	N	national university	10	4
	ここ	ここ	N	here	2	7
+	ごご	午後	N	afternoon, p.m.	3	4
	ございます	ございます (-ARU)	V	exists (polite form of あります) The 〜て form and the informal forms are rarely used today.	5	5
+	こし	腰	N	(lower) back	11	5
	ごじゅうおんひょう	五十音表	N	Chart of Fifty Sounds	2	BTL 1
+	ごしゅじんさま	ご主人様	N	husband (polite)	11	4
+	ごしんせき	ご親戚	N	relative, family (polite)	11	4
	ごぜん	午前	N	morning, a.m.	3	4
	ごぞんじだ↑	ご存知だ↑	Sp. Exp.	know (honorific)	6	6
	こたえてください。	答えてください。	Inst. Exp	Please answer.	0	0
	こたえてください。	PERSONに答えてください。	Inst. Exp	Please answer PERSON.	2	0

272

+	こたえる	答える	V	answer, respond	11	6
	ごちそうさま。	ごちそうさま。	Sp. Exp.	Thank you. (lit. 'It was a feast.')	1	6
+	ごちそうさまでした。	ごちそうさまでした。	Sp. Exp.	Thank you. (lit. 'It was a feast,' formal)	1	6
	こちら	こちら	N	here, this, in this general area, in this direction, this alternative (of two), the speaker's side of a telephone conversation, this person (polite)	2	4
	こちらこそ	こちらこそ	Sp. Exp.	(the pleasure/fault/etc.) is mine	1	10
	こっち	こっち	N	here, in this general area, in this direction, this alternative (of two)	2	7
	こと	こと	N	matter	4	4
	こと	X のこと	Sp. Exp.	it's a matter of X; it means X	3	1
+	ことし	今年	N	this year	4	4
+	ことば	言葉・ことば	N	language, word(s)	10	6
+	こども	こども・子供	N	child	7	2
+	こどものひ	こどもの日	N	Children's Day (BTS 18)	4	4
	ことわざ	ことわざ	N	words of wisdom	1	0
	この	この+ N	Sp. Exp.	this N	3	5
	このあいだ	このあいだ	N	the other day, recently	7	4
	このごろ	この頃	Sp. Exp.	lately, these days	10	2
	このまま	このまま	Sp. Exp.	as it is; without change	12	5
+	こばやし	小林	N	[family name]	3	9R
+	ごはん	ご飯	N	cooked rice or a meal	2	3
+	こまる	困る (-U; 困った)	V	be troubled; be bothered; be embarassed	6	6
	ゴミ	ゴミ	N	trash, garbage	9	1
+	こやま	小山	N	[family name]	12	7R
+	こる	こる (-RU; こった)	V	become stiff	11	5
+	ゴルフ	ゴルフ	N	golf	3	4
+	これ	これ	N	this (thing)	2	1
+	これから	これから	N	from now	2	2
	これで	これで	Sp. Exp.	being this	10	3
	ごろ	TIME+ごろ	Sp. Exp.	about [time]	3	2
+	こわい	恐い・怖い	Adj	scary, frightening	8	5
+	こんかい	今回	N	this time	10	5
+	こんがっき	今学期	N	this term	4	6
+	こんげつ	今月	N	this month	4	4
+	コンサート	コンサート	N	concert	4	4
+	こんしゅう	今週	N	this week	4	4

+	こんど	今度	N	this time, next time	3	4
	こんなに	こんなに	Sp. Exp.	to this extent	9	6
	こんなの	こんなの	Sp. Exp.	this kind (of thing)	8	1
	こんにちは。	こんにちは。	Day1 Phrase	Hello.	0	0
+	こんばん	今晩	N	this evening	4	4
	こんばんは。	こんばんは。	Day1 Phrase	Good evening.	0	0
+	コンビニ	コンビニ	N	convenience store	2	5
	さ	〜さ	Particle	[informal particle checking on whether the other person is following]	12	3
	さ、さあ	さ、さあ	Sp. Exp.	well, well now, so, go on	9	2
	サークル	サークル	N	club	3	1
+	サーシャ	サーシャ	Name	Sasha [given name]	1	1
	さい	〜歳・才	classifier	classifier for naming age	7	2
+	サイダー	サイダー	N	soda	10	3
+	さいとう	斎藤	N	[family name]	3	9R
+	サイフ	サイフ(財布)	N	wallet	3	5
+	さかな	(お)魚	N	fish	10	3
+	さかもと	坂本	Name	Sakamoto [family name]	1	1
	さかもとせんせい	坂本先生	Name	Prof./Dr. Sakamoto	1	1
+	さき	(お)先	N	ahead, previous	4	3
	さきほど	先ほど	N	a while ago, just now	11	5
+	さきょう	左京	N	[family name]	11	9R
+	さくぶん	作文	N	composition, essay, formal writing	10	2
+	さけ	(お)酒	N	sake, alcohol	10	3
+	ささき	佐々木	N	[family name]	3	9R
+	さしあげる	差し上げる↓(-RU; 差し上た)	V	give (to out-group) (humble)	12	6
	さすが	さすが (Noun)	Sp. Exp.	true to (your reputation), what I expected, etc	6	6
+	さつ	〜冊	Classifier	classifier for counting bound volumes	3	5
+	サッカー	サッカー	N	soccer	3	4
+	さっき	さっき	N	a while ago	4	4
+	さっぽろ	札幌	N	Sapporo	9	4
+	さとう	佐藤	N	[family name]	3	9R
+	さびしい・さみしい	寂しい	Adj	lonely	7	1
	さま	〜様	N	[honorific title]	10	3
	さむい	寒い	Adj	cold (climate)	7	1
	さむさ	寒さ	N	the cold	7	1
	さむさにはなれました。	寒さには慣れました。	Sp. Exp.	I got used to to the cold.	7	1
+	さよ(う)なら	さよ(う)なら	Sp. Exp.	goodbye (BTS 11)	1	5

+	さらいげつ	再来月	N	month after next	10	2
	さらいしゅう	再来週	N	week after next	10	2
+	さらいねん	再来年	N	year after next	10	2
	さん	NAME～さん	Title	Mr/s. NAME	1	1
	さん	三・3	Numbers	3	3	2
	ざんねん	残念(な)	N	too bad, regrettable	10	6
	さんぶんのいち	三分の一	Sp. Exp.	one-third	9	2
	じ	～時	Classifier	classifier for naming hours on the clock	3	2
	し・よん	四・4	Numbers	4	3	2
	しあい	試合(する)	N	match, contest, game	10	1
	しあげる	仕上げる (-RU; 仕上げた)	V	finish up, complete	10	2
	ジェーエルシー	JLC	N	JLC	3	1
	ジェシカ	ジェシカ	N	Jessica	12	3
	じかい	次回	N	next time	10	5
	しかた	しかた・仕方	N	way of doing	10	6
+	しかたがない	仕方がない	Sp. Exp.	there's nothing to be done	10	6
	じかん	時間	N	time	3	4
	じかん	～時間	Classifier	classifier for counting hours	4	6
+	シクシク	シクシク(する・痛む)	N	dull continuous pain	11	5
	しけん	試験	N	test	7	3
	しこく	四国	N	Shikoku	9	4
	じこしょうかい	自己紹介(する)	N	self-introduction	6	1
+	しごと	(お)仕事(する)	N	work, job	2	2
+	しごとする	仕事する	V	work	3	2
+	しずか	静か(な)	N	quiet	7	1
+	した	下	N	bottom, under	6	2
+	した	舌	N	tongue	11	5
	しち・なな	七・7	Numbers	7	3	2
+	じっけん	実験(する)	N	experiment	10	2
	しっている	知っている	V	know	6	6
	じつは	実は	Sp. Exp.	actually, in fact	8	5
	しつもん	質問(する)	N	(ask a) question	5	2
	じつようてき	実用的(な)	N	practical	11	3
	しつれい	失礼(な)	N	rude, impolite	10	4
	しつれいします。	失礼します。	Sp. Exp.	Excuse me.	1	5
+	じてんしゃ	自転車	N	bicycle	4	5
	しばらく	しばらく	N	a while, a moment	11	5
	じはん	X時半	Sp. Exp.	half past (hour X) (2:30)	3	2
	じぶん	自分	N	oneself	9	5
+	じぶんてき	自分的(な)	N	like oneself	11	4
	じぶんでは	自分で(は)	Sp. Exp.	on one's own, by oneself (without help)	9	5
+	しまい	X人姉妹	N	X number of sisters (including oneself)	12	5

+	しまう	しまう (-U; しまった)	V	put away	12	2
+	しまい	姉妹	N	sisters	12	5
	しました	しました	V	did	4	3
+	しみず	清水	N	[family name]	3	9R
+	じむしょ	事務所	N	(business) office	9	3
+	しめる	締める (RU; 締めた)	V	wear, put on, fasten (a necktie) (lit. 'tie, tighten')	11	4
	じゃ	じゃ(あ)	Sp. Exp.	So. (informal)	1	9
	じゃあ	じゃあ	Sp. Exp.	well then,	2	8
+	シャーペン	シャーペン	N	mechanical pencil	3	3
	ジャイアンツ	ジャイアンツ	N	Giants	10	1
+	しゃかいがく	社会学	N	sociology	4	2
+	しゃかいじん	社会人	N	a (working) member of society, an employed adult	10	9R
+	しゃかいてき	社会的(な)	N	social	11	4
+	ジャケット	ジャケット	N	jacket	11	3
	しゃしん	写真	N	photo	6	3
+	ジャズ	ジャズ	N	jazz	9	5
+	しゃちょう	社長	N	company president	6	5
+	シャツ	シャツ	N	shirt	11	3
	じゃない	X じゃない	Sp. Exp.	X, isn't it?; X, for sure	10	6
	じゃね。	じゃ(あ)ね。	Sp. Exp.	See you later. (informal)	1	9
	じゃま	(お)邪魔(する)	N	a bother, a nuisance, an obstacle	8	3
	じゃまた。	じゃまた。	Sp. Exp.	See you again. (informal)	1	9
	じゃまたね。	じゃまたね。	Sp. Exp.	See you again. (informal)	1	9
+	シャワー	シャワー	N	shower	9	5
+	しゅう	州	N	state, as in the US	6	1
	じゅう	十 (10〜90)	Numbers	tens (10 through 90)	3	5
	じゅう	十・10	Numbers	10	3	2
	じゅういち	十一・11	Numbers	11	3	2
+	しゅうかん	〜週間	Classifier	classifier for counting weeks	4	6
+	ジュース	ジュース	N	juice	2	3
	しゅうきょう(がく)	宗教(学)	N	religion (religious studies)	4	2
+	しゅうしょく	(ご)就職(する)	N	employment, getting a job	8	1
	じゅうに	十二・12	Numbers	12	3	2
+	しゅうぶんのひ	秋分の日	N	Autumnal Equinox (BTS 18)	4	4
+	しゅうまつ	週末	N	weekend	3	4
	しゅうりつだいがく	州立大学	N	state or public university	10	4
+	じゅぎょう	授業(する)	N	class	3	2
+	しゅくだい	宿題	N	homework	2	2
+	しゅくだいする	宿題する	V	do homework	3	2
+	しゅじん	(ご)主人	N	husband (humble)	7	2
	しゅっしん	(ご)出身	N	birthplace	8	4

+	しゅっちょう	出張	N	business trip	8	6
	しゅみ	趣味	N	hobby	9	5
	じゅんび	準備(する)	N	preparation	10	5
+	しゅんぶんのひ	春分の日	N	Vernal Equinox (BTS 18)	4	4
+	しょう	省	N	provinces in China	6	1
+	しょうがくせい	小学生	N	elementary school student	12	7R
+	しょうがつ	(お)正月	N	New Year's Day/Month (BTS 18)	4	4
+	しょうがっこう	小学校	N	elementary school	9	6
+	しょうがない	しょうがない	Sp. Exp.	there's nothing to be done	10	6
+	しょうきょくてき	消極的(な)	N	passive, unmotivated, pessimistic	11	4
	しょうしょう	少々	Sp. Exp.	a little (polite)	10	3
+	じょうず	上手	N	skillful, good at	6	1
	じょうだん	(ご)冗談	N	joke	8	2
	しょうち	(ご)承知(する)	N	acceptance, consent	11	1
+	しょうテスト	小テスト	N	small test, quiz	12	7R
+	しょうわ	昭和	N	Showa era (1926-1989)	4	4
+	しょうわのひ	昭和の日	N	Showa Day (BTS 18)	4	4
	しょくじ	(お)食事	N	a meal	10	3
+	しょくどう	食堂	N	dining hall, cafeteria	7	1
+	じょし	女子	N	young woman	9	7R
	じょせい	女性	N	woman, girl	12	3
	しょだん	初段	N	first or lowest rank black belt in martial arts, calligraphy, *shōgi*, *igo*, etc.	6	2
+	しょちょう	所長	N	head of a laboratory, research center	6	5
	しょっちゅう	しょっちゅう	Sp. Exp.	frequent, often	10	4
+	しょっぱい	しょっぱい	Adj	salty	10	3
+	しらい	白井	Name	Shirai [family name]	1	1
	しらいです。	NAMEです。	Sp. Exp.	My name is NAME.	1	4
+	しらべる	調べる (-RU; 調べた)	V	investigate, inquire, search	10	5
+	しり	(お)尻	N	buttocks, behind	11	5
+	しりあい	知り合い	N	acquaintance	7	2
+	しりつだいがく	私立大学	N	private university	10	4
+	しる	知る (-U; 知った)	V	find out, know	6	6
	しろ	白	N	white	6	3
+	しろい	白い	Adj	white	3	5
+	しんごう	信号	N	traffic light	7	6
+	しんせき	親戚	N	relative, family (in-group)	11	4
+	しんせつ	(ご)親切(な)	N	kind, gentle	8	5
+	しんせつそう	親切そう(な)	N	looks kind	8	5
	しんぱい	(ご)心配(な)・(する)	N	worry	11	5

	しんぱいをかける	心配をかける	Sp. Exp.	make (someone) worry	11	5
+	すいよう(び)	水曜(日)	N	Wednesday	4	6
	すうがく	数学	N	mathematics	4	2
+	スーツ	スーツ	N	suit	11	2
+	スーパー	スーパー	N	super market	5	4
+	スカート	スカート	N	skirt	11	2
	すき	(お)好き	N	liking, fondness, love	2	3
+	すぎ	過ぎ	N	after, past [time]	3	2
	すぎ(る)	～過ぎ(る)	Sp. Exp.	over- (overeat, overdo, etc.)	11	2
	すきこそもののじょうずなれ	好きこそものの上手なれ	Kotowaza	What one likes, one does well.	9	0
	ズキズキ	ズキズキ(する・痛む)	N	throbbing	11	5
+	すぎる	過ぎる (RU; 過ぎた)	V	exceed, go beyond	11	2
+	すく	空く (-U; 空いた)	V	become empty	8	4
	すぐ	すぐ	N	soon, immediately, right away	5	1
+	すくない	少ない	Adj	few, scarce	10	5
	すごい	すごい	Adj	amazing	2	1
	すこし	少し	N	a little, a few	5	1
+	すし	(お)すし・寿司	N	sushi	2	3
+	すずき	鈴木	N	[family name]	3	9R
+	すずしい	涼しい	Adj	cool (climate)	7	1
	すすめ	(お)勧め	N	recommendation, suggestion	6	6
	すすめる、Xに	Xに勧める・薦める (-RU; 勧めた・薦めた)	V	recommend to X, advise X, encourage X	6	6
	すっごい	すっごい	Adj	really, really	9	6
	ずっと	ずっと	Sp. Exp.	continuously, by far, the whole time	6	5
+	すっぱい	すっぱい	Adj	sour	10	3
	すてき	素敵(な)	N	sharp, nice, good-looking	11	4
	すてる	捨てる (-RU; 捨てた)	V	throw away	9	1
+	スペインご	スペイン語	N	Spanish (language)	3	1
+	スペインじん	スペイン人	N	Spanish (person)	3	1
	スポーツ	スポーツ	N	sport(s)	9	5
+	スポーツのひ	スポーツの日	N	Sports Day (BTS 18)	4	4
+	すませる	済ませる (-RU; 済ませた)	V	finish, get through	10	2
	スマホ	スマホ	N	smartphone	3	3
	すみません。	すみません/すいません。	Sp. Exp.	Excuse me. I'm sorry. Thank you.	1	3
+	すみませんでした。	すみませんでした・すいませんでした。	Sp. Exp.	Sorry/Thank you (for what has happened).	2	2
+	すむ	住む (-U: 住んだ)	V	reside	8	4

	すめばみやこ	住めば都	Kotowaza	Home is where you make it.	7	0
+	する	する (IRR; した)	V	do, play (a game or sport)	2	1
+	する	する	V	wear, put on (jewelry, accessories, make-up)	11	4
	する、Xに	Xにする	Sp. Exp.	decide on X	6	6
	すること	すること	N	something to do	2	8
+	すわる	座る (-U; 座った)	V	sit	6	3
	せ	背	N	back, spine, rear side	6	3
+	せいじんのひ	成人の日	N	Coming of Age Day (BTS 18)	4	4
	せいぶつ	生物	N	biology	6	2
+	せいり	整理（する）	N	sorting, putting in order	9	1
	セーター	セーター	N	sweater	11	3
+	セールス	セールス	N	sales	6	2
+	せかい	世界	N	the world	9	4
	せがたかいひと	背が高い人	Sp. Exp.	tall person/people	6	3
	せき	（お）席	N	seat, (seated) occasion	10	3
	せっきょくてき	積極的（な）	N	active, positive, optimistic	11	4
	ぜったい	絶対（に）	N	absolutely	10	2
+	せつめい	説明（する）	N	explanation	9	3
+	せなか	背中	N	back	11	5
+	ぜひ	是非	Sp. Exp.	by all means	5	5
+	せまい	狭い	Adj	narrow, confined	7	1
	ゼロ・まる・れい	ゼロ・まる・零	Numbers	zero	3	5
	せわ	（お）世話	N	help, aid, assistance	6	4
+	せわする	（お）世話する	V	look after (someone)	12	6
	せん・ぜん	千 (1000〜9000)	Numbers	thousands (1000 〜 9000)	4	1
+	ぜんかい	前回	N	last time	10	5
+	せんがっき	先学期	N	last semester	4	3
+	せんげつ	先月	N	last month	4	3
	せんこう	（ご）専攻（する）	N	major field of study	4	2
+	せんじつ	先日	N	the other day	4	3
+	ぜんじつ	前日	N	the previous day	9	8R
	せんしゅう	先週	N	last week	4	3
	せんせい	NAME 〜先生	Title	Prof./Dr. NAME	1	1
	ぜんぜん	全然	N	not at all, entirely	4	2
+	せんだい	仙台	N	Sendai	9	4
+	せんたく	洗濯（する）	N	laundry	9	1
+	セント	〜セント	Classifier	cent	3	5
	セントルイス	セントルイス	N	St. Louis	8	4
+	せんぱい	先輩	N	senior (BTS 30)	2	8
	ぜんぶ	全部	N	all, everything	5	3
+	ぜんぶで	全部でX	Sp. Exp.	X for everything, X all together	3	5
+	せんめんじょ	洗面所	N	washroom	9	5
+	せんもん	（ご）専門	N	specialization, major	4	2

	せんもんてき	専門的(な)	N	specialized	10	5
	せんりのみちもいっぽから	千里の道も一歩から	Kotowaza	A journey of a thousand miles begins with a single step.	2	0
	そう	そう	N	that way, so	2	5
	そう、そう。	そう、そう。	Sp. Exp.	Right, right; Yes, yes.	3	3
	そういうこと	そういうこと	Sp. Exp.	a thing like that; that kind of thing	10	6
	そうか。	そうか。	Sp. Exp.	Is that so? (expression of awareness)	4	4
	そうか。	そうか。	Sp. Exp.	I see.	7	3
	そうじ	掃除(する)	N	cleaning	9	1
	そうじしたのだれ?	掃除したの誰?	Sp. Exp.	Who is it that cleaned up?	9	1
	そうしていただけますか?	そうしていただけますか?	Sp. Exp.	Can I have you do that?	5	6
	そうしましょう。	そうしましょう。	Sp. Exp.	Let's do it that way.	4	5
+	そうだん	(ご)相談(する)	N	consultation	6	5
	そうだんする	Xに・と相談する	Sp. Exp.	consult with X	6	6
	そうですね(え)	そうですね(え)	Sp. Exp.	(hesitation)	2	7
	そうですねえ	そうですねえ	Sp. Exp.	(to express consideration) let's see	5	3
	そうなんだ。	そうなんだ。	Sp. Exp.	So that's it; I get it now.	7	2
+	そこ	そこ	N	there (near you), that place just mentioned	2	7
+	そちら	そちら	N	there (near you), that (near you), in that general area, in that direction (in your direction), that alternative (of two near you), the other side of a telephone conversation, that person (polite)	2	4
+	そつぎょう	(ご)卒業(する)	N	graduation	8	1
	そっくり	(Xに)そっくり	N	exactly like (X), completely	12	5
+	そっち	そっち	N	there (near you), in that general area, in that direction (in your direction), that alternative (of two near you)	2	7
+	そと	外	N	outside	6	2
+	その	その+N	Sp. Exp.	that N	3	5
	そのうえ	その上	Sp. Exp.	what's more, in addition, plus	11	4
+	そば	そば	N	soba (buckwheat noodles)	2	3
+	そふ	祖父	N	grandfather (in-group)	11	4
+	そぼ	祖母	N	grandmother (in-group)	11	4
	それ	それ	N	that (thing near you)	2	1
	それで、	それで、	Sp. Exp.	then, following that	11	6

	それで、	それで、	Sp. Exp.	and; because of that	12	3
	それとも	それとも	Sp. Exp.	or (else)	9	5
	それに	それに	Sp. Exp.	what's more, besides	7	5
	それにしたら?	それにしたら?	Sp. Exp.	If you did that? (how would it be)	11	2
	それほど	それほど	Sp. Exp.	that much; to that extent	4	1
	それより	それより	Sp. Exp.	leaving that aside, apart from that, more importantly	7	1
+	そんけいご	尊敬語	N	honorific language (BTS 10)	5	5
+	ぞんじる	存じる↓(-U 存じた)	V	know, find out (humble)	6	6
	そんなことない	そんなことない	Sp. Exp.	no such thing	9	6
	そんなに	そんなに	Sp. Exp.	to that extent; so/such a X	8	2
	たい	Verb 〜たい	Adj	want to VERB	6	5
+	だいがく	大学	N	university, college	3	1
+	だいがく、X	X大学	N	X University, X College	3	1
+	だいがくいん	大学院	N	graduate school	3	1
+	だいがくせい	大学生	N	university student	8	9R
+	タイご	タイ語	N	Thai (language)	8	8R
	だいじ	(お)大事(な)	N	important, valuable	7	4
+	たいしょう	大正	N	Taisho era (1912-1926)	4	4
	だいじょうぶ	大丈夫	N	fine, safe, all right	2	1
+	だいすき	大好き	N	very likeable, like very much	2	3
+	たいせつ	大切(な)	N	important, necessary	8	5
+	たいてい	たいてい	Sp. Exp.	usually, as a rule	8	6
+	だいどころ	台所	N	kitchen	9	5
+	だいぶ	だいぶ	Sp. Exp.	a fair amount	9	2
	たいへん	大変(な)	N	tough (to do), awful, terrible	4	3
	タウンシネマ	タウンシネマ	N	Town Cinema	7	6
	たかい	高い	Adj	expensive; Scene 10-6 high, tall	2	7
	たかい	(背が)高い	Adj	tall (in stature)	6	3
+	たかはし	高橋	N	[family name]	3	9R
	だくおん	濁音	N	voiced consonant	5	BTL9
+	たくさん	たくさん	N	a lot, many	3	5
+	たぐち	田口	N	[family name]	11	8R
	だくてん	濁点	N	[diacritical marks]	2	BTL 4
	だけ	〜だけ	Particle	just, only	4	2
	たしか	確か(な)確か	N	sure, certain	8	5
	たしかに	確かに	Sp. Exp.	for sure, certainly	8	5
	だす	出す (-U; 出した)	V	submit, take out (of a container), send out (mail)	5	2
	たすかる	助かる(-U; 助かった)	V	be helped, be saved, be rescued	5	4

	ただ	ただ	N	simply; free of charge	12 4
	ただいま。	ただいま。	Sp. Exp.	I'm home; I'm back.	1 13
+	たちかわ	立川	N	[place name in Tokyo]	9 9R
	たつ	立つ(-U; 立った)	V	stand	6 3
+	たて	縦	N	vertical	11 5
	たてがき	縦書き	N	vertical writing	1 BTL 3
+	たな	棚	N	shelf	12 1
+	たなか	田中	N	[family name]	3 9R
	たのしい	楽しい	Adj	fun	7 4
	たのしみ	（お）楽しみ（な）	N	enjoyment, pleasure	7 2
	たのむ	頼む (-U: 頼んだ)	V	order (at a restaurant, online, etc.), request	6 6
+	たべすぎ	食べ過ぎ	N	think too much	11 2
	たべてるかどうか	食べてるかどうか	Sp. Exp.	whether you're eating or not	12 2
	たべにいく	食べに行く	Sp. Exp.	go to eat	9 2
	たべもの	食べ物	N	food	2 3
	たべる	食べる（-RU; 食べた）	V	eat	2 3
+	たまに	たまに	Sp. Exp.	once in a while	8 6
+	たむら	田村	N	[family name]	10 8R
+	だめ	だめ（な）	N	bad, useless, problematic	3 4
	だれ	だれ・誰	N	who	2 6
	だれかしらない	誰か知らない	Sp. Exp.	don't know who that is	12 3
+	だんし	男子	N	young man	9 7R
	たんじょうび	（お）誕生日	N	birthday	8 1
+	だんせい	男性	N	man, boy	12 3
	チーズ	チーズ	N	cheese	6 3
	チーズ！	チーズ！	Sp. Exp.	Cheese!	6 3
+	ちいさい	小さい	Adj	small	2 7
+	ちいさな	小さな	N	small, little	12 5
+	ちか	地下	N	basement, underground	4 5
+	ちかい	近い	Adj	close	2 7
	ちがう	違う(-U; 違った)	V	different from X	3 6
	ちがう・おなじ	(Xと)違う・同じ	Sp. Exp.	different from/same as X	3 6
+	ちかく	近く	N	nearby, vicinity, neighborhood	6 2
	ちかてつ	地下鉄	N	subway	5 4
	ちがわない	Xと違わない	Sp. Exp.	not different from X	6 6
+	チケット	チケット	N	ticket	3 5
+	ちち	父↓	N	father (humble)	7 2
+	ちちおや	父親	N	father	8 5
+	ちゃいろ	茶色	N	brown	6 3
	ちゃいろのめをしている	茶色の目をしている	Sp. Exp.	has brown eyes	12 3

	ちゃんと	ちゃんと	Sp. Exp.	properly, reliably, satisfactorily	8	1
	ちゅう	X 中	N	while X-ing; in the middle of X-ing; within X	10	2
+	ちゅうがっこう	中学校	N	middle school	9	6
+	ちゅうかりょうり	中華料理	N	Chinese food	10	3
+	ちゅうごく	中国	N	China	6	1
+	ちゅうごくご	中国語	N	Chinese (language)	3	1
+	ちゅうごくじん	中国人	N	Chinese (person)	3	1
+	ちょう	兆	Numbers	trillions (BTS 4)	4	1
+	ちょう・ジャン	張	N	Zhang (Japanese pronunciation: Choo) [Chinese family name]	3	1
+	ちょうさ	調査(する)	N	investigation, survey	10	2
	ちょうど	ちょうど	Sp. Exp.	exactly, precisely, just	9	2
	ちょっと	ちょっと	Sp. Exp.	a little	2	2
	つ	～つ	Classifier	classifier for counting items	5	3
	ついたち	ついたち～三十一日	Numbers	the first ~ the 31st	4	4
	つうやく	通訳(する)	N	interpretation	10	5
	ついて	N について	Sp. Exp.	with regard to N	6	5
	つかう	使う(-U; 使った)	V	use	4	2
	つかってくれたら	使ってくれたら	Sp. Exp.	if you would use it (for me)	12	1
+	つぎ	次	N	next, following	3	4
+	つぎ、がんばろう!	次、頑張ろう!	Sp. Exp.	Do your best next time.	9	9R
+	つきあたり	突き当たり	N	end (of a street, hallway, etc.)	7	6
+	つく	着く(-U; 着いた)	V	arrive	7	6
+	つくえ	机	N	desk	12	1
+	つくる	作る(-U; 作った)	V	make	4	1
+	つける	付ける(-RU; 付けた)	V	attach, apply	11	4
+	つたえる	伝える (-RU; 伝えた)	V	convey a message	11	1
+	つづける	続ける (-RU; 続けた)	V	keep on, continue (something)	10	6
	って	～って	Particle	[topic particle]	3	1
	って・と	QUOTATION+ って・と	particle	[quotation particle]	7	3
+	つとめる	勤める(-RU; 勤めた)	V		9	3
+	つま	妻↓	N	wife (humble)	7	2
+	つまらない	つまらない	Adj	boring	2	7
+	つめたい	冷たい	Adj	cold (to the touch), cold (personality)	7	1
+	つよい	強い	Adj	strong	5	6

Appendix A

283

+	つらい	辛い・つらい	Adj	tough, bitter (experience), painful	7	1
	つれていく	連れて行く	V	take (a person) along	5	4
+	つれてくる	連れて来る	V	bring (a person) along	5	4
+	て	手	N	hand	11	5
	で	〜で	Particle	by means of X	5	4
	で	PLACE で	Particle	[location of activity]	3	4
	で、	で、	Sp. Exp.	and…	12	3
+	ティーシャツ	ティーシャツ	N	T-Shirt	3	5
+	ていしょく	定食	N	set meal	6	6
	ていねい	(ご)丁寧	N	polite	11	1
+	ていねいご	丁寧語	N	formal language (BTS 10)	5	5
	でいらっしゃいます	Noun+ でいらっしゃいます↑	Sp. Exp.	It's [Noun] (honorific)	10	3
+	でかける	出かける (-RU; 出かけた)	V	go out	10	2
	てから	Verb 〜てから	Sp. Exp.	after Verb-ing	9	6
+	できる	できる (-RU; できた)	V	can do, become complete	2	1
+	でぐち	出口	N	exit	6	3
	でございます+	Noun+ でございます+	Sp. Exp.	it's [Noun] (polite)	10	3
+	デザート	デザート	N	dessert	10	3
+	デザイン	デザイン(する)	N	design	6	2
+	テスト	テスト	N	test	2	2
+	てつだう	手伝う (-U; 手伝った)	V	help	4	3
	テニス	テニス	N	tennis	3	4
	では	では	Sp. Exp.	Well then, Act 4-7R [written equivalent of じゃ]	1	5
+	てぶくろ	手袋	N	gloves	11	4
	でも	でも	Sp. Exp.	but, however, and yet	5	1
	でも　じゃなくても	X でも X じゃなくても	Sp. Exp.	whether it's X or not X	5	1
	でも　でも	X でも Y でも	Sp. Exp.	whether it's X or Y	5	1
	でる	出る(-RU; 出た)	V	go out, leave, attend (an event), appear, answer (the phone)	5	4
	てん	〜点	Classifier	point	10	6
	てん	点(、)	N	point, dot	2	BTL 2
+	てんき	天気(がいい)	N	weather (is good)	7	1
+	でんき	電気	N	electricity, light	12	8R
	でんしゃ	電車	N	train	5	4
	てんてん	点々	N	[diacritical marks]	2	BTL 4
+	てんのうたんじょうび	天皇誕生日	N	Emperor's Birthday (BTS 18)	4	4
+	てんのうへいか	天皇陛下	N	emperor (honorific) (BTS 18)	4	4

+	てんぷら	天ぷら	N	tempura	10	3
	でんわ	電話（する）	N	telephone	2	2
+	でんわばんごう	（お）電話番号	N	telephone number (your telephone number)	6	4
	と	〜と(XとY)	Particle	X and Y	3	2
	と	〜と(言います／申します↓／おっしゃいます↑)	Particle	[quotation particle]	6	2
	ど	〜度	Classifier	times, degrees	8	4
	ということは	ということは	Sp. Exp.	that is to say	7	2
+	ドイツ	ドイツ	N	Germany	6	1
+	トイレ	トイレ	N	toilet	2	5
	どう	どう	N	how	2	7
	どういういみ	どういう意味	Sp. Exp.	what do you mean? what does that mean?	11	4
	どうかなあ	どうかなあ	Sp. Exp.	I wonder	9	6
+	とうさん	（お）父さん	N	father	7	2
	どうして	どうして	Sp. Exp.	why	7	3
	どうぞ。	どうぞ。	Sp. Exp.	Go ahead.	1	2
	どうぞよろしく。	どうぞよろしく。	Sp. Exp.	Nice to meet you.	1	4
+	どうぞよろしくおねがいします。	どうぞよろしくお願いします。	Sp. Exp.	Nice to meet you.	1	4
+	とうだい	東大	N	University of Tokyo	11	8R
	とうてん	読点	N	point, dot	2	BTL 2
	どうも。	どうも。	Sp. Exp.	Hello.	1	7
	どうやって	どうやって	Sp. Exp.	(doing) how	9	6
+	どうりょう	同僚	N	co-worker, colleague	3	6
+	とおい	遠い	Adj	far	2	7
+	とおく	遠く	N	distant	7	1
+	とおり	通り	N	way, road, street	7	6
	とか	〜とか	Particle	(things) like, such as	4	2
	とかも	〜とかも	Particle	also (things) like, such as	4	2
+	とき	時・とき	N	time	7	9R
	ときどき	時々	Sp. Exp.	sometimes	8	6
	ときはかねなり	時は金なり	Kotowaza	Time is money.	4	0
	とくい	得意（な）	N	strong point, specialty	10	6
+	どくしょ	読書	N	reading	9	5
+	どくしん	独身	N	single; unmarried	12	5
	とくに	特に	Sp. Exp.	especially	10	2
	どこ	どこ	N	where	2	7
	ところ	ところ	N	place	4	4
+	としょかん	図書館	N	library	3	4
+	どちら	どちら	N	where, which, which direction, which (of two), which person/who (polite)	2	4
	どちらかというと	どちらかと言うと	Sp. Exp.	if I have to say which	12	4

+	どっち	どっち	N	where, which direction, which (of two)	2	7
+	とても	とても	Sp. Exp.	very	2	7
+	とどうふけん	都道府県	N	prefectures (BTS 11)	9	4
	どなた	どなた	N	who (polite)	2	6
+	となり	隣	N	next door, beside	6	2
+	どの	どの+N	Sp. Exp.	which N	3	5
+	ともだち	ともだち	N	friend	3	6
+	どよう(び)	土曜(日)	N	Saturday	4	6
	とりあえず	とりあえず	Sp. Exp.	for now, first of all	10	3
	とる	取る(-U; 取った)	V	take (a class)	4	2
+	とる	撮る(-U; 撮った)	V	take (a photo)	6	3
+	ドル	〜ドル	Classifier	dollar(s) (U.S. currency)	3	5
+	どれ	どれ	N	which (thing)	2	1
+	ドレス	ドレス	N	dress	11	2
	とんでもない	とんでもない	Sp. Exp.	not at all	7	4
	どんどん	どんどん	Sp. Exp.	rapidly, steadily	9	2
+	な	名	N	name	9	8R
	なあ	〜なあ	S. Particle	[sentence particle indicating shared agreement]	2	6
	ないよう	内容	N	content	10	5
	なおる	直る・治る(-U; 直った・治った)	V	get better, get fixed; restore (itself)	7	6
+	なか	中	N	inside	6	2
+	ながい	長い	Adj	long	5	5
	ながさ	長さ	N	length	12	3
+	ながそで	長袖	N	long sleeves	11	3
+	なかた・なかだ	中田	N	[family name]	10	8R
	なかてん	中点(・)	N	raied period	2	BTL 2
	なかなか	なかなか+ affirmative	Sp. Exp.	rather, more than expected	11	2
	なかなか	なかなか〜ない	Sp. Exp.	quite, considerably, rather	8	1
+	なかむら	中村	N	[family name]	3	9R
+	なかやま	中山	N	[family name]	9	9R
+	なく	泣く(-U; 泣いた)	V	cry, weep	8	2
	なさる	なさる↑(-ARU; なさった)	V	do (honorific)	7	4
+	なぜ	何故・なぜ	N	why	7	3
+	なつ	夏	N	summer	8	6
+	なっとう	納豆	N	*natto*, fermented soy beans (BTS 4 FN)	12	2
	なつめそうせき	夏目漱石	N	Natsume Soseki (author, 1867-1916)	9	4
	なつやすみ	夏休み	N	summer vacation/holiday	8	6

	なつやすみのあいだ	夏休みの間	Sp. Exp.	during summer vacation	8	6
	ななころびやおき	七転び八起き	Kotowaza	Fall down seven times, get up eight.	10	0
+	ななめ	斜め	N	diagonal	11	5
+	なにいろ	何色	N	what color	6	3
	なにか・なんか	なにか・何か	Sp. Exp.	something	2	8
+	なにご	何語	N	which language?	3	1
+	なにじん	何人・なに人	N	what nationality	3	1
	なにも	何も	Sp. Exp.	nothing	6	6
+	なは	那覇	N	Naha	9	4
	ナビ	ナビ	N	GPS, navigator	7	6
+	なまえ	（お）名前	N	name (your name)	6	4
+	ならう	習う(-U; 習った)	V	learn	9	5
	ならぶ	Xと・に並ぶ(-U; 並んだ)	V	stand alongside; line up	12	5
	ならんでいるとにてる	並んでいると似てる	Sp. Exp.	look alike standing next to each ogether	12	5
	なる	なる(-U; なった)	V	become	5	6
	なるべく	なるべく	Sp. Exp.	as…as possible	5	1
	なるほど	なるほど	Sp. Exp.	Oh, now I see.	3	1
	なれる	(Xに) 慣れる(-RU; 慣れた)	V	get used/accustomed (to X)	7	1
	なん、なに	何（なん）	N	what	2	3
	なんじ	何時	N	what time	3	2
+	なんで	なんで	N	why	7	3
	なんでしょう。	何でしょう。	Sp. Exp.	What? What could it be?	5	3
	なんとかスーパー	何とかスーパー	Sp. Exp.	so-and-so/such-and-such/something-or-other supermarket	7	6
	なんとなく	なんとなく	Sp. Exp.	somehow or other	12	6
	なんばいもじょうず	何倍も上手	Sp. Exp.	many times better at	9	6
+	なんよう（び）	何曜(日)	N	what day (of the week)?	4	6
	に	～に	Particle	to, towards X	5	4
	に	～に	Particle	[inanimate location particle]	3	6
	に	TIMEに	Particle	[point of time]	3	4
	に	二・2	Numbers	2	3	2
	にあう	(XがYに)似合う(U; 似合った)	V	X looks good on Y	11	2
+	にいさん	（お）兄さん	N	older brother	7	2
+	にがい	苦い	Adj	bitter	10	3
	にがて	苦手(な)	N	weak point, weakness	10	6
+	にく	（お）肉	N	meat	10	3

	にくい	使いにくい	Adj	hard to use	4 5
	にごりてん	濁り点	N	[diacritical marks]	2 BTL 4
	にち・か	～日	Classifier	naming the days of the month; Scene 4-6 counting days	4 4
+	にちじ	日時	N	date and time	7 9R
+	にちよう(び)	日曜(日)	N	Sunday	4 6
+	にっけいじん	日系人	N	person of Japanese heritage	3 1
+	にった	新田	N	[family name]	10 7R
+	にほん	日本(にほん・にっぽん)	N	Japan	6 1
	にほんがく	日本学	N	Japanese studies	4 2
	にほんご	日本語	N	Japanese (language)	3 1
	にほんごクラブ	日本語クラブ	N	Japanese Language Club	3 1
	にほんごではなしましょう。	日本語で話しましょう。	Inst. Exp	Let's speak in Japanese.	2 0
+	にほんじん・にっぽんじん	日本人	N	Japanese (person)	3 1
+	ニュース	ニュース	N	news	3 3
	にる	Xと・に似る (-RU; 似た)	V	look like X; resemble X	12 5
+	にわ	庭	N	garden	9 5
	にん・り	～人	Classifier	classifier for counting people	6 2
+	きょうと	京都	N	Kyoto	9 4
	ね	～ね	S. Particle	[sentence particle indicating agreement]	2 1
	ね?	～ね?	Particle	[particle checking on whether the other person is following]	2 1
	ねえ	～ねえ	S. Particle	[sentence particle assuming shared attitude/opinion]	2 3
+	ねえさん	(お)姉さん	N	older sister	7 2
	ネクタイ	ネクタイ	N	necktie	11 4
+	ねこ	猫	N	cat	12 3
	ねぶそく	寝不足	N	lack of sleep	12 4
	ねむい	眠い	Adj	sleepy	12 4
+	ねる	寝る (-RU; 寝た)	V	sleep, go to bed, lie down	8 1
	ねん	～年	Classifier	classifier for naming the years; Scene 4-6 naming & counting the years	4 4
+	ねんかん	～年間	Classifier	classifier for counting years	6 2
+	ねんせい	～年生	Classifier	classifier for naming grade, class in school	6 1
	さんねんで	３年で	Sp. Exp.	in three years	9 6

	ねんにに、さんかい	年に二、三回	Sp. Exp.	two or three times a year	8	6
	の	の	N	one(s)	3	5
+	ノート	ノート	N	notebook	3	5
+	のう	(お)能	N	Noh (traditional theater)	10	1
+	のちほど	後ほど	N	later	10	8R
	のど	喉	N	throat	8	4
	のどがかわく	喉が渇く	Sp. Exp.	get thirsty	8	4
	のぼる	登る (-U; 登った)	V	climb	7	2
+	のみすぎ	飲み過ぎ	N	eat too much	11	2
+	のみもの	飲み物	N	drink	2	3
+	のむ	飲む・呑む(-U; 飲・呑んだ)	V	drink, swallow (i.e. medicine)	2	3
+	のむ	のむ/呑む (-U; 呑んだ)	V	ingest, swallow	11	5
+	のる	乗る(-U; 乗った)	V	ride, get onboard	5	4
	は	〜は	Particle	[phrase particle indicating contrast]	2	6
	は	Xは	Particle	as for X	3	2
+	は	歯	N	tooth	11	5
+	パーセント	パーセント	N	percent	9	2
+	パートナー	パートナー	N	(romantic) partner	11	4
	はい、	はい、	Inst. Exp	Okay,	0	0
	はい。	はい。	Sp. Exp.	Present. (in roll call); Scene 1-2 Here you are. (handing something over); Scene 1-3 Got it. (accepting something)	1	1
	ばい	〜倍	Classifier	multiple, -fold	9	6
	バイ。	バイ。	Sp. Exp.	Bye. (informal)	1	9
	ばい	倍	N	double, -fold	9	6
	はい、どうぞ。	はい、どうぞ。	Sp. Exp.	Here you go (take it, do it)	1	2
+	ばいてん	売店	N	shop, stand, kiosk	7	1
	バイバイ。	バイバイ。	Sp. Exp.	Bye-bye. (informal)	1	9
	はいる	入る (-U; 入った)	V	go in, enter	9	6
+	はく	履く(U; 履いた)	V	put on, wear (on the legs, such as slacks)	11	2
	はじめて	初めて	N	first time	8	5
	はじめまして。	はじめまして。	Sp. Exp.	How do you do.	6	4
	はじめましょう。	始めましょう。	Inst. Exp	Let's begin.	0	0
+	はじめる	Verb Stem+はじめる (-RU; はじめた)	V	begin X-ing	9	2
+	はじめる	始める(-RU; 始めた)	V	begin (something)	2	2
	ばしょ	場所	N	place	4	4
+	はしる	走る (-U; 走った)	V	run	7	2

Appendix A

+	バス	バス	N	bus	5	4
	バスがある	バスがある	Sp. Exp.	there's a bus	7	1
+	パソコン	パソコン	N	personal computer, laptop	3	6
	はたち	二十歳（はたち）	classifier	20 years old	7	2
	はたらく	働く (-U; 働いた)	V	work	11	6
	はち	八・8	Numbers	8	3	2
	はつおん	発音	N	pronunciation	9	6
	はつか	２０日	N	the twentieth day of the month	4	4
	バッチリ	バッチリ	Sp. Exp.	perfectly, properly, sure thing (informal)	8	1
	はっとりスーパー	服部スーパー	N	Hattori Supermarket	7	6
+	はっぴょう	発表	N	presentation	5	5
+	はな	鼻	N	nose	11	5
	はなし	（お）話	N	talk	6	5
+	はなす	話す (-U; 話した)	V	talk	3	4
	はなれる	Xから・と離れる (-RU; 離れた)	V	be away, separate from	12	2
	はは	母↓	N	mother (humble)	7	2
+	ははおや	母親	N	mother	8	5
	ハヤ！	ハヤ！	Sp. Exp.	Already? So fast? (informal)	9	6
	はやい	早い	Adj	early	3	4
	はやい	速い	Adj	speedy	9	6
	はやく	早く	N	early	12	4
+	はやし	林	N	[family name]	3	9R
	はやす	生やす (-U; 生やした)	V	grow (a beard)	12	5
+	はる	春	N	spring	8	6
	はれる	晴れる(-RU; 晴れた)	V	clear up (of weather)	8	2
	ばん	〜番	Classifier	classifier for namings a number (in a series)	4	4
+	ばん	晩	N	evening	3	4
	ばんきょうしつ	〜番教室	Classifier	classifier for naming a classroom numbers	4	5
	ばんごう	番号	N	number	6	4
+	ばんごはん	晩ごはん	N	dinner	2	3
	はんそで	半袖	N	short sleeves	11	3
+	パンツ	パンツ	N	slacks, pants	11	2
	はんぶん	半分	N	half (of something)	9	2
+	ビール	ビール	N	beer	2	3
+	ひき	〜匹	Classifier	classifier for counting small animals	12	3
	ひく	弾く (-U; 弾いた)	V	play (a stringed instrument)	9	5
	ひくい	低い	Adj	low	10	6
+	ひくい（せが）	（背が）低い	Adj	short (in stature)	6	3

	ひげ	ひげ	N	beard	12	5
+	ひげをはやす	ひげを生やす	Sp. Exp.	grow a beard	12	5
	ひさしぶり	久しぶり	N	a while (since the last time)	10	1
	ひさしぶりに	久しぶりに	Sp. Exp.	for the first time in a while	10	1
+	ひだり	左	N	left	6	2
	びっくりする	(Xに・Adjective-くて)びっくりする	V	be surprised (at X)	7	1
	ピッタリ／ピッタシ	ピッタリ／ピッタシ	N	perfectly, exactly	11	4
	ひつよう	（ご）必要	N	necessary	11	1
+	たりる	足りる (-RU; 足りない)	V	be enough, suffice	12	4
	たら	必要でしたら	Sp. Exp.	if (it's) needed	11	1
	ひと	人（ひと）	N	person	6	3
+	ひどい	ひどい	Adj	cruel, harsh, severe	9	6
	ひとこと	ひとこと	N	something (to say)	6	1
+	ひとり	（お）一人	N	one (person); alone; single	12	5
	すっかり	すっかり	N	completely	12	6
	ずつ	一人ずつ	Sp. Exp.	one (person) at a time	6	2
	ひとりずついってください。	一人ずつ言ってください。	Inst. Exp	Please say it one at a time.	0	0
	ひとりっこ	一人っ子	N	only child	12	5
	ひとりで	一人で	Sp. Exp.	by oneself, alone (lit. 'as one person')	8	1
+	ひま	暇(な)	N	free (time)	8	6
	ひゃく・びゃく・ぴゃく	百 (100〜900)	Numbers	hundreds (100 through 900)	3	5
+	びょういん	病院	N	hospital	5	4
+	びょうき	病気	N	sick	3	2
	ひらがな	平仮名・ひらがな	N	hiragana syllabary	1	BTL 1
+	ヒリヒリ	ヒリヒリ(する・痛む)	N	tender (as a rash)	11	5
+	ひるごはん	（お）昼ごはん	N	lunch	2	3
+	ひるやすみ	昼休み	N	lunch break	12	9R
	ひろい	広い	Adj	spacious, wide	7	1
+	ピンク	ピンク	N	pink	6	3
+	プール	プール	N	pool	7	2
	ふうん	ふうん	Sp. Exp.	hmm	4	2
	フォーマル	フォーマル	N	formal	11	2
	フォント	フォント	N	font	4	5
	ふく	服	N	clothing, outfit	11	2
+	ふくおか	福岡	N	Fukuoka	9	4
	ふくざわだいがく	福沢大学	N	Fukuzawa University	3	1
	ふくしゅう	復習（する）	N	review	5	6
	ふくろ	袋	N	bag	9	1
	ふじさん	富士山	N	Mount Fuji	7	2
+	ふそく	不足（する）	N	insufficiency	12	4
+	ふたご	双子	N	twins	12	5

+	ぶちょう	部長	N	division chief	3	6
+	ぶつり（がく）	物理（学）	N	physics	4	2
+	ふべん	不便（な）	N	inconvenient	7	1
+	ふゆ	冬	N	winter	8	6
	ブライアン・ワン	ブライアン・ワン	Name	Brian Wang	1	1
	ブライアン？	ブライアン？	Sp. Exp.	(Is it/Are you) Brian?	1	7
+	ブラウス	ブラウス	N	blouse	11	2
+	ブラジル	ブラジル	N	Brazil	6	1
+	フラフラ	フラフラ（する）	N	dizzy	11	5
+	フランスご	フランス語	N	French (language)	3	1
+	フランスじん	フランス人	N	French (person)	3	1
+	フリーター	フリーター	N	non-permanent worker	9	3
+	フリーランス	フリーランス	N	freelance, freelancer	9	3
	ふりがな	振り仮名	N	phonetic guide to reading	1	BTL 4
	ふる	降る (-U; 降った)	V	precipitate, fall (i.e., rain)	7	5
+	ふるい	古い	Adj	old	4	1
	プレゼン	プレゼン	N	presentation	5	5
	ふろ	（お）風呂	N	bath	9	5
	ふん・ぷん	～分 (ふん・ぷん), 1分～60分, 何分	Classifier	classifier for naming and counting minute(s)	3	4
+	ぶん	分	N	portion	9	8R
+	ぶんがく	文学	N	literature	4	2
+	ぶんがくてき	文学的（な）	N	literary	11	4
+	ぶんがくぶ	文学部	N	facuty of arts and humanities	6	1
+	ぶんかのひ	文化の日	N	Culture Day (BTS 18)	4	4
+	ふんかん・ぷんかん	～分間	Classifier	classifier for counting minutes	6	2
+	ぶんせき	分析（する）	N	analysis	9	3
+	ぶんぽう	文法	N	grammar	5	6
+	ぶんぼうぐ	文房具	N	stationery	12	1
+	へ	～へ	Particle	to, towards X	5	4
+	ヘアスタイル	ヘアスタイル	N	hairstyle	11	4
+	へいき	平気	N	calm, unconcerned, all right	2	1
	へいきん	平均	N	average	10	6
+	へいせい	平成	N	Heisei era (1989-2019)	4	4
	へえ	へえ	Sp. Exp.	oh, yes? really?	3	5
	ページ	～ページ	Classifier	pages	5	2
	へた	下手	N	unskillful, bad at	6	1
+	べつ	別	N	different, separate, distinct	6	6
+	ペット	ペット	N	pet	12	3
	べつに	別に	Sp. Exp.	(not) particularly	2	8
+	ベトナムご	ベトナム語	N	Vietnamese (language)	8	8R
	へや	部屋	N	room	4	5
+	へん	（この・その・あの）辺	N	(this/that/that) area, vicinity	7	6
	へん	変（な）	N	weird, odd, strange	7	6

+	ペン	ペン	N	pen	3	3
+	べんきょう	勉強（する）	N	study	2	2
+	べんきょうする	勉強する	V	study	3	2
	べんきょうのしかた	勉強の仕方	Sp. Exp.	way of studying	10	6
+	べんきょうぶそく	勉強不足	N	lack of study	12	4
+	べんごし	弁護士	N	lawyer, attorney	9	3
+	べんとう	（お）弁当	N	meal in a box	2	3
	べんり	便利（な）	N	convenient	7	1
	ほう	方	N	way, alternative (of two)	6	3
+	ほうこく	（ご）報告（する）	N	report	6	5
+	ほうこくする	Xに報告する	Sp. Exp.	make a report to X	6	6
+	ぼうし	帽子	N	hat	11	4
	ぼうせん	棒線	N	long vowel symbol	5	BTL2
+	ほうりつ	法律	N	law	9	3
	ホームステイ	ホームステイ	N	homestay	6	1
	ほか	他・外	N	other, else, besides	6	6
	ほかに	ほかに	Sp. Exp.	in addition, besides	7	5
	ぼく	僕	N	I (masculine)	1	7
	ぼく、いちろう。	僕、一郎。	Sp. Exp.	I'm Ichiro. (casual)	1	7
	ほけんしつ	保健室	N	infirmary, clinic	11	5
	ほしい	欲しい（欲しくて）	Adj	want	8	1
	ほしい	〜てほしい/欲しい	Sp. Exp.	want (someone) to X	12	5
+	ポスター	ポスター	N	poster	4	1
+	ほっかいどう	北海道	N	Hokkaido	9	4
	ぼっちゃん	『坊ちゃん』	N	Botchan (novel by Natsume Soseki)	9	4
+	ホテル	ホテル	N	hotel	4	4
	ほど	ほど	Particle	as much as [comparison particle]	6	6
	ほど〜ない	カレーほどすごくない	Sp. Exp.	not as awesome as curry	6	6
+	ほど	思ったほど	Sp. Exp.	more (less) than I thought	10	6
+	ほん	本	N	book	3	5
+	ほん・ぼん・ぽん	〜本	Classifier	classiier for counting long objects	3	5
+	ほんじつ	本日	N	today (formal)	8	7R
+	ほんしゅう	本州	N	Honshu	9	4
+	ほんだ	本田	N	[family name]	10	8R
	ほんと	ほんと	N	short, informal form of ほんとう	7	6
	ほんとう	本当	N	true	4	3
	ほんとうに	本当に	Sp. Exp.	really, truly	10	5
+	ほんや	本屋	N	bookstore	5	4
+	ほんやく	翻訳（する）	N	translation	10	5

	ほんをみないでください。	本を見ないでください。	Inst. Exp	Please don't look at the book.	0	0
	ま(あ)	ま(あ)	Sp. Exp.	hmmm, well, come now, you might say	7	3
	まあ	まあ	Sp. Exp.	I guess [non-commital opinion]	3	1
	まあ!	まあ!	Sp. Exp.	oh!	8	4
+	マーケティング	マーケティング	N	marketing	6	2
	まあまあ	まあまあ	Sp. Exp.	so-so	4	1
+	まい	〜枚	Classifier	classifier for counting thin, flat things	3	5
+	まいあさ	毎朝	N	every morning	8	1
+	まいかい	毎回	N	every time	8	1
+	まいがっき	毎学期	N	every academic term, semester	8	1
+	まいじかん	毎時間	N	every hour	8	1
+	まいしゅう	毎週	N	every week	8	1
+	まいつき	毎月	N	every month	8	1
+	まいとし	毎年	N	every year	8	1
	まいにち	毎日	N	every day	8	1
	まいばん	毎晩	N	every evening	8	1
	まいる	参る↓(-U; 参った)	V	go, come (humble)	5	5
+	まえ	前	N	before [time]; Scene 6-3 front	3	2
+	まえだ	前田	N	[family name]	10	8R
	まかせてください。	任せてください。	Sp. Exp.	Leave it to me. Let someone do it.	5	3
	まかせる	任せる(-RU; 任せた)	V	leave it to someone else, let someone else do it	5	3
	まがる	曲がる (-U; 曲がった)	N	turn, make a turn	7	6
	まさか	まさか	Sp. Exp.	No way. Never. (interjection)	7	6
	まじ	まじ	N	really, truly, honestly (very informal)	9	6
	まじ?	まじ?	Sp. Exp.	Really? Truly?	9	6
+	まじめ	真面目(な)	N	diligent, serious	8	5
+	まじめそう	真面目そう(な)	N	looks diligent, serious	8	5
+	まずい	まずい	Adj	awkward, unappetizing, unpleasant; Scene 9-6 awful, disgusting, unappetizing	9	5
	ますます	ますます	Sp. Exp.	more and more, less and less	9	4
	また	また	Sp. Exp.	again	1	9
	まだ	まだ	Sp. Exp.	still, yet	6	1

+	またあとで	またあとで	Sp. Exp.	again later	3	4
	またせる	待たせる (-RU; 待たせた)	V	make someone wait	10	3
	まちがえる	間違える (-RU; 間違えた)	V	mistake (something), make a mistake or error (on something)	10	4
+	まつ	待つ (-U; 待った)	V	wait	3	2
	まっすぐ	まっすぐ	N	straight	7	6
	まったく	まったく	Sp. Exp.	good grief (expression of exasperation)	9	1
+	まつもと	松本	N	[family name]	3	9R
	まつやま	松山	N	Matsuyama (a city in Ehime Prefecture)	9	4
	まで	〜まで	Particle	up to, until; Scene 5-4 as far as X	4	4
	までに	TIME 〜までに	Particle	by TIME X	5	5
+	まど	窓	N	window	6	3
+	マネージャー	マネージャー	N	manager	6	2
	まま	まま		as is, condition	12	5
	まよう	迷う (-U; 迷った)	V	become confused, lost	6	6
+	マラソン	マラソン	N	marathon	7	2
	まる	丸 (。)	N	circle, period	2	BTL 2
	まん	万	Numbers	10,000s	4	1
+	まんが	漫画	N	comics, *manga*	12	1
+	マンション	マンション	N	condominium	7	6
+	まんなか	真ん中	N	middle	6	3
+	ミーティング	ミーティング	N	meeting	2	2
+	みえる	見える (-RU; 見えた)	V	appear, be visible	6	3
	みぎ	右	N	right	6	2
	みぎ、じゃなくひだり	右、じゃなく左	Sp. Exp.	right, I mean left	6	3
	みぎからでいい	右からでいい	Sp. Exp.	from the right is good	6	2
	みじかい	短い	Adj	short	5	5
+	みず	(お)水	N	water	2	3
	ミズーリ	ミズーリ	N	Missouri	8	4
+	みずた	水田	N	[family name]	10	8R
+	みせ	店	N	store, shop	6	2
+	みせる	見せる (-RU; 見せた)	V	show	5	5
	みち	道	N	street	7	6
	みてください。	見てください。	Inst. Exp	Please look at it.	2	0
	みどり	緑	N	green	6	3
+	みどりのひ	緑の日	N	Green Day (BTS 18)	4	4
	みなさん	みなさん	N	everyone (out group); Scene 6-1 (used in addressing a group)	3	7R

295

+	みみ	耳	N	ear	11	5
+	みる	見る(-RU; 見た)	V	look, watch	3	4
+	ミルク	ミルク	N	milk	2	3
+	みんな	みんな	N	everyone, all	3	4
+	みんなで	みんなで	Sp. Exp.	all together	3	4
	みんなでいってください。	みんなで言ってください。	Inst. Exp	Please say it all together.	0	0
	むかえ	迎え	N	greeting, welcome	12	4
	むかえる	迎える (-RU; 迎えた)	V	go to meet; welcome	12	4
+	ムカムカ	ムカムカ(する)	N	nauseated; queasy	11	5
+	むこう	向こう	N	opposite side, other side, over there	6	2
+	むずかしい	難しい	Adj	hard, difficult	2	7
	むずかしくなりました。	難しくなりました。	Sp. Exp.	It became difficult.	5	6
+	むすこ	息子↓	N	son (humble)	7	2
+	むすこさん	息子さん	N	son	7	2
+	むすめ	娘↓	N	daughter (humble)	7	2
+	むすめさん	娘さん	N	daughter	7	2
+	むね	胸	N	chest	11	5
+	むらかみ	村上	N	[family name]	9	9R
+	むらさき	紫	N	purple	6	3
+	むらた	村田	N	[family name]	10	8R
	むり	無理(な)	N	impossible, unreasonable	9	5
	むりする	無理する	V	try/work too hard, overdo	11	5
	め	～目	Classifier	classifier for naming numbers in a series	5	6
+	め	目	N	eye	11	5
	めい	～名	Classifier	classifier for counting people (formal)	10	3
	めいさま	～名様	Classifier	classifier for counting people (polite)	10	3
	めいし	名刺	N	business card	6	4
+	めいじ	明治	N	Meiji era (1868-1912)	4	4
	めいわく	(ご)迷惑(な)・(する)	N	trouble, bother	7	4
+	めいわくになる	(ご)迷惑になる	Sp. Exp.	become an annoyance	7	4
+	めうえ	目上	N		9	8R
+	めした	目下	N		9	8R
	めいわくをかける	(ご)迷惑をかける	Sp. Exp.	cause someone trouble	7	4
+	メール	メール	N	email	6	4
+	メガネ	メガネ	N	eyeglasses	11	4
+	メキシコ	メキシコ	N	Mexico	6	1
	めざまし(どけい)	目覚まし(時計)	N	alarm (clock)	8	1
	めずらしい	珍しい	Adj	unusual, rare	7	3

	メチャ	メチャ	Sp. Exp.	absurd, really, extreme (slang)	9	6
	メニュー	メニュー	N	menu	10	3
	めはくちほどにものをいい	目は口ほどに物を言い	Kotowaza	Eyes say as much as the words.	11	0
+	めん	麺	N	noodles	10	3
	めんせつ	面接(する)	N	interview (for a job)	11	2
	めんせつにきる	面接に着る	Sp. Exp.	wear t an interview	11	2
+	めんどう	面倒(な)	N	trouble(some), care, attention	8	5
+	めんどうそう	面倒そう(な)	N	looks troublesome	8	5
+	めんどくさい	めんどくさい	Adj	bothersome, tiresome	8	5
	メンバー	メンバー	N	member	6	1
	も	〜も	Particle	also, too	3	6
	もう	もう	Sp. Exp.	already	6	1
	もう!	もう!	Sp. Exp.	Really!	8	2
	もういちどきいてください。	PERSON にもう一度聞いてください。	Inst. Exp	Please ask PERSON again.	2	0
	もういちまい	もう一枚	Sp. Exp.	one more sheet	6	3
	もういっかいいってください。	もう一回言ってください。	Inst. Exp	Please say it again.	0	0
+	もうしあげる	申し上げる (-RU; 申し上げた)	V	say, tell	11	1
	もうしつたえる	申し伝える (-RU; 申し伝えた)	V	convey a message	11	1
	もうしわけありません。	申し訳ありません・ないです。	Sp. Exp.	I'm sorry.	5	3
+	もうしわけありませんでした。	申し訳ありませんでした・なかったです。	Sp. Exp.	I'm sorry (for what happened).	5	3
	もうしわけございません↓。	申し訳ございません↓。	Sp. Exp.	I am terribly sorry. (lit. 'I have no excuse.')	6	4
	もうしわけない	申し訳ない	Sp. Exp.	I'm very sorry	12	4
+	もうす	申す↓(-U; 申した)	V	say (humble)	6	2
+	もうちょっと	もうちょっと	Sp. Exp.	a little more	6	3
+	もくよう(び)	木曜(日)	N	Thursday	4	6
	もし	もし	Sp. Exp.	if, supposing	11	1
	もしかしたら	もしかしたら	Sp. Exp.	by some chance; maybe	12	6
+	もしかすると	もしかすると	Sp. Exp.	by some chance; maybe	12	6
	もちろん	もちろん	Sp. Exp.	of course	5	1
	もつ	持つ (-U)	V	hold, have, carry	5	3
+	もっていく	持っていく	V	take (a thing)	5	3
	もってきていただけますか?	持ってきていただけますか?	Sp. Exp.	Can I have you bring it?	5	3
	もってくる	持ってくる	V	bring (a thing)	5	3
	もっと	もっと	Sp. Exp.	More	6	3

	もっとおおきなこえではなしてください。	もっと大きな声で話してください。	Inst. Exp	Please talk louder.	0	0
+	もどる	戻る (-U; 戻った)	V	go back	7	6
	もの	もの	N	thing (tangible)	6	6
+	もの	もの	N	thing (tangible)	11	4
	もらう	もらう (-U; もらった)	V	get, receive	11	5
	もらっちゃって	もらっちゃって	Sp. Exp.	take, get	12	2
+	モリス	モリス	Name	Morris [family name]	1	1
+	もんだい	問題	N	problem	10	6
+	やかましい	やかましい	Adj	noisy, boisterous, annoying	8	5
	やぎ	八木	N	Yagi [family name] (Ms. Yagi is Sasha's supervisor)	1	11
+	やきとり	焼き鳥	N	yakitori	2	3
+	やきにく	焼肉	N	*yakiniku* (grilled meat)	10	3
	やきゅう	野球	N	baseball	10	1
+	やさい	(お)野菜	N	vegetable	10	3
+	やさしい	優しい	Adj	kind, nice, gentle	8	5
+	やさしい	易しい	Adj	easy	2	7
	やさしそう	優しそう(な)	N	looks nice, looks kind	8	5
+	やすい	安い	Adj	inexpensive, cheap	2	7
+	やすこ	安子	N	[given name]	12	9R
	やすい	使いやすい	Adj	easy to use	4	5
+	やすだ	安田	N	[family name]	12	9R
	やすみ	(お)休み	N	day off, vacation	3	2
	やすみのとき	休みの時	Sp. Exp.	during one's vacation; when one is on vacation	8	6
+	やすむ	休む (-U; 休んだ)	V	take a break, go on vacation/holiday	6	5
	やっきょく	薬局	N	pharmacy	7	6
	やっぱり・やはり	やっぱり・やはり	Sp. Exp.	as expected, sure enough	3	2
	やばい	やばい	Adj	troublesome, dangerous, awesome, extreme (as an interjection, 'awful, crap, oh no')	9	5
+	やま	山	N	mountain	9	9R
+	やまぐち	山口	N	[family name]	3	9R
+	やました	山下	N	[family name]	9	9R
	やましたさん	山下さん	N	Mr/s. Yamashita	4	3
+	やまだ	山田	N	[family name]	3	9R
+	やまなか	山中	N	[family name]	9	9R
	やまもと	山本	N	[family name]	3	9R
	やめる	止める・辞・やめる (-RU; やめた)	V	stop, quit (something)	8	2
	やる	やる(-U; やった)	V	do (less formal than する)	5	2
+	やる	やる(-U; やった)	V	give	12	6

298

+	ゆうがた	夕方	N	evening	9	2
+	ゆうびんきょく	郵便局	N	post office	5	4
	ゆうめい	有名(な)	N	famous	9	4
	ゆうめい	Xで有名	Sp. Exp.	well-known for X	9	4
+	ゆき	雪	N	snow	3	6
+	ゆきこ・せつこ	雪子	N	[given name]	12	8R
	ゆっくりする	(ご)ゆっくり	N	slow, relaxed	8	3
	ゆっくりする	ゆっくりする	V	relax, take it easy	8	3
+	ゆび	指	N	finger	11	5
+	ゆびわ	指輪	N	ring	11	2
	ゆめ	夢	N	dream	10	6
	ゆめをみる	夢を見る	V	have (see) a dream	10	6
	よ	〜よ	S. Particle	[sentence particle indicating certainty]	2	2
+	ヨーロッパ	ヨーロッパ	N	Europe	8	4
	よう(び)	〜曜(日)	Classifier	days of the week	4	6
	ようこそ。	ようこそ。	Sp. Exp.	Welcome. (greeting)	8	3
	よかったら	よかったら	Sp. Exp.	if it's all right	2	3
	よくわかりませんけど……	よくわかりませんけど……	Sp. Exp.	I'm not sure but…	3	6
	よこ	横	N	side, horizontal	11	5
	よこがき	横書き	N	horizontal writing	1	BTL 3
	よこになる	横になる	Sp. Exp.	lie down	11	5
+	よしだ	吉田	N	[family name]	3	9R
	よしだうんそう	吉田運送	N	Yoshida Transport	6	4
+	よしゅう	予習(する)	N	prepare for a lesson	5	6
	よね	〜よね	S. Particle	[sentence particle indicating shared certainty]	3	6
+	よびすて	呼び捨て	N	callig someone without a title (BTS 2)	1	1
	よぶ	呼ぶ (-U; 呼んだ)	V	call, invite	5	5
+	よみ	読み	N	reading	5	6
	よみかき	読み書き	N	reading and writing	5	6
+	よむ	読む(-U; 読んだ)	V	read	2	3
	よやく	予約(する)	N	reservation	10	3
	より	より	Particle	compared to [comparison particle]	6	6
	より	思ったより	Sp. Exp.	to the extent I thought	10	6
+	よる	夜	N	evening	9	1
	よる	寄る(-U; 寄った)	V	get close to, drop by, lean on	6	3
	よるがた	夜型	N	night person	12	4
	よろこぶ	喜ぶ(-U; 喜んだ)	V	be delighted, be pleased	5	5
	よろこんで	喜んで	Sp. Exp.	delighted	5	5
	よろこんで	喜んで	Sp. Exp.	happily, with pleasure	12	6
+	よろしい	よろしい	Adj	good (polite)	2	1

+	よろしかったら	よろしかったら	Sp. Exp.	if it's all right (polite)	2	3
	よろしく	よろしく	Sp. Exp.	thanks; please treat me favorably	2	1
	よろしくおねがいします。	よろしくお願いします。	Sp. Exp.	Nice to meet you.	1	4
	よろしければ	よろしければ	Sp. Exp.	if you would like, if it pleases you	5	5
	よわい	弱い	Adj	weak	5	6
	よんでください。	読んでください。	Inst. Exp	Please read it.	2	0
+	ラーメン	ラーメン	N	ramen (noodles)	2	3
+	らいがっき	来学期	N	next semester	4	4
+	らいげつ	来月	N	next month	4	4
+	らいしゅう	来週	N	next week	4	4
+	らいねん	来年	N	next year	4	4
+	らく	楽(な)	N	easy, comfortable	7	1
	ランチ	ランチ	N	lunch, lunch special	6	6
	ランチよりカレーのほうがおすすめ	ランチよりカレーの方がお勧め	Sp. Exp.	curry rather than the lunch special is the recommendation	6	6
+	リーダー	リーダー	N	leader	6	2
+	りっぱ	立派(な)	N	splendid, elegant	12	5
+	リビング	リビング	N	living room	9	5
+	りゅうがく	留学(する)	N	study abroad	6	1
+	りゅうがくせい	留学生	N	study abroad student	6	1
	りゅうがくせいセンター	留学生センター	N	International Student Center	6	1
+	りょう	寮	N	dormitory	2	5
	りょうかい	了解(する)	N	understanding, consent, agreement	5	1
	りょうしん	(ご)両親	N	parents	8	4
+	りょうり	X料理	N	x-cuisine	10	3
+	りょうり	(お)料理(する)	N	cooking	9	5
	りょこう	旅行(する)	N	travel	9	3
	リラックス	リラックス(する)	N	relax	9	4
+	ルームメート	ルームメート	N	roommate	3	6
	るいはともをよぶ	類は友を呼ぶ	Kotowaza	Birds of a feather flock together.	8	0
+	るす	留守	N	away from home or work	6	5
	ルビ	ルビ	N	phonetic guide to reading	1	BTL 4
	れいごうごうにい、はちきゅうのななななにいれい	０５５２、８９の７７２０	Sp. Exp.	(0552) 89-7720	6	4
	れいじ	零時	Numbers	midnight (0 o'clock)	3	2
+	れいわ	令和	N	Reiwa era (2019-present)	4	4
	れきし	歴史	N	history	4	2

+	れきしてき	歴史的(な)	N	historical	11	4
+	レストラン	レストラン	N	restaurant	4	4
	レセプション	レセプション	N	reception	5	5
+	レポート	レポート	N	report	2	2
+	れんしゅう	練習(する)	N	practice, rehearse	5	6
+	れんしゅうぶそく	練習不足	N	lack of practice	12	4
	れんらく	(ご)連絡	N	contact, communication	4	4
+	れんらくさき	連絡先	N	contact information	6	4
+	ローマじ	ローマ字	N	romanization	12	7R
	ろく	六・6	Numbers	6	3	2
+	ロシアご	ロシア語	N	Russian (language)	3	1
+	ロシアじん	ロシア人	N	Russian (person)	3	1
+	ロビー	ロビー	N	lobby	3	4
	ろんぶん	論文	N	thesis	10	2
	わ	〜羽	Classifier	classifier for counting birds and rabbits	12	3
	わーい	わーい	Sp. Exp.	wow! (surprise)	12	1
	わあ	わあ	Sp. Exp.	wow	2	3
+	ワイシャツ	ワイシャツ	N	dress shirt (for men)	11	2
	わかい	若い	Adj	young	12	5
	わからないこと	分からないこと	Sp. Exp.	things/matters one doesn't understand	10	5
	わかりました。	わかりました。	Sp. Exp.	Understood.	2	4
	わかる	わかる (-U; わかった)	V	understand	2	1
	わざわざ	わざわざ	Sp. Exp.	specially	8	4
+	わしょく	和食	N	Japanese food	10	3
	わすれもの	(お)忘れ物	N	forgotten thing	8	2
+	わすれる	忘れる (-RU; 忘れた)	V	forget	8	2
	わだい	話題	N	subject, topic of conversation	8	2
+	わたし	私	N	I (gentle)	1	7
+	わたしてき・ぼくてき	私/僕的(な)	N	like me	11	4
+	わたなべ	渡辺	N	[family name]	3	9R
+	わらう	笑う (-U; 笑った)	V	laugh	8	2
	わりと	わりと	Sp. Exp.	relatively	4	5
+	わるい	悪い	Adj	bad	7	4
	わるいゆめ	悪い夢	Sp. Exp.	nightmare	10	6

Appendix B: Japanese-English glossary by Act and Scene

List of abbreviations

N = Noun
V = Verb
Adj = Adjective
Sp. Exp. = Special Expressions

	すめばみやこ	住めば都	Kotowaza	Home is where you make it.	7	0
	キャンパス	キャンパス	N	campus	7	1
+	とおく	遠く	N	distant	7	1
	べんり	便利(な)	N	convenient	7	1
+	ふべん	不便(な)	N	inconvenient	7	1
+	らく	楽(な)	N	easy, comfortable	7	1
+	しずか	静か(な)	N	quiet	7	1
	さむさ	寒さ	N	the cold	7	1
+	きもち	気持ち	N	feeling, sensation	7	1
+	てんき	天気	N	weather	7	1
+	しょくどう	食堂	N	dining hall, cafeteria	7	1
+	カフェテリア	カフェテリア	N	cafeteria	7	1
+	ばいてん	売店	N	shop, stand, kiosk	7	1
+	エイティーエム	ATM	N	ATM	7	1
	なれる	(Xに)慣れる(-RU; 慣れた)	V	get used/accustomed (to X)	7	1
	びっくりする	(Xに)びっくりする	V	be surprised (at X)	7	1
+	かよう	通う(-u; 通った)	V	commute	7	1
	ひろい	広い	Adj	spacious, wide	7	1
+	せまい	狭い	Adj	narrow, confined	7	1
	さむい	寒い	Adj	cold (climate)	7	1
+	つめたい	冷たい	Adj	cold (to the touch), cold (personality)	7	1

302

+	あつい	暑い	Adj	hot (weather, climate)	7	1
+	あつい	熱い	Adj	hot (non-weather, non-climate)	7	1
	あたたかい	暖かい・温かい	Adj	warm (climate, personality)	7	1
+	すずしい	涼しい	Adj	cool (climate)	7	1
	くらい	暗い	Adj	dark	7	1
	あかるい	明るい	Adj	light, bright	7	1
	きもちがいい	気持ちがいい	Adj	good feeling	7	1
+	てんきがいい	天気がいい	Adj	the weather is good	7	1
	きつい	きつい	Adj	severe, intense	7	1
+	つらい	辛い・つらい	Adj	tough, bitter (experience), painful	7	1
+	うれしい	うれしい / 嬉しい	Adj	happy, glad	7	1
+	かなしい	悲しい	Adj	sad	7	1
+	さびしい・さみしい	寂しい	Adj	lonely	7	1
+	ありがたい	ありがたい	Adj	grateful, thankful	7	1
	うん	うん	Sp. Exp.	yes (informal)	7	1
	ううん	ううん	Sp. Exp.	no (informal)	7	1
	さむさ	寒さ	Sp. Exp.	coldness	7	1
	さむさにはなれました。	寒さには慣れました。	Sp. Exp.	I got used to to the cold.	7	1
	あたたかくてきもちがいい	暖かくて気持ちがいい	Sp. Exp.	warm and good feeling	7	1
	バスがある	バスがある	Sp. Exp.	there's a bus	7	1
	それより	それより	Sp. Exp.	leaving that aside, apart from that, more importantly	7	1
	びっくりする	(X に・Adjective-くて) びっくりする	Sp. Exp.	be surprised (at X)	7	1
	ふじさん	富士山	N	Mount Fuji	7	2
+	プール	プール	N	pool	7	2
+	カラオケ	カラオケ	N	karaoke	7	2
+	マラソン	マラソン	N	marathon	7	2
	たのしみ	（お）楽しみ（な）	N	enjoyment, pleasure	7	2
	おとうとさん	弟さん	N	younger sister	7	2
+	いもうとさん	妹さん	N	younger brother	7	2
	にいさん	（お）兄さん	N	older brother	7	2
	ねえさん	（お）姉さん	N	older sister	7	2
+	きょうだい	（ご）兄弟	N	brothers, siblings	7	2
+	かあさん	（お）母さん	N	mother	7	2
+	とうさん	（お）父さん	N	father	7	2
+	おくさん	奥さん	N	wife	7	2
+	しゅじん	（ご）主人	N	husband	7	2

+	むすめさん	娘さん	N	daughter	7	2
+	むすこさん	息子さん	N	son	7	2
+	かぞく	(ご)家族	N	family	7	2
+	おとうと	弟↓	N	younger brother (humble)	7	2
+	いもうと	妹↓	N	younger sister (humble)	7	2
+	あに	兄↓	N	older brother (humble)	7	2
+	あね	姉↓	N	older sister (humble)	7	2
	はは	母↓	N	mother (humble)	7	2
+	ちち	父↓	N	father (humble)	7	2
+	つま	妻↓	N	wife (humble)	7	2
+	おっと	夫↓	N	husband (humble)	7	2
+	むすめ	娘↓	N	daughter (humble)	7	2
+	むすこ	息子↓	N	son (humble)	7	2
+	おとな	おとな・大人	N	adult	7	2
+	こども	こども・子供	N	child	7	2
+	あかちゃん	赤ちゃん	N	baby	7	2
+	おとこのこ	男の子	N	boy	7	2
+	おんなのこ	女の子	N	girl	7	2
+	せんぱい	先輩	N	senior	7	2
+	こうはい	後輩	N	junior	7	2
+	しりあい	知り合い	N	acquaintance	7	2
	のぼる	登る (-U; 登った)	V	climb	7	2
+	くだる	下る(-U; 下った)	V	come/go down from	7	2
+	はしる	走る (-U; 走った)	V	run	7	2
	およぐ	泳ぐ(-U; 泳いだ)	V	swim	7	2
	さい	〜歳・才	classifier	classifier for naming age	7	2
	はたち	二十歳(はたち)	classifier	20 years old	7	2
	ということは	ということは	Sp. Exp.	that is to say	7	2
	いくんだ。	行くんだ。	Sp. Exp.	The fact is, I'm going.	7	2
	そうなんだ。	そうなんだ。	Sp. Exp.	So that's it; I get it now.	7	2
	しけん	試験	N	test	7	3
	おくれる	遅れる (-RU; 遅れた)	V	become late, run late	7	3
	めずらしい	珍しい	Adj	unusual, rare	7	3
	きびしい	厳しい	Adj	strict, severe, intense	7	3
	って・と	QUOTATION + って・と	particle	[quotation particle]	7	3
	かなり	かなり	Sp. Exp.	quite, considerably	7	3
	ま(あ)	ま(あ)	Sp. Exp.	hmmm, well, come now, you might say	7	3
	そうか。	そうか。	Sp. Exp.	I see.	7	3
	どうして	どうして	Sp. Exp.	why	7	3
+	なぜ	何故・なぜ	N	why	7	3
+	なんで	なんで	N	why	7	3

	このあいだ	このあいだ	N	the other day, recently	7	4
	めいわく	（ご）迷惑（な）・（する）	N	trouble, bother	7	4
	かげん	（お）加減	N	personal condition	7	4
+	ぐあい	具合	N	condition	7	4
	だいじ	（お）大事（な）	N	important, valuable	7	4
	かける	かける (-RU; かけた)	V	cause (lit. 'hang (something)'	7	4
	おもう	思う (-U; 思った)	V	think	7	4
	なさる	なさる↑(-ARU; なさった)	V	do (honorific)	7	4
	たのしい	楽しい	Adj	fun	7	4
+	わるい	悪い	Adj	bad	7	4
+	ぐあいがいい・わるい	具合がいい・悪い	Adj	be in a good/bad condition	7	4
	めいわくをかける	（ご）迷惑をかける	Sp. Exp.	cause someone trouble	7	4
+	めいわくになる	（ご）迷惑になる	Sp. Exp.	become an annoyance	7	4
	とんでもない	とんでもない	Sp. Exp.	not at all	7	4
	おかげさまで	おかげさまで	Sp. Exp.	thanks to you	7	4
	おだいじに	お大事に	Sp. Exp.	take care	7	4
	あるき	歩き	N	walk	7	5
	あつまる	集まる (-U; 集まった)	V	get together, assemble	7	5
	ふる	降る (-U; 降った)	V	precipitate, fall (i.e., rain)	7	5
	おなじ	同じX	Sp. Exp.	the same X	7	5
	それに	それに	Sp. Exp.	what's more, besides	7	5
	ほかに	ほかに	Sp. Exp.	in addition, besides	7	5
	あるくひと	歩く人	Sp. Exp.	people who (will) walk	7	5
	タウンシネマ	タウンシネマ	N	Town Cinema	7	6
+	えいがかん	映画館	N	movie theater	7	6
	みち	道	N	street	7	6
+	とおり	通り	N	way, road, street	7	6
+	へん	（この・その・あの）辺	N	(this/that/that) area, vicinity	7	6
	まっすぐ	まっすぐ	N	straight	7	6
	こうさてん	交差点	N	intersection	7	6
+	しんごう	信号	N	traffic light	7	6
+	つきあたり	突き当たり	N	end (of a street, hallway, etc.)	7	6
+	かど	角	N	corner	7	6
	ナビ	ナビ	N	GPS, navigator	7	6
	へん	変（な）	N	weird, odd, strange	7	6
	ほんと	ほんと	N	short, informal form of ほんとう	7	6
	やっきょく	薬局	N	pharmacy	7	6
+	こうばん	交番	N	police box	7	6

	はっとりスーパー	服部スーパー	N	Hattori Supermarket	7	6
+	マンション	マンション	N	condominium	7	6
	あいだ	間	N	interval, space between	7	6
	まがる	曲がる (-U; 曲がった)	N	turn, make a turn	7	6
+	もどる	戻る (-U; 戻った)	V	go back	7	6
+	つく	着く(-U; 着いた)	V	arrive	7	6
	なおる	直る・治る(-U; 直った・治った)	V	get better, get fixed; restore (itself)	7	6
	おかしい	おかしい	Adj	funny, weird, odd, strange	7	6
+	あぶない	危ない	Adj	dangerous	7	6
	あれ?	あれ?	Sp. Exp.	What? Huh?	7	6
	まさか	まさか	Sp. Exp.	No way. Never. (interjection)	7	6
	なんとかスーパー	何とかスーパー	Sp. Exp.	so-and-so/such-and-such/something-or-other supermarket	7	6
	あいだ	XとYの間	Sp. Exp.	between X and Y	7	6
+	とき	時・とき	N	time	7	9R
+	にちじ	日時	N	date and time	7	9R
	るいはともをよぶ	類は友を呼ぶ	Kotowaza	Birds of a feather flock together.	8	0
	たんじょうび	(お)誕生日	N	birthday	8	1
+	そつぎょう	(ご)卒業(する)	N	graduation	8	1
+	けっこん	(ご)結婚(する)	N	wedding, marriage	8	1
+	しゅうしょく	(ご)就職(する)	N	employment, getting a job	8	1
	めざまし(どけい)	目覚まし(時計)	N	alarm (clock)	8	1
	こえ	声	N	voice	8	1
+	おと	音	N	sound	8	1
	まいにち	毎日	N	every day	8	1
+	まいしゅう	毎週	N	every week	8	1
+	まいつき	毎月	N	every month	8	1
+	まいじかん	毎時間	N	every hour	8	1
+	まいがっき	毎学期	N	every academic term/semester	8	1
+	まいとし	毎年	N	every year	8	1
+	まいかい	毎回	N	every time	8	1
	まいあさ	毎朝	N	every morning	8	1
	まいばん	毎晩	N	every evening	8	1
	あける	開ける (-RU; 開けた)	V	open (something)	8	1
	あたる	当たる (-U: 当たった)	V	hit on target	8	1
	おきる	起きる(-RU; 起きた)	V	wake up, rise	8	1
+	ねる	寝る (-RU; 寝た)	V	sleep, go to bed, lie down	8	1

+	きこえる	聞こえる (-RU; 聞こえた)	V	be audible	8	1
	ほしい	欲しい (欲しくて)	Adj	want	8	1
	おたんじょうびおめでとう(ございます)。	お誕生日おめでとう（ございます）。	Sp. Exp.	Happy birthday. (lit. 'Congratulations on your birthday.')	8	1
	あけてみる	開けてみる	Sp. Exp.	try opening it and see	8	1
	あたり！	当たり！	Sp. Exp.	right (on target)!; you got it!	8	1
	こんなの	こんなの	Sp. Exp.	this kind (of thing)	8	1
	バッチリ	バッチリ	Sp. Exp.	perfectly, properly, sure thing (informal)	8	1
	ひとりで	一人で	Sp. Exp.	by oneself, alone (lit. 'as one person')	8	1
	なかなか	なかなか〜ない	Sp. Exp.	quite, considerably, rather	8	1
	いろいろ	いろいろ(な)	Sp. Exp.	various	8	1
	ちゃんと	ちゃんと	Sp. Exp.	properly, reliably, satisfactorily	8	1
	わすれもの	（お）忘れ物	N	forgotten thing	8	2
	きっぷ	切符	N	ticket(s)	8	2
	うそ	嘘	N	lie	8	2
	じょうだん	（ご）冗談	N	joke	8	2
	いや	嫌（な）	N	disagreeable, unpleasant	8	2
	わだい	話題	N	subject, topic of conversation	8	2
	やめる	止める・辞・やめる (-RU; やめた)	V	stop, quit (something)	8	2
+	わすれる	忘れる (-RU; 忘れた)	V	forget	8	2
+	おぼえる	覚える (-RU; 覚えた)	V	remember, memorize	8	2
+	わらう	笑う (-U; 笑った)	V	laugh	8	2
+	なく	泣く (-U; 泣いた)	V	cry, weep	8	2
	はれる	晴れる(-RU; 晴れた)	V	clear up (of weather)	8	2
+	くもる	曇る (-U; 曇った)	V	get cloudy	8	2
	かえる	変える(-RU; 変えた)	V	change (something)	8	2
	そんなに	そんなに	Sp. Exp.	to that extent; so/such a X	8	2
	もう！	もう！	Sp. Exp.	Really!	8	2
	じゃま	（お）邪魔（する）	N	a bother, a nuisance, an obstacle	8	3
	えんりょ	（ご）遠慮（する）	N	restraint	8	3
	ゆっくりする	（ご）ゆっくり	N	slow, relaxed	8	3

307

	あがる	上がる (-U; 上がった)	V	rise, go up, enter a house	8	3
	ゆっくりする	ゆっくりする	V	relax, take it easy	8	3
	ようこそ。	ようこそ。	Sp. Exp.	Welcome. (greeting)	8	3
	ごえんりょなく	ご遠慮なく	Sp. Exp.	without reservation	8	3
	おみやげ	お土産おみやげ	N	souvenir, gift	8	4
+	ヨーロッパ	ヨーロッパ	N	Europe	8	4
+	アフリカ	アフリカ	N	Africa	8	4
+	オーストラリア	オーストラリア	N	Australia	8	4
+	いわい	（お）祝い	N	congratulations, celebration	8	4
	かし	（お）菓子	N	sweets, candy	8	4
	しゅっしん	（ご）出身	N	birthplace	8	4
	ミズーリ	ミズーリ	N	Missouri	8	4
	セントルイス	セントルイス	N	St. Louis	8	4
	りょうしん	（ご）両親	N	parents	8	4
	のど	喉	N	throat	8	4
+	おなか	お腹	N	abdomen, stomach	8	4
	すむ	住む (-U: 住んだ)	V	reside	8	4
	かわく	渇く/乾く (-U; かわいた)	V	become dry	8	4
+	すく	空く (-U; 空いた)	V	become empty	8	4
	いれる	入れる/いれる (-RU; いれた)	V	put (something) in; brew or infuse (tea)	8	4
	いれる	淹れる/いれる (-RU; いれた)	V	brew or infuse (tea)	8	4
	ど	〜度	Classifier	times, degrees	8	4
	まあ！	まあ！	Sp. Exp.	oh!	8	4
	わざわざ	わざわざ	Sp. Exp.	specially	8	4
	いらしたこと	いらしたこと	Sp. Exp.	have gone; the experience of having gone	8	4
	おちゃをいれる	お茶を淹れる	Sp. Exp.	brew or infuse tea	8	4
	のどがかわく	喉が渇く	Sp. Exp.	get thirsty	8	4
+	おなかがすく	お腹が空く	Sp. Exp.	get hungry	8	4
	おかまいなく	お構いなく	Sp. Exp.	don't go to any bother	8	4
	やさしそう	優しそう(な)	N	looks nice, looks kind	8	5
+	げんき	元気(な)	N	healthy, energetic	8	5
+	げんきそう	元気そう(な)	N	looks healthy, energetic	8	5
+	まじめ	真面目(な)	N	diligent, serious	8	5
+	まじめそう	真面目そう(な)	N	looks diligent, serious	8	5
+	しんせつ	（ご）親切(な)	N	kind, gentle	8	5
+	しんせつそう	親切そう(な)	N	looks kind	8	5
+	めんどう	面倒(な)	N	trouble(some), care, attention	8	5

+	めんどうそう	面倒そう(な)	N	looks troublesome	8	5
	けっこう	結構(な)	N	nice, wonderful, quite, enough, sufficient (often by implication 'no thank you')	8	5
	はじめて	初めて	N	first time	8	5
+	たいせつ	大切(な)	N	important, necessary	8	5
	きゃく	(お)客(様)	N	guest, customer, client	8	5
	おや	親	N	parent	8	5
+	ははおや	母親	N	mother	8	5
+	ちちおや	父親	N	father	8	5
	たしか	確か(な)	N	sure, certain	8	5
+	やさしい	優しい	Adj	kind, nice, gentle	8	5
+	こわい	恐い・怖い	Adj	scary, frightening	8	5
	うるさい	うるさい	Adj	annoying, loud, noisy, tiresome	8	5
+	やかましい	やかましい	Adj	noisy, boisterous, annoying	8	5
+	めんどくさい	めんどくさい	Adj	bothersome, tiresome	8	5
	じつは	実は	Sp. Exp.	actually, in fact	8	5
	ふうん	ふうん	Sp. Exp.	hmmm	8	5
	たしかに	確かに	Sp. Exp.	for sure, certainly	8	5
	しょうがつ	(お)正月	N	New Year	8	6
	なつやすみ	夏休み	N	summer vacation/holiday	8	6
+	はる	春	N	spring	8	6
+	なつ	夏	N	summer	8	6
+	あき	秋	N	autumn, fall	8	6
+	ふゆ	冬	N	winter	8	6
	あいだ	間	N	during; between	8	6
+	きゅうか	休暇	N	break, holiday	8	6
+	ひま	暇(な)	N	free (time)	8	6
+	しゅっちょう	出張	N	business trip	8	6
	おやこうこう	親孝行	N	filial piety (a Confucian virtue); dedication to parents	8	6
+	おやふこう	親不孝	N	lack of filial piety	8	6
	かい	〜回	Classifier	times, instances	8	6
	やすみのとき	休みの時	Sp. Exp.	during one's vacation; when one is on vacation	8	6
	かならず	必ず	Sp. Exp.	without fail, always, without exception	8	6
+	たいてい	たいてい	Sp. Exp.	usually, as a rule	8	6
	ときどき	時々	Sp. Exp.	sometimes	8	6

+	たまに	たまに	Sp. Exp.	once in a while	8	6
	なつやすみのあいだ	夏休みの間	Sp. Exp.	during summer vacation	8	6
	ねんにに、さんかい	年に二、三回	Sp. Exp.	two or three times a year	8	6
	いっかいも	一回も number + も + neg	Sp. Exp.	not a single time	8	6
+	ほんじつ	本日	N	today (formal)	8	7R
+	ベトナムご	ベトナム語	N	Vietnamese (language)	8	8R
+	タイご	タイ語	N	Thai (language)	8	8R
+	インドネシアご	インドネシア語	N	Indonesian (language)	8	8R
+	だいがくせい	大学生	N	university student	8	9R
	すきこそもののじょうずなれ	好きこそものの上手なれ	Kotowaza	What one likes, one does well.	9	0
	ゴミ	ゴミ	N	trash, garbage	9	1
	そうじ	掃除(する)	N	cleaning	9	1
+	せいり	整理(する)	N	sorting, putting in order	9	1
+	せんたく	洗濯(する)	N	laundry	9	1
+	よる	夜	N	evening	9	1
	ふくろ	袋	N	bag	9	1
	すてる	捨てる (-RU; 捨てた)	V	throw away	9	1
+	かたづける	片付ける(-RU; 片付けた)	V	clean (something) up, tidy up	9	1
+	あらう	洗う(-U; 洗った)	V	wash	9	1
	あやまる	謝る(-U; 謝った)	V	apologize	9	1
	おく	置く(-U: 置いた)	V	put, place, position	9	1
	そうじしたのだれ？	掃除したの誰？	Sp. Exp.	Who is it that cleaned up?	9	1
	まったく	まったく	Sp. Exp.	good grief (expression of exasperation)	9	1
	はんぶん	半分	N	half (of something)	9	2
+	てん	点	N	point(s), score	9	2
+	パーセント	パーセント	N	percent	9	2
	おわり	終わり	N	the end	9	2
	おひる	お昼	N	noon, lunch time	9	2
+	ゆうがた	夕方	N	evening	9	2
	いく	行く(-U; 行った)	V	cover (as in a task)	9	2
	かたづく	片付く(-U; 行片付いた)	V	be in order; be finished; be taken care of	9	2
+	おわる	Verb Stem + おわる (-U; おわった)	V	finish X-ing	9	2
+	はじめる	Verb Stem + はじめる (-RU; はじめた)	V	begin X-ing	9	2
	さんぶんのいち	三分の一	Sp. Exp.	one-third	9	2
+	だいぶ	だいぶ	Sp. Exp.	a fair amount	9	2

	さ、さあ	さ、さあ	Sp. Exp.	well, well now, so, go on	9	2
	どんどん	どんどん	Sp. Exp.	rapidly, steadily	9	2
	ちょうど	ちょうど	Sp. Exp.	exactly, precisely, just	9	2
	たべにいく	食べに行く	Sp. Exp.	go to eat	9	2
	かんぱい	乾杯(する)	N	toast	9	3
+	じむしょ	事務所	N	(business) office	9	3
+	けんきゅうしょ	研究所	N	research institute	9	3
+	こうむいん	公務員	N	public servant, government worker	9	3
	かいしゃいん	会社員	N	company employee	9	3
+	アルバイト	アルバイト(する)	N	part-time work, part-timer	9	3
+	フリーランス	フリーランス	N	freelance, freelancer	9	3
+	べんごし	弁護士	N	lawyer, attorney	9	3
+	エンジニア	エンジニア	N	engineer	9	3
+	フリーター	フリーター	N	non-permanent worker	9	3
	りょこう	旅行(する)	N	travel	9	3
	かんけい	関係(する)	N	relationship	9	3
+	けんちく	建築	N	architecture	9	3
+	きょういく	教育(する)	N	education	9	3
+	あいてぃー	IT	N	IT	9	3
+	ほうりつ	法律	N	law	9	3
	きょうみ	興味	N	interest	9	3
+	ぶんせき	分析(する)	N	analysis	9	3
+	せつめい	説明(する)	N	explanation	9	3
	あそび	遊び	N	play, fun	9	3
	あそぶ	遊ぶ (-RU; 遊んだ)	V	play	9	3
+	つとめる	勤める(-RU; 勤めた)	V		9	3
	かんぱい!	乾杯!	Sp. Exp.	Cheers!	9	3
	かんけいの	X 関係の Y	Sp. Exp.	Y related to X	9	3
	きょうみがある	X に興味がある	Sp. Exp.	have an interest in X	9	3
+	せかい	世界	N	the world	9	4
+	くに	国	N	the nation	9	4
	しこく	四国	N	Shikoku	9	4
+	ほんしゅう	本州	N	Honshu	9	4
+	きゅうしゅう	九州	N	Kyushu	9	4
+	ほっかいどう	北海道	N	Hokkaido	9	4
+	おきなわ	沖縄	N	Okinawa	9	4
	まつやま	松山	N	Matsuyama (a city in Ehime Prefecture]	9	4
+	さっぽろ	札幌	N	Sapporo	9	4
+	せんだい	仙台	N	Sendai	9	4
+	かなざわ	金沢	N	Kanazawa	9	4
+	ふくおか	福岡	N	Fukuoka	9	4

+	おおさか	大阪	N	Osaka	9	4
+	きょうと	京都	N	Kyoto	9	4
+	なは	那覇	N	Naha	9	4
	おんせん	温泉	N	hot spring	9	4
	リラックス	リラックス(する)	N	relax	9	4
	ゆうめい	有名(な)	N	famous	9	4
	ぼっちゃん	『坊ちゃん』	N	Botchan (novel by Natsume Soseki)	9	4
	なつめそうせき	夏目漱石	N	Natsume Soseki (author, 1867-1916)	9	4
	のなかでいちばんいってみたいの	[Category] の中で一番行ってみたいの	Sp. Exp.	within/among [category] the one I want to go to most	9	4
	うちで	X, Y, Z のうちで	Sp. Exp.	among X, Y, and Z	9	4
	うちで3つつの	三つのうちで	Sp. Exp.	among three	9	4
	う〜ん	う〜ん	Sp. Exp.	umm	9	4
	ゆうめい	X で有名	Sp. Exp.	well-known for X	9	4
	ますます	ますます	Sp. Exp.	more and more, less and less	9	4
+	とどうふけん	都道府県	N	prefectures (BTS 11)	9	4
	しゅみ	趣味	N	hobby	9	5
+	けんどう	剣道	N	kendo	9	5
	おんがく	音楽	N	music	9	5
	スポーツ	スポーツ	N	sport(s)	9	5
+	りょうり	(お)料理(する)	N	cooking	9	5
+	どくしょ	読書	N	reading	9	5
+	ゲーム	ゲーム	N	game(s)	9	5
+	え	絵	N	drawing, picture	9	5
	えんか	演歌	N	*enka* (a popular ballad style of singing)	9	5
	うた	歌	N	song	9	5
+	ジャズ	ジャズ	N	jazz	9	5
+	クラシック	クラシック	N	classical (music)	9	5
	むり	無理(な)	N	impossible, unreasonable	9	5
	ふろ	(お)風呂	N	bath	9	5
+	シャワー	シャワー	N	shower	9	5
+	だいどころ	台所	N	kitchen	9	5
+	にわ	庭	N	garden	9	5
+	リビング	リビング	N	living room	9	5
+	せんめんじょ	洗面所	N	washroom	9	5
+	げんかん	玄関	N	entry way	9	5
	じぶん	自分	N	oneself	9	5
	ひく	弾く (-U; 弾いた)	V	play (a stringed instrument)	9	5
+	ならう	習う(-U; 習った)	V	learn	9	5

	うたう	歌う (-U; 歌った)	V	sing	9	5
+	かく	描く(-U; 描いた)	V	draw, paint, sketch	9	5
+	あびる	浴びる (-RU; 浴びた)	V	take (a shower) (lit. 'bathe in' or 'be covered in')	9	5
	きがつく	X に気がつく(-U; 気がついた)	V	notice X	9	5
+	おもいだす	思い出す (-U; 思い出した)	V	remember	9	5
	やばい	やばい	Adj	troublesome, dangerous, awesome, extreme (as an interjection, 'awful, crap, oh no')	9	5
+	まずい	まずい	Adj	awkward, unappetizing, unpleasant	9	5
	それとも	それとも	Sp. Exp.	or (else)	9	5
	きくのせんもん	聞くの専門	Sp. Exp.	listening is my specialty	9	5
	じぶんでは	自分で(は)	Sp. Exp.	on one's own, by oneself (without help)	9	5
+	しょうがっこう	小学校	N	elementary school	9	6
+	ちゅうがっこう	中学校	N	middle school	9	6
	まじ	まじ	N	really, truly, honestly (very informal)	9	6
	ばい	倍	N	double, -fold	9	6
	はつおん	発音	N	pronunciation	9	6
	はいる	入る (-U; 入った)	V	go in, enter	9	6
	はやい	速い	Adj	speedy	9	6
	うまい	上手い・美味い・旨い・うまい	Adj	delicious, skillful	9	6
+	まずい	まずい	Adj	awful, disgusting, unappetizing	9	6
+	えらい	偉い	Adj	excellent, distinguished, admirable	9	6
+	ひどい	ひどい	Adj	cruel, harsh, severe	9	6
	すっごい	すっごい	Adj	really, really	9	6
	ばい	～倍	Classifier	multiple, -fold	9	6
	てから	Verb ～てから	Sp. Exp.	after Verb-ing	9	6
	ハヤ!	ハヤ!	Sp. Exp.	Already? So fast? (informal)	9	6
	まじ?	まじ?	Sp. Exp.	Really? Truly?	9	6
	どうやって	どうやって	Sp. Exp.	(doing) how	9	6
	ねんで	３年で	Sp. Exp.	in three years	9	6

	こんなに	こんなに	Sp. Exp.	to this extent	9	6
	どうかなあ	どうかなあ	Sp. Exp.	I wonder	9	6
	なんばいもじょうず	何倍も上手	Sp. Exp.	many times better at	9	6
	そんなことない	そんなことない	Sp. Exp.	no such thing	9	6
	メチャ	メチャ	Sp. Exp.	absurd, really, extreme (slang)	9	6
+	き	木	N	wood, tree	9	7R
+	おかね	お金	N	money	9	7R
+	だんし	男子	N	young man	9	7R
+	じょし	女子	N	young woman	9	7R
+	きょうこ	今日子	N	[female given name]	9	7R
+	めうえ	目上	N		9	8R
+	こうこうせい	高校生	N		9	8R
+	かわかみ	川上	N	[family name]	9	8R
+	な	名	N	name	9	8R
+	ぜんじつ	前日	N	the previous day	9	8R
+	めした	目下	N		9	8R
+	きのした	木下	N	[family name]	9	8R
+	ぶん	分	N	portion	9	8R
+	むらかみ	村上	N	[family name]	9	9R
+	かみむら・うえむら	上村	N	[family name]	9	9R
+	きむら	木村	N	[family name]	9	9R
+	たちかわ	立川	N	[place name in Tokyo]	9	9R
+	やま	山	N	mountain	9	9R
+	やました	山下	N	[family name]	9	9R
+	うえやま	上山	N	[family name]	9	9R
+	なかやま	中山	N	[family name]	9	9R
+	やまなか	山中	N	[family name]	9	9R
+	かわなか	川中	N	[family name]	9	9R
	つぎ、がんばろう！	次、頑張ろう！	Sp. Exp.	Do your best next time.	9	9R
	ななころびやおき	七転び八起き	Kotowaza	Fall down seven times, get up eight.	10	0
	やきゅう	野球	N	baseball	10	1
+	かぶき	歌舞伎	N	kabuki (traditional theater)	10	1
+	のう	（お）能	N	noh (traditional theater)	10	1
+	えいが	映画	N	movies	10	1
	しあい	試合(する)	N	match, contest, game	10	1
	ジャイアンツ	ジャイアンツ	N	Giants	10	1
	ひさしぶり	久しぶり	N	a while (since the last time)	10	1
	いこう	行こう	V	let's go	10	1
	かっておきますので	買っておきますので	Sp. Exp.	because/so I'll buy X ahead of time	10	1

	ひさしぶりに	久しぶりに	Sp. Exp.	for the first time in a while	10	1
	ろんぶん	論文	N	thesis	10	2
	ぜったい	絶対(に)	N	absolutely	10	2
+	けんきゅう	研究(する)	N	research	10	2
+	さくぶん	作文	N	composition, essay, formal writing	10	2
+	じっけん	実験(する)	N	experiment	10	2
+	ちょうさ	調査(する)	N	investigation, survey	10	2
+	うんてん	運転(する)	N	driving (a car)	10	2
	ちゅう	X中	N	while X-ing; in the middle of X-ing; within X	10	2
+	いちにちじゅう	一日中	N	all day	10	2
	さらいしゅう	再来週	N	week after next	10	2
+	さらいげつ	再来月	N	month after next	10	2
+	さらいねん	再来年	N	year after next	10	2
	しあげる	仕上げる (-RU; 仕上げた)	V	finish up, complete	10	2
+	すませる	済ませる (-RU; 済ませた)	V	finish, get through	10	2
+	おわらせる	終わらせる (-RU; 終わらせた)	V	finish (something), close (something)	10	2
+	でかける	出かける (-RU; 出かけた)	V	go out	10	2
	このごろ	この頃	Sp. Exp.	lately, these days	10	2
	とくに	特に	Sp. Exp.	especially	10	2
	よやく	予約(する)	N	reservation	10	3
	せき	(お)席	N	seat, (seated) occasion	10	3
	しょくじ	(お)食事	N	a meal	10	3
+	にく	(お)肉	N	meat	10	3
+	さかな	(お)魚	N	fish	10	3
+	やさい	(お)野菜	N	vegetable	10	3
+	てんぷら	天ぷら	N	tempura	10	3
+	めん	麺	N	noodles	10	3
+	やきにく	焼肉	N	*yakiniku* (grilled meat)	10	3
+	わしょく	和食	N	Japanese food	10	3
+	ちゅうかりょうり	中華料理	N	Chinese food	10	3
+	りょうり	X料理	N	X-cuisine	10	3
	メニュー	メニュー	N	menu	10	3
	アルコール	アルコール	N	alcohol, alcoholic beverage	10	3
	オレンジジュース	オレンジジュース	N	orange juice	10	3
+	サイダー	サイダー	N	soda	10	3
+	コーラ	コーラ	N	cola	10	3
+	さけ	(お)酒	N	sake, alcohol	10	3

+	デザート	デザート	N	dessert	10	3
+	くだもの	果物	N	fruit	10	3
	うかがう	伺う↓ (-U; 伺った)	V	inquire, hear	10	3
	またせる	待たせる (-RU; 待たせた)	V	make someone wait	10	3
	おまたせする	お待たせする↓	V	make someone wait	10	3
	あまい	甘い	Adj	sweet	10	3
+	からい	辛い	Adj	spicy	10	3
+	しょっぱい	しょっぱい	Adj	salty	10	3
+	すっぱい	すっぱい	Adj	sour	10	3
+	にがい	苦い	Adj	bitter	10	3
	めい	～名	Classifier	classifier for counting people (formal)	10	3
	めいさま	～名様	Classifier	classifier for counting people (polite)	10	3
	いらっしゃいませ。	いらっしゃいませ。	Sp. Exp.	Welcome.	10	3
	さま	～様	N	[honorific title]	10	3
	でいらっしゃいます	Noun + でいらっしゃいます↑	Sp. Exp.	It's [Noun] (honorific)	10	3
	でございます+	Noun + でございます+	Sp. Exp.	It's [Noun] (polite)	10	3
	しょうしょう	少々	Sp. Exp.	a little (polite)	10	3
	おまちください。	お待ちください。	Sp. Exp.	Please wait.	10	3
	おまたせいたしました。	お待たせいたしました。	Sp. Exp.	sorry to make you wait	10	3
	おしょくじのほう	お食事の方	Sp. Exp.	the food part of your order	10	3
	うかがって↓おります↓。	伺って↓おります↓。	Sp. Exp.	We've heard. We've received.	10	3
	おきまりでしょうか。	お決まりでしょうか。	Sp. Exp.	Have you decided?	10	3
	とりあえず	とりあえず	Sp. Exp.	for now, first of all	10	3
	これで	これで	Sp. Exp.	being this	10	3
	かしこまりました。	かしこまりました↓。	Sp. Exp.	Understood.	10	3
	クリントンだいがく	クリントン大学	N	Clinton University	10	4
	しゅうりつだいがく	州立大学	N	state or public university	10	4
+	けんりつだいがく	県立大学	N	prefectural university	10	4
+	こくりつだいがく	国立大学	N	national university	10	4
+	しりつだいがく	私立大学	N	private university	10	4
+	けんしゅう	研修(する)	N	training	10	4
+	インターン	インターン	N	intern	10	4
	しつれい	失礼(な)	N	rude, impolite	10	4

	まちがえる	間違える (-RU; 間違えた)	V	mistake (something), make a mistake or error (on something)	10	4
	しょっちゅう	しょっちゅう	Sp. Exp.	frequent, often	10	4
	あるかもしれません。	あるかもしれません。	Sp. Exp.	There may be.	10	4
	いったとき	言った時	Sp. Exp.	when I have said	10	4
	つうやく	通訳(する)	N	interpretation	10	5
+	ほんやく	翻訳(する)	N	translation	10	5
	きんちょう	緊張(する)	N	tension, nervousness	10	5
	せんもんてき	専門的(な)	N	specialized	10	5
	ないよう	内容	N	content	10	5
	じかい	次回	N	next time	10	5
+	こんかい	今回	N	this time	10	5
+	ぜんかい	前回	N	last time	10	5
	じゅんび	準備(する)	N	preparation	10	5
	しらべる	調べる (-RU; 調べた)	V	investigate, inquire, search	10	5
+	きにする	気にする	V	care about, be bothered, worry	10	5
	おおい	多い	Adj	a lot, many, numerous	10	5
+	すくない	少ない	Adj	few, scarce	10	5
	わからないこと	分からないこと	Sp. Exp.	things/matters one doesn't understand	10	5
	ほんとうに	本当に	Sp. Exp.	really, truly	10	5
	きちんと	きちんと	Sp. Exp.	precisely, neatly, accurately, as it should be	10	5
	ゆめ	夢	N	dream	10	6
+	もんだい	問題	N	problem	10	6
	こくご	国語	N	Japanese (lit. 'national') language	10	6
+	がいこくご	外国語	N	foreign language	10	6
+	ことば	言葉・ことば	N	language, word(s)	10	6
	とくい	得意(な)	N	strong point, specialty	10	6
	にがて	苦手(な)	N	weak point, weakness	10	6
	いっしょうけんめい	一生懸命	N	all out, for all one is worth	10	6
	へいきん	平均	N	average	10	6
	いか	以下	N	below	10	6
+	いじょう	以上	N	above	10	6
	しかた	しかた・仕方	N	way of doing	10	6
	ざんねん	残念(な)	N	too bad, regrettable	10	6
	がっかり	がっかり(な)・(する)	N	feel disappointment, lose hear	10	6
	ゆめをみる	夢を見る	V	have (see) a dream	10	6

317

	かえってくる	返ってくる	V	come back (inanimate)	10	6
+	うける	受ける (-RU; 受けた)	V	receive; catch; be given	10	6
+	あきらめる	諦める (-RU; 諦めた)	V	be reconciled, give up	10	6
+	つづける	続ける (-RU; 続けた)	V	keep on, continue (something)	10	6
	ひくい	低い	Adj	low	10	6
+	たかい	高い	Adj	high, tall	10	6
	くやしい	悔しい	Adj	frustrating, annoying	10	6
	てん	〜点	Classifier	point, dot	10	6
	げんきない	元気ない	Sp. Exp.	have no energy	10	6
	わるいゆめ	悪い夢	Sp. Exp.	nightmare	10	6
	そういうこと	そういうこと	Sp. Exp.	a thing like that; that kind of thing	10	6
	おもったより	思ったより	Sp. Exp.	to the extent I thought	10	6
+	おもったほど	思ったほど	Sp. Exp.	more (less) than I thought	10	6
	いか・いじょういじょう	X以下・以上	Sp. Exp.	below/above X	10	6
	べんきょうのしかた	勉強の仕方	Sp. Exp.	way of studying	10	6
+	しょうがない	しょうがない	Sp. Exp.	there's nothing to be done	10	6
+	しかたがない	仕方がない	Sp. Exp.	there's nothing to be done	10	6
	じゃない	Xじゃない	Sp. Exp.	X, isn't it?; X, for sure	10	6
+	えいこく	英国	N	England	10	7R
+	えいいち	英一	N	[male given name]	10	7R
+	えいこ・ひでこ	英子	N	[female given name]	10	7R
+	おいそがしいなか	お忙しい中	Sp. Exp.	when you are busy	10	7R
+	にった	新田	N	[family name]	10	7R
+	なかた・なかだ	中田	N	[family name]	10	8R
+	たなか	田中	N	[family name]	10	8R
+	ほんだ	本田	N	[family name]	10	8R
+	むらた	村田	N	[family name]	10	8R
+	かねだ	金田	N	[family name]	10	8R
+	まえだ	前田	N	[family name]	10	8R
+	うえだ	上田	N	[family name]	10	8R
+	かわた	川田	N	[family name]	10	8R
+	たがわ	田川	N	[family name]	10	8R
+	たむら	田村	N	[family name]	10	8R
+	みずた	水田	N	[family name]	10	8R
+	のちほど	後ほど	N	later	10	8R

+	あけましておめでとうございます	明けましておめでとうございます	Sp. Exp.	Happy New Year	10	8R
+	あいだ	会田	N	[family name]	10	9R
+	しゃかいじん	社会人	N	a (working) member of society, an employed adult	10	9R
	めはくちほどにものをいい	目は口ほどに物を言い	Kotowaza	Eyes say as much as the words.	11	0
	きかくぶ	企画部	N	planning division	11	1
+	かいはつぶ	開発部	N	development division	11	1
	えいぎょうぶ	営業部	N	operations division	11	1
	ていねい	(ご)丁寧	N	polite	11	1
	ひつよう	(ご)必要	N	necessary	11	1
	しょうち	(ご)承知(する)	N	acceptance, consent	11	1
	もうしつたえる	申し伝える (-RU; 申し伝えた)	V	convey a message	11	1
+	もうしあげる	申し上げる (-RU; 申し上げた)	V	say, tell	11	1
	つたえる	伝える (-RU; 伝えた)	V	convey a message	11	1
	かわる	Xと・に代わる (-U; 代わった)	V	switch over to X (on the telephone)	11	1
	もし	もし	Sp. Exp.	if, supposing	11	1
	ひつようでしたら	必要でしたら	Sp. Exp.	if (it's) needed	11	1
	ふく	服	N	clothing, outfit	11	2
+	ワイシャツ	ワイシャツ	N	dress shirt (for men)	11	2
+	ブラウス	ブラウス	N	blouse	11	2
+	スカート	スカート	N	skirt	11	2
+	パンツ	パンツ	N	slacks, pants	11	2
+	スーツ	スーツ	N	suit	11	2
+	ドレス	ドレス	N	dress	11	2
+	ゆびわ	指輪	N	ring	11	2
+	イヤリング	イヤリング	N	earring	11	2
	めんせつ	面接(する)	N	interview (for a job)	11	2
+	インタビュー(する)	インタビュー(する)	N	interview (television, media, also job)	11	2
+	がっかい	学会	N	academic conference	11	2
	フォーマル	フォーマル	N	formal	11	2
+	カジュアル	カジュアル	N	casual	11	2
+	たべすぎ	食べ過ぎ	N	eat too much	11	2
+	のみすぎ	飲み過ぎ	N	drink too much	11	2
+	かんがえすぎ	考え過ぎ	N	think too much	11	2
+	はく	履く(U; 履いた)	V	put on, wear (on the legs, such as slacks)	11	2
+	すぎる	過ぎる (RU; 過ぎた)	V	exceed, go beyond	11	2
	にあう	(XがYに)似合う(U; 似合った)	V	X looks good on Y	11	2

+	こい	濃い	Adj	dark colored, thick, strong (flavor, possibility)	11	2
+	うすい	薄い	Adj	light colored, thin, dilute, weak (taste, probability)	11	2
	すぎ(る)	〜過ぎ(る)	Sp. Exp.	over- (overeat, overdo, etc.)	11	2
	めんせつにきる	面接に着る	Sp. Exp.	wear to an interview	11	2
	なかなか	なかなか + affirmative	Sp. Exp.	rather, more than expected	11	2
	それにしたら?	それにしたら?	Sp. Exp.	If you did that (how would it be)?	11	2
	きせつ	季節	N	season	11	3
	はんそで	半袖	N	short sleeves	11	3
+	ながそで	長袖	N	long sleeves	11	3
+	シャツ	シャツ	N	shirt	11	3
	セーター	セーター	N	sweater	11	3
+	ジャケット	ジャケット	N	jacket	11	3
	オーバー	オーバー	N	coat	11	3
	じつようてき	実用的(な)	N	practical	11	3
	かさねる	重ねる(-RU; 重ねた)	V	put on top	11	3
	きる	着る (-RU; 着た)	V	wear, put on	11	3
	かわる	変わる(-U; 変わった)	V	change, switch	11	3
	きせつによって	季節によって	Sp. Exp.	depending on the season	11	3
	かさねることにして(い)る	重ねることにして(い)る	Sp. Exp.	usually layer (habit)	11	3
	すてき	素敵(な)	N	sharp, nice, good-looking	11	4
+	おしゃれ	おしゃれな(な)	N	stylish	11	4
	ネクタイ	ネクタイ	N	necktie	11	4
+	くつ	靴	N	shoes	11	4
+	アクセサリー	アクセサリー	N	accessory	11	4
+	ぼうし	帽子	N	hat	11	4
+	てぶくろ	手袋	N	gloves	11	4
+	メガネ	メガネ	N	eyeglasses	11	4
+	ヘアスタイル	ヘアスタイル	N	hairstyle	11	4
+	もの	もの	N	thing (tangible)	11	4
+	パートナー	パートナー	N	(romantic) partner	11	4
+	しんせき	親戚	N	relative, family (in-group)	11	4
+	そぼ	祖母	N	grandmother (in-group)	11	4
+	そふ	祖父	N	grandfather (in-group)	11	4
+	おじ	伯父/叔父	N	uncle (in-group)	11	4

+	おば	伯母/叔母	N	aunt (in-group)	11	4
+	いとこ	いとこ	N	cousin (in-group)	11	4
	おくさま	奥様	N	wife (polite)	11	4
+	ごしゅじんさま	ご主人様	N	husband (polite)	11	4
+	ごしんせき	ご親戚	N	relative, family (polite)	11	4
+	おじいさん・おじいさま	おじいさん/お祖父様	N	uncle (polite)	11	4
+	おばあさん/おばあさま	おばあさん/お祖母様	N	aunt (polite)	11	4
+	おいとこさん	おいとこさん	N	cousin (polite)	11	4
+	かれ	彼	N	he, boyfriend	11	4
+	かのじょ	彼女	N	she, girlfriend	11	4
	イメージ	イメージ	N	image	11	4
	ピッタリ／ピッタシ	ピッタリ／ピッタシ	N	perfectly, exactly	11	4
	いみ	意味	N	meaning	11	4
	せっきょくてき	積極的(な)	N	active, positive, optimistic	11	4
+	しょうきょくてき	消極的(な)	N	passive, unmotivated, pessimistic	11	4
+	しゃかいてき	社会的(な)	N	social	11	4
+	れきしてき	歴史的(な)	N	historical	11	4
+	ぶんがくてき	文学的(な)	N	literary	11	4
+	じぶんてき	自分的(な)	N	like oneself	11	4
+	わたしてき・ぼくてき	私・僕的(な)	N	like me	11	4
	おいわい	お祝い	N	congratulations, celebration, gift	11	4
+	かぶる	被る (U; 被った)	V	wear, put on (one's head, such as a hat)	11	4
+	しめる	締める (RU; 締めた)	V	wear, put on, fasten (a necktie) (lit. 'tie, tighten')	11	4
+	かける	掛ける (RU; 掛けた)	V	wear, put on (glasses, buttons) (lit. 'hang, suspend')	11	4
+	つける	付ける(-RU; 付けた)	V	attach, apply	11	4
+	する	する	V	wear, put on (jewelry, accessories, make-up)	11	4
+	カッコいい	カッコいい	Adj	good-looking, stylish, cool	11	4
	そのうえ	その上	Sp. Exp.	what's more, in addition, plus	11	4
	おもい	[person] + 思い	Sp. Exp.	thoughtful about [person]	11	4

Appendix B

321

	どういういみ	どういう意味	Sp. Exp.	what do you mean? what does that mean?	11	4
	さきほど	先ほど	N	a while ago, just now	11	5
	きゅう	急(な)	N	sudden	11	5
	ズキズキ	ズキズキ(する・痛む)	N	throbbing	11	5
+	シクシク	シクシク(する・痛む)	N	dull, continuous pain	11	5
+	ヒリヒリ	ヒリヒリ(する・痛む)	N	tender (as a rash)	11	5
+	カサカサ	カサカサ(する・になる)	N	dry	11	5
+	フラフラ	フラフラ(する)	N	dizzy	11	5
+	ムカムカ	ムカムカ(する)	N	nauseated; queasy	11	5
	しばらく	しばらく	N	a while, a moment	11	5
	ほけんしつ	保健室	N	infirmary, clinic	11	5
	クリニック	クリニック	N	clinic	11	5
	あたま	頭	N	head	11	5
+	くび	首	N	neck	11	5
+	かた	肩	N	shoulder	11	5
+	こし	腰	N	(lower) back	11	5
+	て	手	N	hand	11	5
+	うで	腕	N	arm	11	5
+	ゆび	指	N	finger	11	5
+	あし	足/脚	N	feet/ leg	11	5
+	せなか	背中	N	back	11	5
+	むね	胸	N	chest	11	5
+	しり	(お)尻	N	buttocks, behind	11	5
+	かお	顔	N	face	11	5
+	め	目	N	eye	11	5
+	みみ	耳	N	ear	11	5
+	はな	鼻	N	nose	11	5
+	くち	口	N	mouth	11	5
+	は	歯	N	tooth	11	5
+	した	舌	N	tongue	11	5
	よこ	横	N	side, horizontal	11	5
+	たて	縦	N	vertical	11	5
+	ななめ	斜め	N	diagonal	11	5
	しんぱい	(ご)心配(な)・(する)	N	worry	11	5
+	こる	こる (-RU; こった)	V	become stiff	11	5
+	いたむ	痛む (-U; 痛んだ)	V	become painful	11	5
	もらう	もらう (-U; もらった)	V	get, receive	11	5
+	のむ	のむ/呑む (-U; 呑んだ)	V	ingest, swallow	11	5
	むりする	無理する	V	try/work too hard, overdo	11	5
	いたい	痛い	Adj	painful	11	5
+	かゆい	痒い	Adj	itchy	11	5
	きゅうに	急に	Sp. Exp.	suddenly	11	5

+	きもちがわるい	気持ちが悪い	Sp. Exp.	feel unwell; sickening, unpleasant, revolting	11	5
	あまり・あんまり + affirmative	あまり・あんまり + affirmative	Sp. Exp.	so, to such an extent	11	5
	よこになる	横になる	Sp. Exp.	lie down	11	5
	しんぱいをかける	心配をかける	Sp. Exp.	make (someone) worry	11	5
	あいづち	相槌	N	back-channeling (nods, interjections and the like that indicate one is paying attention)	11	6
	けっか	結果	N	result	11	6
	はたらく	働く (-U; 働いた)	V	work	11	6
+	うつ	打つ (-U; 打った)	V	hit, insert	11	6
+	こたえる	答える	V	answer, respond	11	6
+	それで、	それで、	Sp. Exp.	then, following that	11	6
+	あいづちをうつ	相槌を打つ	Sp. Exp.	provide back-channel comments and nods	11	6
+	おせわさま	お世話様	Sp. Exp.	your kindness	11	7R
+	えきまえ	駅前	Sp. Exp.	in front of the station	11	8R
+	とうだい	東大	N	University of Tokyo	11	8R
+	たぐち	田口	N	[family name]	11	8R
+	かわぐち	川口	N	[family name]	11	8R
+	うきょう	右京	N	[family name]	11	9R
+	さきょう	左京	N	[family name]	11	9R
	かわいいこにはたびをさせよ	可愛い子には旅をさせよ	Kotowaza	If you love your child, send them out into the world.	12	0
+	キャラ(クター)	キャラ(クター)	N	(fictional) character	12	1
+	ぶんぼうぐ	文房具	N	stationery	12	1
+	まんが	漫画	N	comics, *manga*	12	1
+	つくえ	机	N	desk	12	1
+	いす	椅子	N	chair	12	1
+	たな	棚	N	shelf	12	1
+	いっぱい	いっぱい	N	a lot, much, full	12	1
+	かす	貸す(-U; 貸した)	V	lend, rent (to someone)	12	1
	くれる	くれる (-RU; くれた)	V	give (to in-group)	12	1
+	くださる	くださる↑(-ARU; くださった)	V	give (to in-group) (honorific)	12	1
	つかってくれたら	使ってくれたら	Sp. Exp.	if you would use it (for me)	12	1
	わーい	わーい	Sp. Exp.	wow! (surprise)	12	1
+	おん	恩	N	benevolence, favor (BTS 1)	12	BTS 1
+	ぎり	義理	N	obligation (BTS 1)	12	BTS 1
	おくる	送る (-U; 送った)	V	send	12	2

+	うけとる	受け取る (-U; 受け取った)	V	take, accept	12	2
+	しまう	しまう (-U; しまった)	V	put away	12	2
	はなれる	Xから・と離れる (-RU; 離れた)	V	be away, separate from	12	2
	もらっちゃって	もらっちゃって	Sp. Exp.	take, get	12	2
	たべてるかどうか	食べてるかどうか	Sp. Exp.	whether you're eating or not	12	2
	きっと	きっと	Sp. Exp.	surely, undoubtedly	12	2
+	なっとう	納豆	N	*natto*, fermented soy beans (BTS 4 FN)	12	2
	ジェシカ	ジェシカ	N	Jessica	12	3
	がんこ	頑固(な)	N	stubborn	12	3
	かみ	髪	N	hair	12	3
+	け	毛	N	fur	12	3
	ながさ	長さ	N	length	12	3
+	からだ	体・身体・からだ	N	body	12	3
	じょせい	女性	N	woman, girl	12	3
+	だんせい	男性	N	man, boy	12	3
+	ペット	ペット	N	pet	12	3
+	いぬ	犬	N	dog	12	3
+	ねこ	猫	N	cat	12	3
+	かう	飼う (飼った)	V	keep (a pet or other animal)	12	3
+	ひき	〜匹	Classifier	classifier for counting small animals	12	3
+	わ	〜羽	Classifier	classifier for counting birds and rabbits	12	3
	おとなしい	おとなしい	Adj	laidback, quiet, docile	12	3
+	かしこい	賢い	Adj	clever, smart	12	3
+	あたまが・のいい	頭が・のいい	Adj	intelligent	12	3
	さ	〜さ	Particle	[informal particle checking on whether the other person is following]	12	3
	だれかしらない	誰か知らない	Sp. Exp.	don't know who that is	12	3
	ちゃいろのめをしている	茶色の目をしている	Sp. Exp.	has brown eyes	12	3
	で、	で、	Sp. Exp.	and…	12	3
	それで、	それで、	Sp. Exp.	and; because of that	12	3
	むかえ	迎え	N	greeting, welcome	12	4
	はやく	早く	N	early	12	4
+	おそく	遅く	N	far	12	4
	よるがた	夜型	N	night person	12	4
	あさがた	朝型	N	morning person	12	4
	ただ	ただ	N	simply; free of charge	12	4

	ねぶそく	寝不足	N	lack of sleep	12	4
+	べんきょうぶそく	勉強不足	N	lack of study	12	4
+	れんしゅうぶそく	練習不足	N	lack of practice	12	4
+	ふそく	不足(する)	N	insufficiency	12	4
	むかえる	迎える (-RU; 迎えた)	V	go to meet; welcome	12	4
+	たりる	足りる (-RU; 足りない)	V	be enough, suffice	12	4
	ねむい	眠い	Adj	sleepy	12	4
	きてくださってありがとうございます。	来てくださってありがとうございます。	Sp. Exp.	Thank you for coming.	12	4
+	きてくれてありがとう(ございます)。	来てくれてありがとう(ございます)。	Sp. Exp.	Thanks for coming.	12	4
	きていただいて	来ていただいて	Sp. Exp.	getting you to come	12	4
	もうしわけない	申し訳ない	Sp. Exp.	I'm very sorry	12	4
	あさにつよい	朝に強い	Sp. Exp.	morning type (lit. 'strong in the morning')	12	4
	どちらかというと	どちらかと言うと	Sp. Exp.	if I have to say which	12	4
	おおきな	大きな	N	large, big	12	5
+	ちいさな	小さな	N	small, little	12	5
+	りっぱ	立派(な)	N	splendid, elegant	12	5
+	きょうじゅ	教授	N	professor (academic rank)	12	5
	まま	まま		as is, condition	12	5
	そっくり	そっくり	N	exactly like, completely	12	5
	ひげ	ひげ	N	beard	12	5
	いがい	X以外	N	outside of X; besides X	12	5
	ひとりっこ	一人っ子	N	only child	12	5
+	しまい	姉妹	N	sisters	12	5
	きょうだい	X人兄弟	N	X number of siblings (including oneself)	12	5
+	しまい	X人姉妹	N	X number of sisters (including oneself)	12	5
+	かぞく	X人家族	N	X number in a family (including oneself)	12	5
+	ふたご	双子	N	twins	12	5
+	ひとり	(お)一人	N	one (person); alone; single	12	5
+	どくしん	独身	N	single; unmarried	12	5
	はやす	生やす (-U; 生やした)	V	grow (a beard)	12	5
	ならぶ	Xと・に並ぶ(-U; 並んだ)	V	stand alongside; line up	12	5
	にる	Xと・に似る (-RU; 似た)	V	look like X; resemble X	12	5
	わかい	若い	Adj	young	12	5

325

	このまま	このまま	Sp. Exp.	as it is; without change	12	5
	ほしい	～てほしい/欲しい	Sp. Exp.	want (someone) to X	12	5
	そっくり	Xにそっくり	Sp. Exp.	look exactly like X	12	5
+	ひげをはやす	ひげを生やす	Sp. Exp.	grow a beard	12	5
	ならんでいるとにてる	並んでいると似てる	Sp. Exp.	look alike standing next to each other	12	5
	あんない	(ご)案内(する)	N	show around	12	6
	すっかり	すっかり	N	completely	12	6
+	せわする	(お)世話する	V	look after (someone)	12	6
	あげる	あげる/上げる (-RU; あげた)	V	give (to out-group)	12	6
+	さしあげる	差し上げる↓(-RU; 差し上た)	V	give (to out-group) (humble)	12	6
+	やる	やる (-U; やった)	V	give	12	6
	いくことになりました。	行くことになりました。	Sp. Exp.	It has been decided I will go.	12	6
	なんとなく	なんとなく	Sp. Exp.	somehow or other	12	6
	もしかしたら	もしかしたら	Sp. Exp.	by some chance; maybe	12	6
+	もしかすると	もしかすると	Sp. Exp.	by some chance; maybe	12	6
	よろこんで	喜んで	Sp. Exp.	happily, with pleasure	12	6
	あんないしてあげる	案内してあげる	Sp. Exp.	I'll do you the favor of showing you around	12	6
+	おしらせ	お知らせ	N	announcement, notice (lit. 'letting know')	12	7R
+	ローマじ	ローマ字	N	romanization	12	7R
+	しょうテスト	小テスト	N	small test, quiz	12	7R
+	しょうがくせい	小学生	N	elementary school student	12	7R
+	こやま	小山	N	[family name]	12	7R
+	おやま	小山	N	[family name]	12	7R
+	おがわ	小川	N	[family name]	12	7R
+	おだ	小田	N	[family name]	12	7R
+	きょうかい	教会	N	church	12	7R
+	でんき	電気	N	electricity, light	12	8R
+	がんねん	元年	N	first year (of a new era)	12	8R
+	おおあめ	大雨	N	heavy rain	12	8R
+	おおゆき	大雪	N	heavy snow	12	8R
+	ゆきこ・せつこ	雪子	N	[given name]	12	8R
+	やすだ	安田	N	[family name]	12	9R
+	やすこ	安子	N	[given name]	12	9R
+	ひるやすみ	昼休み	N	lunch break	12	9R

Index

academic major 4-2 BTS 6
accent アクセント Introduction
adjective 2-1 BTS 1; formal affirmative non-past 〜いです 2-1 BTS 1; formal affirmative past 〜かったです 4-1 BTS 1; formal negative non-past 〜くないです、〜くありません 2-1 BTS 1; formal negative past 〜くなかったです、〜くありませんでした 4-1 BTS 1; informal affirmative non-past 〜い 2-3 BTS 15; informal affirmative past 〜かった 4-1 BTS 1; informal negative non-past 〜くない 2-6 BTS 25; informal negative past 〜くなかった 4-1 BTS 1; polite お〜 6-5 BTS 17; -sa form 〜さ 7-1 BTS 2; stem 〜く 2-1 BTS 1, 12-4 BTS 10; stem 〜くなる 5-6 BTS 14
affirmative/negative: affirmative adjective forms 〜いです、〜かったです 2-1 BTS 1, 2-3 BTS 15, 4-1 BTS 1; affirmative noun *desu* forms です、でした 2-1 BTS 1, 4-1 BTS 1, 2-5 BTS 18, 3-4 BTS 18, 4-3 BTS 14; affirmative verb forms 〜ます、〜ました 2-1 BTS 1, 4-1 BTS 1; negative adjective forms 〜くないです、〜くありません、〜くなかったです、〜くありませんでした 2-1 BTS 1, 4-1 BTS 1, 2-6 BTS 25; negative noun *desu* forms じゃないです、じゃありません、じゃなかったです、じゃありませんでした 2-1 BTS 1, 4-1 BTS 1, 2-6 BTS 25; negative verb forms 〜ないです、〜ません、なかったです、〜ませんでした 2-1 BTS 1, 4-1 BTS 1
affirming 2-1 BTS 5
aimai 曖昧 4-2 BTS 12
aizuchi 相槌 8-5 BTS 14
apologizing 10-2 BTS 5
appearance 8-5 BTS 12
approximation 4-1 BTS 5, 8-6 BTS 16

borrowed words 5-7 BTL 3
bowing お辞儀 Introduction
business communication: business cards 名刺 6-4 BTS 14; emails 11-7 BTL 1; phone conversations 11-1 BTS 2

calendar 4-4 BTS 18
classifier 3-2 BTS 9; multiple in a sentence 5-3 BTS 6; naming *vs.* counting 4-6 BTS 29
clothing 11-2 BTS 4
colors 6-3 BTS 11
commands 5-1 BTS 2; negative 8-2 BTS 4
commuting 7-1 BTS 3
comparison: three or more items 〜が一番 9-4 BTS 10; two items より、ほど 6-6 BTS 24, 10-6 BTS 12
compliments 9-6 BTS 18, 11-4 BTS 8
compounds 4-5 BTS 25
conditional 〜たら 11-1 BTS 1, 11-2 BTS 5, 11-4 BTS 9, 11-5 BTS 12, 11-6 BTS 15
consonants, long 促音 Introduction; (hiragana) 3-9 BTL 2; (katakana) 5-7 BTL 10

daroo だろう 8-5 BTS 13
dependence 甘え 5-6 BTS 15
deshoo でしょう 4-1 BTS 2, 4-2 BTS 12, 5-2 BTS 3
diacritics 濁点 2-9 BTL 4
double consonants (hiragana) 促音 (っ) 3-9 BTL 2
double consonants (katakana) 促音 (ッ) 5-7 BTL 10
double-*ga* 〜が〜が 4-6 BTS 27

echo question 2-2 BTS 7
embedded question 12-2 BTS 4, 12-3 BTS 6
existence (inanimate) 2-8 BTS 29
explanation *no de* 〜ので 10-1 BTS 3

family 家族 7-2 BTS 6, 11-4 BTS 11, 12-5 BTS 15
female speech style 8-3 BTS 9
fonts フォント 3-9 BTL 5
formal/informal 2-1 BTS 1, 7-1 BTS 1, 7-3 BTS 10; formal adjective forms 2-1 BTS 1, 4-1-BTS 1; formal noun *desu* forms 2-1 BTS 1, 4-1-BTS 1; formal *-te* form 〜まして 6-4 BTS 16; formal verb forms 2-1 BTS 1, 4-1-BTS 1; informal adjective forms 2-3 BTS 15, 2-6 BTS 25, 4-1 BTS 1; informal noun *desu* forms 2-1 BTS 1, 2-5 BTS 18, 2-6 BTS 25, 3-4 BTS 18, 4-3 BTS 14; informal verb forms 2-6 BTS 25, 7-1 BTS 1, 7-3 BTS 8
fractions 9-2 BTS 6
frequency expressions 8-6 BTS 15
furigana ふりがな 1-15 BTL 4

genkooyooshi 原稿用紙 1-15 BTL 5
gifts 8-4 BTS 11

handaku-on (hiragana) 半濁音 3-9 BTL 4
handwritten characters 2-9 BTL 3
hesitation noises 2-2 BTS 8
hiragana 平仮名 2-9 BTL 1
holidays 4-4 BTS 18
humble verb 謙譲語 6-5 BTS 21
humor ユーモア 8-2 BTS 6

informal *see* formal/informal
interjections 9-6 BTS 16
inverted sentence 3-6 BTS 32
invitations 招待 2-2 BTS 1

kango (Chinese borrowed words) 漢語 9-8 BTL 3
kanji readings 漢字 1-15 BTL 2, 7-7 BTL 10, 7-8 BTL 11, 7-8 BTL 13, 7-9 BTL 15, 8-7 BTL 2, 8-8 BTL 3
katakana 片仮名 5-7 BTL 1
keyboard input 4-7 BTL 3, 7-8 BTL 14
ko-so-a-do series こそあど 2-1 BTS 2, 2-4 BTS 17, 2-7 BTS 28, 3-5 BTS 22, 8-1 BTS 2, 10-6 BTS 15
koto こと 10-5 BTS 9; *koto ni naru* ことになる 12-6 BTS 19; *koto ni suru* ことにする 11-3 BTS 7; sentence + *koto* ことがある・ない 8-4 BTS 10; *sono koto* そのこと 4-4 BTS 16;

tte/to iu koto って・ということ 12-1 BTS 2; *X no koto* 〜のこと 3-1 BTS 5
kun-yomi 訓読み 1-15 BTL 2

loanwords 外来語 3-3 BTS 14

male speech style 8-3 BTS 9
manner expression 4-1 BTS 3, 5-1 BTS 2
-mashoo form 〜ましょう 3-2 BTS 8, 10-1 BTS 2
mono もの 9-5 BTS 14
mora 拍 Introduction
multiplication 9-6 BTS 17

names 名前 1-4 BTS 8, 1-7 BTS 14, 3-9 BTS 6
n desu, んです 6-5 BTS 19, 7-2 BTS 4, 7-6 BTS 18, 7-7 BTL 2, 8-2 BTS 5, 9-1 BTS 2, 12-4 BTS 14
negating 2-1 BTS 5
negative *see* affirmative/negative
negative questions 3-2 BTS 12
noun 2-1 BTS 1
noun *desu*: formal affirmative non-past です 2-1 BTS 1; formal affirmative past でした 4-1 BTS 1; formal negative non-past じゃないです、じゃありません 2-1 BTS 1; formal negative past じゃなかったです、じゃありませんでした 4-1 BTS 1; informal affirmative non-past だ 2-5 BTS 18, 3-4 BTS 18; informal affirmative past だった 4-3 BTS 14; informal negative non-past じゃない 2-6 BTS 25; informal negative past じゃなかった 2-6 BTS 25

occupations 9-3 BTS 7
okurigana 送り仮名 7-8 BTL 12
omoiyari 思いやり 3-4 BTS 16, 7-4 BTS 11
onomatopoeia オノマトペ 11-5 BTS 14
on-yomi 音読み 1-15 BTL 2

particle 3-1 BTS 4; *dake* だけ 4-2 BTS 9; *de* (means) で 5-4 BTS 9; *de* (place) で 3-4 BTS 15; *ga* が 4-3 BTS 13; *ga* (double *ga*) が 4-6 BTS 2; *ga* (sentence *ga*) が 2-4 BTS 16; *ka* (noun *ka* noun *(ka))* か 6-6 BTS 23; *kara* から 4-4 BTS 22; *kara* (reason) から 5-5 BTS 12; *kedo, keredo, kedomo, keredomo* けど、けれど、けども、けれども 2-4 BTS 16; *made* まで 4-4 BTS 22, 5-5 BTS 13; *made ni* までに

Index

5-5- BTS 13; *mo* も 3-6 BTS 31; multiple 4-2 BTS 10; *na* (connecting nouns) な 3-1 BTS 2; *ni* (decisions) に 6-6 BTS 28; *ni* (location) に 3-6 BTS 30; *ni* (time) に 3-4 BTS 20; *ni/e* (location) に、へ 5-4 BTS 8; *no* (connecting nouns) の 3-1 BTS 2, 3-6 BTS 29; *no de* ので 10-1 BTS 3; [noun + particle] as question 4-2 BT 7; *o* を 4-5 BTS 24, 4-7 BTL 2; *o* (location) を 7-6 BTS 17; particle + *desu* 4-4 BTS 23, 6-2 BTS 5; question word + *mo* 6-6 BTS 22; *sa* さ 12-3 BTS 7; *shi* (sentence *shi*) し 9-3 BTS 9; *to* と 3-2 BTS 10; *to* (noun *to* sentence) と 6-6 BTS 25; *to* (sentence *to* sentence) と 12-4 BTS 13; *to issho ni* と一緒に 3-4 BTS 17; *to/tte* (quotations) と、って 7-3 BTS 9; *toka* とか 4-2 BTS 8, 10-6 BTS 11; *tte* って 3-1 BTS 4; *wa* は 2-6 BTS 22, 3-2 BTS 7

particle (sentence particle) 2-1 BTS 3; *ka, ne* か、ね 2-1 BTS 3; multiple: *ka naa, ka nee* かなあ、かねえ 2-6 BTS 24, 3-6 BTS 33; *nee* ねえ 2-3 BTS 14; *nee, naa* ねえ、なあ 2-6 BTS 23; *yo* よ 2-2 BTS 6

permission ～て(も)いい 5-1 BTS 2

polite adjective *see* adjective

politeness 敬語 5-5 BTS 10, 6-4 BTS 15, 10-3 BTS 6

polite prefixes 8-3 BTS 8

polite request ～ていただけますか 5-3 BTS 5

punctuation 句読点 2-9 BTL 2, 10-9 BTL 1

questions without *ka* 4-4 BTS 15

quotation marks 9-8 BTL 1

quotations 7-3 BTS 9

radicals (kanji radicals) 部首 7-9 BTL 15

ritual language 1-4 BTS 7, 1-6 BTS 13

romanization ローマ字 Introduction

self, words for 1-7 BTS 15

self-introduction 自己紹介 1-4 BTS 7, 1-10 BTS 20, 6-1 BTS 4

sentence modifier 7-5 BTS 14, 9-1 BTS 1

spoken language (*vs.* written language) 話しことば、書きことば 4-7 BTL 1

story telling 11-6 BTS 15

-tara form ～たら *see* conditional

tategaki (vertical writing) 縦書き 1-15 BTL 3

-te form ～て 5-1 BTS 1, 2, 5-2 BTS 4; informal command 6-3 BTS 10; manner expressions 5-1 BTS 2; *-te hoshii* ～てほしい 12-5 BTS 17; *-te (mo) ii* ～て(も)いい 5-1 BTS 2; *-te (i)masu* ～て(い)ます 6-1 BTS 1; *-te kara* ～てから 9-6 BTS 15; *-te kimasu/ikimasu* ～てきます・いきます 5-4 BTS 7, 9-2 BTS 5; *-te miru* ～てみる 8-1 BTS 1; *-te mo* ～ても 5-1 BTS 2; *-te oku* ～ておく 10-1 BTS 1; *-te shimau* ～てしまう 12-2 BTS 5

time, relative 4-4 BTS 18

time expressions 3-2 BTS 9

titles 1-1 BTS 2, 1-7 BTS 14

togetherness 10-3 BTS 7

transitive verb *-te aru* ～てある 9-1 BTS 3

transportation *see* commuting

verb 2-1 BTS 1; formal affirmative non-past ～ます 2-1 BTS 1; formal affirmative past ～ました 4-1 BTS 1; formal negative non-past ～ないです、～ません 2-1 BTS 1; formal negative past ～なかったです、～ませんでした 4-1 BTS 1; giving and receiving 12-1 BTS 1, 12-4 BTS 9, 12-6 BTS 18; informal affirmative non-past ～る 7-1 BTS 1; informal affirmative past ～た 7-1 BTS 8; informal negative non-past ～ない 2-6 BTS 25; informal negative past ～なかった 7-1 BTS 8; root 7-1 BTS 1; stem 3-2 BTS 8; stem as noun 7-5 BTS 13

visiting 8-3 BTS 7

voiced consonants 濁音: (hiragana) 2-9 BTL 4; (katakana) 5-7 BTL 9

vowels, long 長音: (hiragana) Introduction, 2-9 BTL 5; (katakana) 5-7 BTL 2

word order 4-6 BTS 28

written language (*vs.* spoken language) 書きことば、話しことば 4-7 BTL 1, 12-7 BTL 1

yokogaki (horizontal writing) 横書き 1-15 BTL 3

yoo-on 拗音: (hiragana) や、ゆ、よ 3-9 BTL 3; (katakana) ャ、ュ、ョ 6-7 BTL 5